THIS PLACE IS WHO WE ARE

May 2023

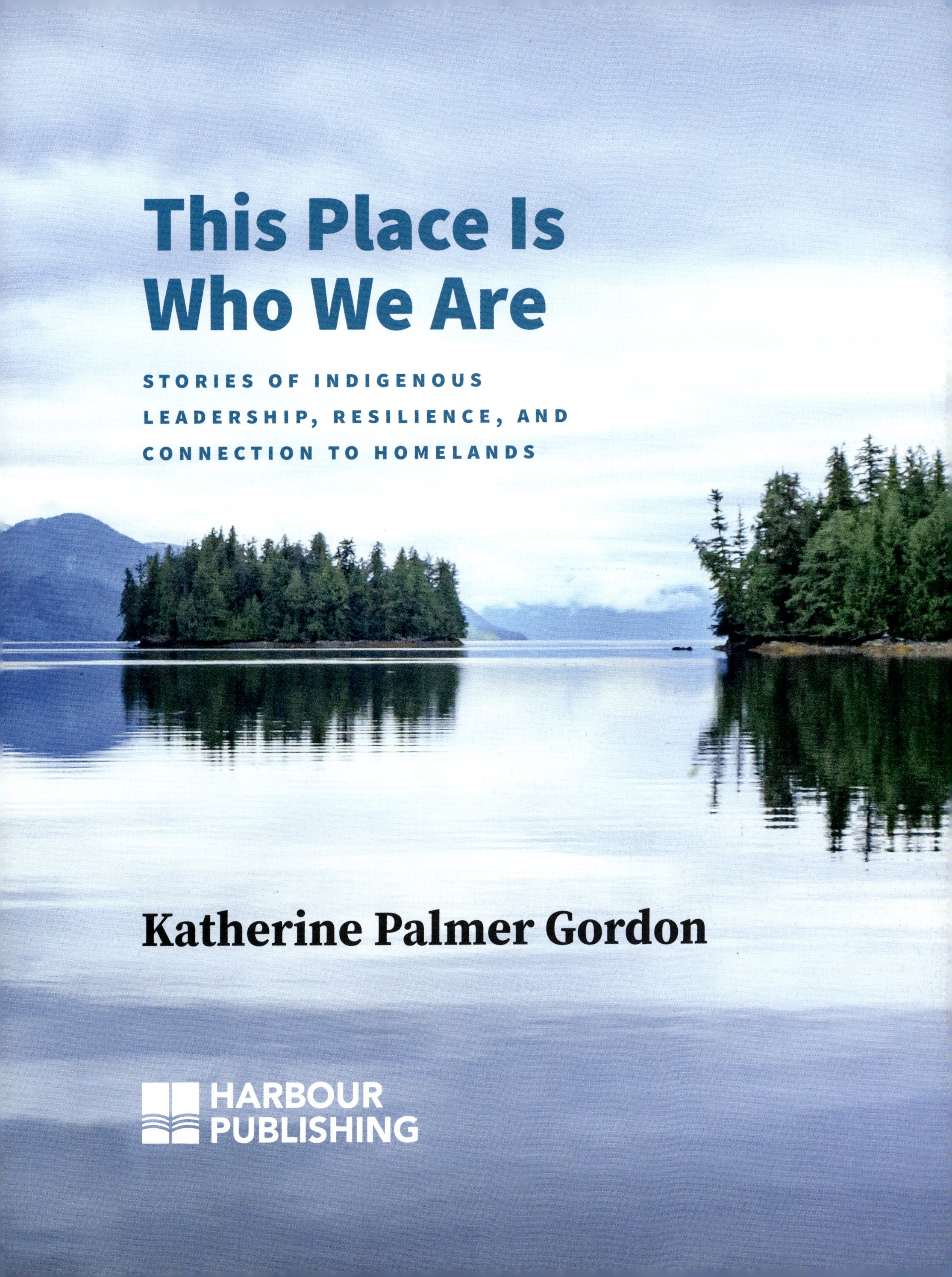

This Place Is Who We Are

STORIES OF INDIGENOUS LEADERSHIP, RESILIENCE, AND CONNECTION TO HOMELANDS

Katherine Palmer Gordon

HARBOUR PUBLISHING

Title page photo: Rescue Bay Conservancy, Susan Island, central coast, BC.

Page 2 photo: Princess Royal Island, east of Hecate Strait on the northern BC coast.

Page 223 photo: A quiet moment for a coastal wolf in Gitga'at homelands.

Page 226 photo: School of herring in Haíłzaqv territorial waters.

1 2 3 4 5 — 27 26 25 24 23

HARBOUR PUBLISHING CO. LTD.

P.O. Box 219, Madeira Park, BC, V0N 2H0

www.harbourpublishing.com

MAP on page x courtesy of Coast Funds

EDITED by Alicia Hibbert

INDEXED by Catherine Plear

COVER AND TEXT DESIGN by Libris Simas Ferraz / Onça Publishing

COVER PHOTOGRAPH courtesy of Swan Bay Rediscovery Camp (Rachel Singleton-Poster)

PRINTED AND BOUND in South Korea

PRINTED with vegetable-based ink on paper certified by the Forest Stewardship Council®

HARBOUR PUBLISHING acknowledges the support of the Canada Council for the Arts, the Government of Canada, and the Province of British Columbia through the BC Arts Council.

Canada

Canada Council for the Arts | Conseil des arts du Canada

British Columbia Arts Council

British Columbia

MIX
Paper | Supporting responsible forestry
FSC www.fsc.org FSC® C140526

LIBRARY AND ARCHIVES CANADA CATALOGUING IN PUBLICATION

Title: This place is who we are : stories of Indigenous leadership, resilience, and connection to homelands / Katherine Palmer Gordon.

Names: Gordon, Katherine, 1963- author.

Description: Includes bibliographical references and index.

Identifiers: Canadiana (print) 20220479755 | Canadiana (ebook) 20220479852 | ISBN 9781990776137 (softcover) | ISBN 9781990776144 (EPUB)

Subjects: LCSH: Indigenous peoples—British Columbia. | LCSH: Human ecology—British Columbia. | LCSH: Indigenous peoples—British Columbia—Social conditions.v

Classification: LCC E78.B9 G67 2023 | DDC 971.1004/97—dc23

Dedication

This book is, naturally, first and foremost dedicated with immense gratitude to all the people who have shared their voices and stories in its pages, and their families, their Elders, leaders, communities, and Nations.

There are two other people whom I would also like to acknowledge. Merv Child, former chair of Coast Funds, is a tireless advocate and worker for the rights of the Indigenous Peoples whose homelands span the central and north coast of what is now known as British Columbia. Gilakas'la, Merv, for supporting the idea of this book right from the beginning.

The late David "Dave" Mannix was the first chief executive of Coast Funds and a fierce protector of the people, places, and principles he cared about and the individuals he loved. He is a sorely missed friend and "big brother." I know that he would be very proud of this book and all of the people involved in bringing it to life.

Table of Contents

Facing page: Raven at Taaw (Tow Hill), on X̱aaydaga Gwaay.yaay/X̱aayda Gwaay (Haida Gwaii).

Following spread: Lava beds at Anhluut'ukwsim Lax̱mihl Angwinga'asanskwhl Nisg̱a'a (Nisg̱a'a Memorial Lava Bed Park).

"We are not apart from nature; we are a part *of* it. We are part of the same ecosystem. What's best for the ecosystem is therefore best for everything in it, us included."

—Mansell Griffin, Nisga'a Lisims Government's director of lands and resources, 2021

Gitwinksihlkw Canyon City
Ts'im K'ol'hl Da oots'ip
Fishery Bay
Laxgalts'ap
Greenville
T'áalan Stl'áng Lepas Bay
Masset
Gaw Tlagee
Old Massett
Burns Lake
Kitimat
Tsee-Motsa Kitamaat
q̓axλálisela Douglas Channel
Gardner Canal
HlGaagilda Skidegate
Txałgiu
Hartley Bay
Princess Royal Island
HECATE STRAIT
Huchsduwachsdu
Nuyem Jees
Kitlope Heritage Conservancy
Kiis Gwaay Burnaby Island
'Laanas Dagang.a Swan Bay
Klemdulxk Klemtu
Swindle Island
Gwaii Haanas
National Park Reserve and
Haida Heritage Site
Nuxalk Bella Coola
NUXALK RIVER
Wáglísla Bella Bella
Koeye Conservancy
Calvert Island
Smith Inlet
T'akus Takush
Ba'as
Blunden Harbour
U'kwanalis
Kingcome
Viner
Sound
Tsawatti
Knight Inlet
Tsulquate
Port Hardy
Gwa-yas-dums
Gilford Island
Port McNeill
'Yalis
Alert Bay
JOHNSTONE STRAIT
Loughborough
Inlet
Glamax'tw
Tyee Spit
Campbell
River
Tsable River
Area Enlarged
Canada
YT
NT
NU
BC
AB
SK
MB
ON
QC
NL
NB
PE
NS
Hudson
Bay
Vancouver
Ottawa
Toronto
Pacific
Ocean
Atlantic
Ocean
USA

A Unique and Wondrous Place

The central and north coast of what settlers refer to as British Columbia in Canada, a vast region which spans the homelands of more than two dozen First Nations, is one of the largest remaining coastal temperate rainforests in the world. In their co-authored essay "From Conflict to Collaboration," Arthur Sterritt and Merran Smith describe that unique and wondrous place, and its people, this way:[1]

> Extending from Bute Inlet north to the British Columbia–Alaska border, and including Haida Gwaii, [the area comprises] 74,000 square kilometres (28,500 square miles). Here, trees up to one thousand years old tower as high as skyscrapers. Valley bottoms sustain more biomass than any other terrestrial ecosystem on earth. Streams and rivers sustain twenty per cent of the world's wild salmon. Forests, marine estuaries, inlets, and islands support tremendous biological diversity, including grizzly bears, black bears, white Kermode bears (also known as Spirit Bears), unique wolf populations, six million migratory birds, and a multitude of unique botanical species.
>
> For millennia, these riches of the [forest] have supported equally rich human cultures. The central and north coast and the archipelago of Haida Gwaii are the unceded traditional territory of more than two dozen coastal First Nations. Historically, First Nations carefully managed the abundant natural resources of both land and sea, relying on their knowledge of seasonal cycles to harvest a wide variety of resources without depleting them. They had absolute power over their traditional territories, resources and right to govern, to make and enforce laws, to decide citizenship and to manage their lands, resources and institutions.

Place Names and Frequently Used Terms

Places and place names

Various villages, towns, cities, and geographic locations are mentioned in this book. In the interests of space, narrative flow, and avoiding repetition, I have not specifically described where these places are every time. Many readers will be familiar with some of them already, of course. To assist those who are not, a map has been included on page x. I have also used original names for places as much as possible; these names have not been displaced by the application of non-Indigenous names and are still in current use. Existing geographic place names are also included for ease of reference.

There is one name I have refrained from using for the most part and that is the term "The Great Bear Rainforest." It is not an Indigenous name, but a term coined in the late 1990s by the environmental movement on the west coast of Canada. The intention was to raise local and international awareness of this ecologically threatened region on the central and north coast of what is now known as British Columbia, and to build support for protecting it from unsustainable resource extraction, especially logging of the area's old-growth forests.

In the course of writing this book, very few people I interviewed used this term. Whereas some embrace it, I learned that it is not a name that is appreciated by all First Nations people in relation to their homelands in this part of the province. Some of the people who shared their stories in this book had great difficulty with the term because of painful experiences they associate with it. To respect that reality, I have opted not to use the term except where it forms part of the name of an organization, an agreement, regulation, or statute, or in one case, the name of a film.

Language and orthography

The orthography (spelling and fonts) of original Indigenous languages continues to evolve over time. Indigenous people are engaged in language reclamation work with Elders who have retained their languages. Increasingly they are able to access and interpret archival records of their languages, which allows them to re-establish correct original orthographies through technology that is becoming more sophisticated. For example, although it has been common to write Tsimshian in the past, it is now more appropriate to write Ts'msyen. Where once we might have written Liqwiltokw, as you will see in Chapter Six, it now appears as Ligʷiłdaxʷ.

For the purposes of this book, I accept complete responsibility and apologize wholeheartedly for any spellings or orthographies I have used that are out-of-date or incorrect. I encourage readers to do their own research and seek the necessary permissions if wishing to use these terms. For those to whom some of the terms may be new or unfamiliar, audio clips on the "First Voices" website offer the opportunity to hear the correct pronunciation of words and phrases and to learn their meanings.

Frequently used terms

Various terms are also repeated in almost every story. For the same reasons given relating to place names, I have set out here brief explanations of the most common terms rather than repeat them in each of the stories. In the capitalization of various terms throughout the book, Gregory Younging's *Elements of Indigenous Style: A Guide for Writing By and About Indigenous Peoples* has been used for guidance.

- Aboriginal Title and law: The Aboriginal Title and Rights of the Indigenous Peoples of Canada are recognized in Section 35 of the *Constitution Act* of 1982. Aboriginal law refers to jurisprudence within the colonial legal system of Canada that describes and determines where, what, and how Aboriginal Title and Rights may be exercised. Original Indigenous laws, some of which are described in this book, predate Canada's legal system and have not been usurped by it.
- Department of Indian Affairs (DIA): The federal government ministry with responsibility for policies relating to Indigenous Peoples in Canada was split into two departments in 2017. Responsibilities are now divided between Crown-Indigenous Relations and Northern Affairs Canada (CIRNAC) and Indigenous Services Canada (ISC). It is referenced in this book as DIA (Department of Indian Affairs).
- Eulachon: There are numerous different English spellings (such as oolichan) for this small anadromous fish that migrates annually upstream in the spring to spawn in many coastal rivers in British Columbia. They are prized by First Nations for their social, trade, and nutritional values. Their name in the relevant language is used by interviewee preference in different chapters.
- Guardians, Guardian Watchmen, Indigenous Guardians: Some of the people in this book have been or continue to work as Guardians for their Nations. These Guardians monitor, manage, and steward their lands and waters on behalf of their Nations. They are often referred to as the "eyes and ears" of their Nations out in their territories. Some operate in networks, for example, through the Coastal First Nations Great Bear Initiative[2] and the Ha-ma-yas Stewardship Network.[3]

- Hereditary Chief(s): Whereas most First Nations are governed by an elected Chief and Council (see below) the vital role of hereditary chieftainship has never been displaced by the *Indian Act* system (again, see below). The term "hereditary Chief," however, is in itself an impoverished English rendering of what is in reality a far more complex, sophisticated, and generous system of inherited or transmitted responsibilities for the wellbeing of both people and places. That can best be understood by reading what people have to say about the role in these stories, explained in their terms rather than mine.
- Indian reserve, Indian Band, Band Council, Chief Councillor, Chief and Council: these are all statutory terms under the 1867 *Indian Act* of Canada and included here to provide context to the content of the stories in this book.
  - "Indians" are people registered as "Indians" under the *Indian Act*, and Indian Bands are registered groups of such individuals, often called members.
  - Reserves or Indian reserves are parcels of land held in the name of the federal government and set aside under the *Indian Act* for use by Indian Bands.
  - Band Councils govern the reserve lands and the Band. Their members are typically elected. Councils are normally headed by elected Chiefs or Chief Councillors.
- Potlatch: Each Nation has its own term for the Potlatch, an event that is commonly misunderstood by non-Indigenous people. Deeply significant, a Potlatch can be held for many different cultural reasons, including recognizing life events, decision-making, conflict avoidance and resolution, problem solving, justice, the passing forward of names, and other such matters.
- Indian residential school system: the government-sanctioned system that forcibly removed Indigenous children from their homes and sent them to church-run institutions, often far from home, where many of them suffered terrible abuse. Thousands did not survive.[4]

Difficult content and caring for yourself

The stories in this book include content that could trigger a range of feelings and thoughts. Difficult topics are discussed or briefly mentioned that may surface trauma, including residential schools, Sixties Scoop, addictions, environmental devastation, and missing and murdered Indigenous women and girls. Indigenous people who need additional support within Canada can contact the Hope for Wellness Help Line at 1-855-242-3310. Non-Indigenous people may wish to access mental health supports available in their province or country.

FOREWORD

We Have Always Been Here

My name is Dallas Smith. I am a citizen of the Tlowitsis Nation, connected to the homelands of the Kwak̓wala-speaking peoples that span the southern portion of the central and north coast of what is referred to as the province of British Columbia, in Canada. My mother comes from Ha̲xwa'mis (Wakeman Sound) and Tsax̱is (Fort Rupert). My father comes from Gwa-yas-dums (Gilford Island) and Qalagwees (Turnour Island). I was born and raised in the town of White Rock, near Vancouver, and only came to live in my territory in my early twenties. It has always been my ancestral home; this is the place that I say I am from.

Our people have protected and managed our territories for fourteen thousand years and more. We have always been a functioning and thriving part of the ecosystems we live within and have sustained ourselves from them throughout that whole time, keeping our lands and waters and ourselves healthy and strong.

Much of that was interrupted by the colonization of Canada and its impacts on us, on our autonomy, our resilience, our fluency in our languages, and more than one hundred years of being disconnected from our stewardship of our homelands and the ways in which we took care of each other. That part of our history is better understood these days by Canadians. What is less well-known is that our people have for decades been working unceasingly to reconnect to our lands and waters and our Indigenous ways of being and to reassume our rightful place in our territories. The door to so much positive change has opened as a result of all that work. This more contemporary history provides important context to the individual stories in this book.

I also believe that this journey we have been taking over the past few decades needs to be understood as part of our broader story as Indigenous Peoples in Canada. That is because, as author Katherine Palmer Gordon writes in the Gwa'sala-'Nakwaxda'xw story in Chapter Two: "This is a story of defiance of seemingly impossible odds and of overcoming the worst of human experiences. It is a story of courage, strength, resilience, and determination. Above all, it is a story of the triumph of culture over colonization, hope over great hardship, and love over immense loss."

I could not agree more. The journey has been a powerful but challenging one, but the destination looks more promising than it has for a long time. Non-Indigenous people, companies, organizations, and governments are finally understanding and accepting the work we are doing to return to that way of living in our homelands and restoring our stewardship roles within them. I am really proud to have been part of the journey and the work since the beginning, despite the challenges. Let me tell you a little bit of that story and about some of those challenges.

In 1992 the government of British Columbia announced the start of a new lands and resource management planning approach for the province, including the central and north coast. Competition and conflict over access to the valuable natural resources of this region[5] had existed since the earliest days of colonization. But as the turn of the twenty-first century approached, tensions were steadily increasing between government land-use regulators, the environmental sector, and resource industries, who all had different ambitions for the area.

By that time, our homelands had already begun to show scary evidence of the impact of the post-colonial approach to resource management. Our old-growth forests were under threat from commercial logging as forestry companies pushed hard into the region from the south. Water quality was suffering. Wildlife populations had started to fall dramatically. Commercial fishing became more and more of a struggle. Every First Nations community in the region was suffering economically, with unemployment rates averaging seventy per cent, and in some places, as much as eighty per cent.

As part of the work to develop land and resource management plans (the LRMP process), the provincial government said that it would consult public stakeholders for input into how plans in their regions should operate. They included First Nations in that category, despite the fact that we had never ceded our Rights and Title in our territories. We have never

Coast Funds chair Dallas Smith

considered ourselves to be mere stakeholders. We have always been governments of our territories and we certainly didn't intend to approach the LRMP discussions on anything other than a government-to-government basis. Our perspective on land and resource planning and use in our homelands was also simple: return autonomy and responsibility for resource management and protection in our territories to us.

This was before the days of the *Delgamuukw* decision[6] in the Supreme Court of Canada, however, and as far as the government was concerned—at least at the beginning—we were just another group they had to talk to. By 1995 the consultation process was under way, and I was appointed as a Kwakwaka'wakw representative. It was a real eye-opener for me, learning about how many different groups were in our traditional territories and what they were doing there. It wasn't just resource extraction industries like logging and commercial fishing companies. There were commercial marine operators, recreational groups, tourism operators, municipalities, environmentalists, and community groups, among others, and they all wanted different things out of our homelands. Most of all, they didn't want anyone to get in the way of them doing those things. That included First Nations.

For our people, these were simply places that sustained us and always have. We went to different places where we could get halibut or dig for shellfish. We harvested trees for our Big Houses or for other cultural purposes. Often we just harvested the bark or single planks and left the trees living and healthy. We hunted animals for food. We respected all of these living things and we never took too much. We knew where to go, what to look for, what to leave alone, how to behave respectfully in our natural world. We knew what was required to manage these areas so as to continue to sustain us over the long term as well as future generations of our people.

For us, it was a way of behaving in our homelands that assumed we are a part of the natural world, not separate from it. These days that approach is sometimes described as "ecosystem-based management" or EBM. EBM recognizes and embraces human interaction with the ecosystems we live in rather than excluding human activity. But long before it was called that, in our ways of protecting and using our resources, First Nations were employing ecosystem-based management as a resource sustainability strategy.

It is a way of thinking that is not just about conservation—as that term typically gets used in the context of land protection—but also about managing resource extraction and use and human wellbeing as inseparable parts of a whole rather than in silos. How can you treat conservation and human use of natural resources as separate things and still keep the land healthy? This is the way of thinking we brought to the LRMP process.

We also realized we needed to be proactive rather than reactive. We had to be able to say to the government, "We aren't here just to answer *your* questions. Here are our questions, and *you* need to answer them before you plan on doing anything in our territories." To be able to do that we needed our own territorial land-use and marine plans so that we could make decisions about whether or not to support other activities in our homelands.

Of course, this same way of thinking, about how lands and people and wellbeing are interconnected, underpinned all of our plans. That was true even if we had different approaches in our territories and different strengths and diverse ways of managing our challenges. If your community was located in a heavily industrialized place like Campbell River or the Kitimat Valley, you faced different considerations than a Nation living in a place like Hartley Bay or Bella Bella or Klemtu. But ultimately we all had the same vision of healing ourselves and protecting our territories, exercising our autonomy, improving our cultural, social, and physical wellbeing, and regaining, in contemporary terms, the levels of prosperity that we had always enjoyed prior to colonization.

Many of us spent the best part of a decade discussing with the provincial government and the environmentalists, and all of these other stakeholders, how to achieve that vision in our territories and to advance the human wellbeing of our communities. Finally, in 2006, the provincial government committed to end logging in more than two million hectares of the region, roughly one-third of the total area, protecting the forest in new conservancies and biodiversity areas which supported cultural uses and sustainable economic activities by the First Nations.

Let me be clear. That wasn't a perfect outcome by any means. Most of that protection took place in the northern part of the region despite efforts to protect the important places in the south as well. The government was not prepared to halt logging in Knight Inlet, for example. To say that remains a sore point with the Nations from that area is a huge understatement. The K̲wik̲wa̲sut̓inux̲w Hax̲wa'mis Nation, for example, say they feel excluded from and utterly betrayed by the process. This remains a source of continuing pain for them as they witness the ongoing extraction of resources from and degradation of the ecosystems in their homelands.

Another outcome of the work was the establishment through various partnerships of an organization called Coast Funds. Working with private donors we raised $60 million for a new conservation fund in the names of First Nations with territories spanning the region. We were able to match this with contributions from the governments of BC and Canada to create another $60 million fund for the First Nations to invest in sustainable economic development.

It was a completely novel approach called conservation financing or "project finance for permanence" (PFP), a model described in environmental terms as being "designed to create the conditions needed for permanent, sustainable conservation of globally important ecosystems." Coast Funds, of which I took on the role of chair in 2021, is the world's first PFP initiative. It was also an important stepping-stone to help us to put back into action our own ways of taking care of our territories and of ourselves, using all of the principles and values our Elders have passed down to us over millennia and applying them to our twenty-first-century realities.

In the fifteen years since it was established, Coast Funds has attracted global interest as a model that is being replicated in other parts of the world. There is good reason for that interest. By the beginning of 2022 the First Nations had invested over $100 million of our funds in more than four hundred conservation and sustainable economic development initiatives in our homelands, including habitat restoration, establishment of stewardship and integrated resource management departments and Guardian programs, business and community planning, acquisition of tourism and sustainable forestry businesses, shellfish aquaculture start-ups, and much more. We have also leveraged more than three times as much independent investment through external partnerships. The revenues from those investments are helping pay for cultural, social, and environmental programs in our communities, as well as educational scholarships and job training opportunities.

These are all outstanding achievements. But again, as all too often is the case in reaching these types of agreements and outcomes, the price has been too high for some. In the establishment of Coast Funds, the private funders who contributed capital were very focussed on protected areas and on the implementation of EBM, so signing on to the new provincial land-use plans was a condition of accessing that capital. Not every First Nation thought that was appropriate, especially if those plans did not include sufficient protection of their homelands, and some rejected the condition.

Unsurprisingly, given their experience in those years, the K̲wik̲wa̱sut̓inux̱w Hax̱wa'mis Nation was among those Nations who resisted the condition strongly. As a result, for more than a decade they did not have access to any conservation funds nor a significant portion of the economic development fund. In 2019 the K̲wik̲wa̱sut̓inux̱w Hax̱wa'mis Nation signed the Hith'alis Agreement with the BC government setting out principles for EBM implementation in their territory. That not only unlocked their allocation of provincial government funding for the first time but garnered an additional contribution to Coast Funds to build their new stewardship endowment. They are working now to grow their funds, start a Guardian program, educate private funders about the need to change colonial approaches to funding—the difference that will make to First Nations is phenomenal, as the story of Nawalakw that Maxwiyalidizi K'odi Nelson recounts in Chapter Ten shows—and reach further agreements with the province on the recognition of their Rights and Title, amongst many other initiatives that they are leading.

It is also important to understand the decision to enter into the Hith'alis Agreement was not made lightly by the K̲wik̲wa̱sut̓inux̱w Hax̱wa'mis. Private donors yet again did not contribute to the new stewardship endowment for the K̲wik̲wa̱sut̓inux̱w Hax̱wa'mis. There are also several other Nations that still have no access to a conservation endowment, despite signing land-use agreements and agreeing to EBM principles.

All of this illustrates why, as I have already noted, we are neither at the beginning of this story nor the end. There remains a great deal of reconciliation and healing to do, as people like K̲ii'iljuus (Barbara Wilson) tells author Katherine Palmer Gordon in the Introduction to this book.

Barbara also emphasizes that to be meaningful, reconciliation is not about making peace with other governments but about re-establishing our essential connections to our homelands. At this stage of the story, all of the First Nations are continuing the journey toward that vision of reconciliation and reconnection to our lands in different ways and on our terms. The story now is also about the next generation. The "elder statesmen" of that early work are all still doing what they can to better the lives of their people. Now, the next generation is stepping up to the plate to do the work: people like Wei Wai Kum Chief Councillor and economic development professional Christopher Roberts; Jess H̓áusṫI, a formidable force to be dealt with; and Trevor Russ, vice-president, Council of the Haida Nation.

We also have so many young people becoming fully qualified as Guardians of our homelands, our "eyes and ears" on the lands and waters, implementing our land- and marine-use plans through the Nations' Guardian stewardship programs. Many of them were out-of-work commercial fishermen when they started earning their technical stewardship qualifications, so they already knew the territory very well. That's been such a success and we are so proud of that transition. More and more of our young people are also earning university degrees and doctorates in science, engineering, accounting, and business. It's heartwarming, inspiring, and exciting.

When you talk to the First Nations in our homelands these days, the kinds of stories you hear are the personal stories that showcase this incredible journey we have all taken in the last few decades and the vision for the future. Indigenous people are doing this in diverse ways, including the people whose voices Katherine has brought to the pages of this beautiful book. These individuals talk about their connection to their homelands and their Nations' efforts to increase the wellbeing of those homelands and their people through careful stewardship and thoughtful investments. They talk about the cultural significance of their work. Most of all, they reflect on their dreams for the future. They are mindful of ensuring that the generations following in their footsteps will thrive in their homelands as our ancestors have always done since time immemorial.

As the shared and unique histories I have already recounted and all these stories illustrate, this is not an easy journey, nor is it one in which every Nation or every individual chooses to follow the same route. In "A Different Life," for example, Haisla Chief Crystal Smith describes her drive as a young, passionate leader to help her Nation overcome and heal from the devastating environmental, cultural, and social impacts of overwhelming land loss and industrialization in Haisla territory. Crystal talks about what makes her who she is and some of the many challenges she has faced, both as an individual and a leader.

Everyone makes their own decisions about what pathway to take to wellbeing in their territories, and Crystal and the people in whose footsteps she is following have made theirs. Most readers of this book will be familiar with the Haisla Nation's decision, made before Crystal became Chief in 2017, to work toward healing and restoration of the wellbeing of their people by investing in a liquid natural gas (LNG) partnership in their territory. That approach has set the Haisla apart from many other First Nations. The cost has been high to all concerned in terms of their connections with each other.

As Katherine points out in other chapters, many Indigenous Peoples, including the Gitga'at, the Haíłzaqv Nation, and the Council of the Haida Nation, have fought strenuously against oil or gas development in or potentially affecting their homelands. They have done so both in court and on the front lines of protests against heavy industrial development in their territories. The painful consequences of these opposing forces continue to be writ large in terms of damaged relationships and disputes between the Nations and individuals concerned.

It is important, I believe, for readers of this book to understand these challenges and their consequences, and to acknowledge the intensely painful part that the impacts of colonization continue to play in the lives of all of the Indigenous people who share their stories in this book. Wei Wai Kum Chief Councillor Christopher Roberts' community in Campbell River, for example, is also surrounded by commercial and industrial development. As he points out in "A Ligʷiłdaxʷ Bottom Line," nothing could have prepared him for just how challenging it would be to take on the role of Chief Councillor and implement his vision for a future in which the cultural, environmental and economic wellbeing of his community would be seamlessly woven together. "The challenge for us," says Christopher, "is how we strike that balance of a strong cultural identity, rooted in all those values that set us apart, without it being all about commerce and being successful economically. Every Nation has this dilemma, but I think that being in such an intense urban setting adds another dynamic altogether."

Facing page: Salmon travelling upriver, north central coast of BC.

By contrast, in "A Voice for the Bears" Katherine describes how members of the Kitasoo/Xai'xais Nations, including ten-year-old Mercedes Robinson Neasloss, explained at a public hearing held in their community of Klemtu that fossil fuel development in or near their territory would threaten their whole way of life, and argued that no such development should ever take place in or near their homelands. Similarly, in "Haíɫzaqv Unfettered," the trauma experienced by the Haíɫzaqv Nation after an oil spill near a sacred site in their territory illustrates why people like Jess H̓áusi̓I, Chief Marilyn Slett, and the other individuals in that story have fought so hard against oil and gas development on the coast.

The people in all of the stories in this book, including the individuals who share their stories in "Stl'mstaliwa—The Whole Human Experience" and "The Work of Tx̱eemsim," disparate as they all are in the approaches they have taken to wellbeing, have a common thread that binds them: their understanding of the integral interconnection of people, land, and wellbeing. They also demonstrate in their different ways the opportunities that await us as we reconnect to our homelands and regain our wellbeing as Indigenous Peoples.

The work that everyone is doing is not just challenging, but inspiring and powerful. It is truly my honour to stand among so many people whom I hold in the highest respect as they share their stories of resiliency and power in this book. Reading them gives me great hope for the future and for all of our generations yet unborn. Gilakas'la!

—Dallas Smith, 2022

INTRODUCTION

This Place Is Who We Are

In 2007, I was introduced by my friend and colleague David Mannix to the central and north coast region of what is referred to as British Columbia, including X̱aaydaga Gwaay.yaay/X̱aayda Gwaay (Haida Gwaii), and the wonderful people living in that region.

Dave, who was the first chief executive of Coast Funds, asked me to help with some of the work required to get the still relatively new organization up to full speed. Working with Dave and his small team of staff over the next eight years, I travelled many times from my home on Gabriola Island, near Nanaimo on Vancouver Island, to visit communities in the region. There I witnessed firsthand the work Indigenous Peoples in those communities are doing to improve the lives and wellbeing of their people and of the health of the environment in which they live.

These visits were educational, awe-inspiring, heart-warming, and motivational. At times, they were heartbreaking; from many of the people I was privileged to meet I learned about the continuing, debilitating, and often tragic impacts of colonial policies and actions upon them and their communities. So much healing is still required in these communities from the consequences of colonization, a reality that is all too often overlooked by their non-Indigenous neighbours.

"Sometimes it's hard to understand the extent of the healing that is needed," reflects K̲ii'iljuus (Barbara Wilson), "when what people mostly see are such dynamic, energetic leaders fighting so powerfully for our rights and speaking with such enthusiasm about the work we are doing to reconnect to our lands. But the need for healing and recovery is immense." The X̱aayda, and all the other First Nations connected to the central and north coast, are also driven in their work by their passion for their future generations, says Barbara. "I have one great-granddaughter already and another on the way. I don't want the land left in a mess for them. That's certainly my driver. That's why I am doing this work."

During my visits to the region, I witnessed just what such passionate people can achieve despite the challenges that face them when they have a clear vision, the will, and the opportunity to be—as 'Cúagilákv Jess H̓áusi̓I puts it in Chapter Four of this book—completely unfettered in their identity and ways of being. I heard stories that were tragic. I also heard many that were immensely uplifting. I met cultural leaders on the frontlines of revitalizing their languages, teaching their children and youth their history, reconnecting their people to their identity, and helping them heal from the past. I listened to devoted Chiefs, Elders, and other leaders who had such love in their hearts for their communities it was impossible not to be moved by their words.

In 2015 I told Merv Child, then the chair of Coast Funds, that I would like to write a book sharing these important stories through the voices of the people involved. Merv, a citizen of the Dzawada̱'enux̱w First Nation and a qualified lawyer, had been on the board of Coast Funds since its inception, and chair for eight years. Merv liked the idea of a book of this kind and enthusiastically encouraged me to do it.

Another four years would pass, however, before I finally sat down at my desk to begin work in earnest on this book. I opened a blank document on my laptop and typed at the top: "This Place Is Who We Are." That was only intended to be a working title until the book was completed. However, as a starting point, it was a phrase that captured neatly what I hoped the stories in the book would eventually convey in different ways: that people, the places that they and their forebears are from, and the wellbeing of both—physical, social, environmental, economic, spiritual, and cultural—are inseparable.

As is evident, *This Place Is Who We Are* became the final title. For the Indigenous people whose voices grace these pages, it is crystal-clear that the places they are from are utterly embedded in their identity. Taking care of their homelands, based on ancient values and ways of being and behaving toward their natural environment and each other, is as natural as breathing to them; the connection between people and place and wellbeing an everyday reality.

Indeed, the interconnection of people and place, and humanity's intimate relationship with our natural environment, are concepts so utterly

Gunner Point, in Sunderland Channel looking west toward Johnstone Strait (just north of Sayward/ Kelsey Bay).

fundamental in an Indigenous framework they essentially go without saying; or they would, if not for the evidence that much of the non-Indigenous world appears to have largely forgotten those concepts. The term "resource management" in its deployment in western governance has instead become synonymous with exploitation over sustenance and short-term profit over planning for the future. This is a recipe, if it continues unchecked, for an inevitable ecological and human disaster of epic proportions.

"We're in such a crisis in the world globally," observes renowned ethnobotanist Nancy J. Turner, professor emeritus at the University of Victoria, who has worked with many Indigenous Peoples over the course of her distinguished career. "In our western mainstream society, we're very self-satisfied that we have all the answers when we don't, and we're paying for it in all of these different ways now. It's like a pandemic of environmental loss and destruction. We have to change our ways. We have to be less acquisitive of things and we have to change our values, what we see as important in life, and start valuing nature more."

The twenty-first-century consequences of accelerating climate change have been brutally illustrated in recent times. Devastating wildfires raged through British Columbia in the summer of 2021, and flooding and mudslides took lives, destroyed homes, and severely damaged significant provincial transportation infrastructure in November that year. Unsustainable resource extraction and use is rapidly reaching a point of no return. There has never been a greater incentive for human beings to reflect on our collective and individual approaches to the natural environment.

It is also more than time to look to proven success in that regard. In November 2019 researchers at the University of British Columbia in Vancouver published a study demonstrating that lands managed and protected by Indigenous Peoples enjoy as much as forty per cent greater biodiversity than those managed by non-Indigenous government agencies and organizations.[7] In an article published a few months later, co-authors La'goot Spencer Greening, a Gitga'at doctoral scholar, Jess H̓áust̓I, and Nicole Morven from the Nisg̱a'a Nation—all of whom share their stories in this book—pointed out:[8] It's worth noting a key difference between Western and Indigenous resource management practices: Indigenous practices have been tested and refined over millennia; Western practices in North America go back less than five hundred years...for over fourteen thousand years in North America, Indigenous peoples were able to live in ways that did not threaten ecosystems and food populations like we see today."

In "A Voice for the Bears" Kitasoo/Xai'xais stewardship officer Vernon Brown re-emphasizes that point. "Our environmental and cultural laws didn't come into existence overnight. Along the way, there's been a lot of learning—from observation, trial and error, and from events beyond anyone's control." Human nature being what it is, says Vernon, Indigenous people made mistakes just like anyone else. "We have stories of famine, of war, floods, of overuse, and of hard lessons learned." But through all of that learning, his ancestors adapted as the landscape and the oceans changed. "Today, we're still adapting to change. For example, we now have to be adaptive conservationists because so many of our resources have been taken from the ocean and from our forests. We have no choice but to adapt and to keep adapting."

It is an adaptive approach that has also been forced to deal with what Nancy Turner describes as "invisible loss"[9]: the impacts of colonial decision-making and resource management policy on cultural values and lifestyle, on traditional knowledge, on identity, and on physical and emotional wellbeing. “Invisible losses [are] by their very nature unrecognized and unacknowledged. Acknowledging, respecting, and addressing the historical, current, and potential future invisible losses of First Nations communities is essential to sustainability,” Turner concludes unequivocally, “for all of us.”

It is clear that none of the stories in this book can be told without recounting these kinds of losses, all linked to the impacts of colonization. Since the arrival of European settlers in the 1600s, and continuing today, Indigenous Peoples in Canada have survived genocidal government policy, mass expropriation of land, denial of identity, the atrocities of the residential school system, grievous racism, and a systematic assault on culture, language, and original Indigenous laws, governance, and practices. As Jess Ḣáusƛ̓ points out, it remains a continuing struggle to recover from all of this while at the same time trying to work toward a better future. These efforts are further embattled whenever some fresh trauma hits an Indigenous community, as in 2016, for example, when an articulated barge carrying 100,000 litres of diesel fuel and oil sank at Q̓vúqvái (Gale Pass), an immensely important Haíɫzaqv food-harvesting and cultural site.

“I realized at that time,” says Jess, “that you can’t separate the really difficult and traumatic parts of our history as a people, the ways in which we’ve been regulated off our own territory since contact and the ways that social and cultural systems have been fragmented by colonization, from the way we respond to situations like that happening.” That is equally true of how Indigenous Peoples approach better environmental management in their territories, and the improved wellbeing of their people in a contemporary context.

In the face of all this, to describe their resilience as remarkable is a massive understatement. Although the age-old adaptive stewardship practices and responsibilities that Vernon Brown describes were severely disrupted by the policies and laws of colonizing governments, Indigenous Peoples have steadfastly held onto much of their ancient knowledge and the laws that have governed their ways of life since time immemorial. With increasing strength in recent decades, using all the tools at their disposal and building on all the work their forebears have already done in this regard, they have continued the work of reconnecting to their homelands and restoring and healing them from the environmental impacts of colonization.

They are also exercising those original roles and practices and approaching conservation, sustainable resource use and development, and community wellbeing as a natural whole rather than as separate or distinct objectives. They are functioning, as Mansell Griffin points out in Chapter Three, as part of their ecosystems rather than separately from them, interacting intimately with the resources available to nurture and sustain them and employing management principles and practices that ensure there will always be sufficient resources not only for themselves but for future generations.

The personal stories shared in this book showcase all of these ways of thinking, values, ideas, challenges, and opportunities, in various rich and illuminating ways. In "Stl'mstaliwa—The Whole Human Experience," cultural teacher Snxakila (Clyde Tallio), describes his pathway to stl'mstaliwa, the full human experience of being in balance physically, emotionally, intellectually and spiritually. "We believe that every human being should strive to be in balance, not only with themselves but with the environment, in all of those four ways," he says.

Gwa'sala-'Nakwaxda'xw hereditary and former elected Chief Paddy Walkus talks in "This Sacred Connection" about his personal journey to recovery from the impacts of government oppression and how he has devoted more than forty years of his life to leading his people along a pathway to healing and prosperity. "Our old people gave us guidance in how to survive," says Paddy. "I believe it is so critical for our people that we go back to those values and teachings. Everything we do must be sustainable. We cannot just take and take. Everything must still be here one thousand years from now."

In "Our Homelands Build Us Up and Make Us Strong," multiple X̲aayda voices explain what their Rediscovery camps are doing to heal and empower their youth by reconnecting them to their lands and waters. "The difference that Rediscovery makes is huge," observes Gwaliga Hart. "The children find their voice; they find the pride within themselves and who they are in their culture." Children who are healthy and self-confident, he believes, are the future champions of not only X̲aayda Gwaay but the world. "They can be whatever and whoever they want to be." Similarly, Jess H̓áusƚI talks in "Haíłzaqv Unfettered" about her vision that future generations will never suffer the impacts of colonization but instead will be free to exercise their cultural and environmental laws with pride and power. "When I think about the future for my kids," says Jess, "I am unbelievably happy. It is such a gift to be Haíłzaqv, in all the ways that manifests in their lives."

Nisg̱a'a fisheries monitoring coordinator Nicole Morven speaks about her work for the Nisg̱a'a Nation in "The Work of Tx̱eemsim" and reflects upon the ancient relationship of Nisg̱a'a people with salmon, Saak (eulachon or oolichan) and other fish species of K̲'alii-Aksim Lisims (the Nass River). Her relationship with K̲'alii-Aksim Lisims as a descendant of Tx̱eemsim, the supernatural being who brought light and hope to the Nisg̱a'a in time immemorial, is both ancestral and existential. "The river and the fish are in my bones," she says simply.

In "A Ligʷiłdaxʷ Bottom Line," Wei Wai Kum Chief Christopher Roberts describes the challenges and opportunities of an urban First Nation looking for a pathway to prosperity while protecting the environment and along with it ancient Ligʷiłdaxʷ history and living cultural values. "It was clear to me from the beginning," observes Christopher, "that reconciling who the Wei Wai Kum are as Indigenous people and our ambitions for prosperity, wellbeing and self-determination could not be focussed solely on our participation in the economy." Haisla Chief Councillor Crystal Smith also describes her drive as a leader to overcome the environmental, cultural, and social impacts of overwhelming land loss and industrialization in Haisla territory, in "A Different Life." It's not an easy role. "It's a rollercoaster," she admits. "You have your good times and you have your bad times. But every day, I get a reminder of why I love what I do. For me, ultimately, it is my opportunity to help change our story."

"The Children Are Our Reason for Breathing" is about the efforts of Dzawada̱'enux̱w hereditary Chief Maxwiyalidizi K'odi Nelson to build a healing centre and ecolodge in K̲wik̲wa̱sut̓inux̱w Ha̱x̱wa'mis homelands, combining revenues from the lodge with social and environmental programs for Musgamakw Dzawada̱'enux̱w youth and adults alike. "I ran away from wellness in my own life for so many years," says K'odi. "Having seen what being out on the land could do, and the healing that gave me, I wanted to share that with our people and our children."

"A Voice for the Bears" centres on young Kitasoo/Xai'xais woman Mercedes Robinson Neasloss, who embodies all the power and strength of her ancestors. Mercedes has worked hard to give a voice to the wildlife and, in doing so, to the Nation she hopes to serve one day in the future (possibly as a teacher—at this stage of her life, it is difficult to know what path she will follow). She is certain of one thing, however. "The biggest lessons in my life so far," she said in 2020, "are to always respect the territory, and to protect the land and the bears, because we have so much to learn from them, and so that future generations will always have the opportunity to enjoy what we have."

Finally, in "Gugwilx'ya'ansk—We Are Living It," Spencer Greening describes how he is working with his people to implement ayaawx and adaawx, Ts'msyen law and oral history. For Gitk'a'ata, this is based on inherited and learned responsibility rather than accumulation of individual wealth and power; wealth is measured by generosity rather than the accumulation of material goods. Community, environmental, and economic wellbeing are achieved through following Ts'msyen law and practice: just "living it" the Gitga'at way.

These stories celebrate resilience, healing, cultural strength, and love of land, identity, ancestors, and each other. Who these people are and what they have experienced is immensely inspiring. What they have to say is powerful and compelling. As humanity moves into the most challenging global environmental era that we have experienced in millennia, their love of the landscape and of their place in it offers a different and hopeful way to see the future: one in which we are able to successfully live with nature and use the planet's resources to sustain ourselves physically, culturally, and economically.

These are also all, ultimately, just beautiful stories about good people working hard for their communities, their homelands, the future and, as revered Gwawaenuk hereditary Chief Kwa̱nkwa̱nxwalege Wakas (Robert Joseph) says, "of all the generations yet unborn." There has never been a better time to listen to these voices, and their inspiring stories about how respect and love for the places that identify who they are will help sustain not only their people, but all of us.

—Katherine Palmer Gordon, 2022

Stl'mstaliwa—The Whole Human Experience

CHAPTER ONE

"In our It7Nuxalkmc language," says Snxakila, "'stl'mstaliwa' means to have the full human experience: to be physically, emotionally, intellectually, and spiritually balanced. We believe that every human being should strive to be in balance, not only with themselves but with the environment in all of those four ways."

Stl'mstaliwa is a foundational phrase in Snxakila's It7Nuxalkmc lexicon. It serves as a framework for a personal way of living and behaving. Stl'mstaliwa also speaks in fundamental terms to both his identity and his connection to the place that he is from. A citizen of the Nuxalk Nation, Snxakila was born in the Bella Coola valley and raised on reserve in the village of Q'umk'uts'. Located where the Nuxalk (Bella Coola) River empties into the North Bentinck Arm of Burke Channel, the small town of just over eight hundred residents has become the contemporary home of the Nuxalk Nation. Snxakila's forebears lived in Ats'aaxlh (South Inlet), in the village of Talyu, one of the four territories of the Nuxalk Nation.[10] As such, Snxakila is Talyuumc as well as Nuxalkmc.

Now in his mid-thirties, Snxakila is deeply engaged in his own personal journey of stl'mstaliwa. It is one that began nineteen years ago: an exploration into understanding not only who he is as a Nuxalkmc human being, but of the landscape in which he and his fellow Nuxalkmc citizens and their ancestors before them have lived and thrived for millennia.

"The more teachings we hear, the more we potlatch and do ceremony and witness community, we really start to awaken. It is right there in the word stl'mstaliwa. It reminds us of what it means to be human beings, that we're constantly seeking to awaken. It is really beautiful."

—Snxakila (Clyde Tallio), Nuxalk Nation, January 2021

Facing page: Nascall Bay, Dean Channel, northeast of Bella Coola.

Snxakila (Clyde Tallio) speaking in the Thorsen Creek Conservancy, an area of cultural heritage significance to the Nuxalk.

It is a journey that has taken him back into his people's original history, empowering him to appreciate these things more fully and to see his place in the world increasingly clearly. "Nuxalk is the name of our river and so when we say we are Nuxalkmc," explains Snxakila, "we are saying we are the people of the Bella Coola River." In that name is embedded who the Nuxalk are and what connects them to the land. "When our migrating human ancestors settled here, it was this land that formed the Nuxalk culture, the Nuxalk way of being, the Nuxalk world view. When we walk this land, we are walking in the footprints of our ancestors. When we see our land, we see more than just a beautiful place. We see how it came to be this beautiful place through following those footprints and understanding the stories of our ancestors.

"In our tradition of smayusta, our ancestral creation stories," he continues, "we have origins for everything. In the very first part of our smayusta, it said that the territory, the land, the four realms, were all prepared for us. The spirit guardians, the animals, the birds, the sea life, the medicines, the trees, the plants, the soils, all were prepared and ready. Each in their own room in the Creator's house, the first ancestors were made. They were carved from the cosmic tree (the Milky Way), the tree of the upper world, the great tree of life, and were each given spirit and breath. The carvings came alive. These first ancestors were given names, tools, teachings, technologies, and when they were ready, the Creator told them to look to the walls of his house. Hanging on the walls were animal, bird and sea creature cloaks, the Crests. The first ancestors wrapped themselves in the cloaks and transformed. The Creator

opened the sky and, guided by the eyelashes of the sun, they descended to the mountaintops. They removed the cloaks, which floated back to the upper world.

"There were four generations of these supernatural ancestors, from the first to come to earth to the first to become mortal beings after the first generation. This reflects the four living generations in our society at any given time: the youth, from birth to twenty years of age; the working adults, from twenty to forty years of age; the leadership, from forty to sixty years of age; and the Elders after that," explains Snxakila. "Each of these phases of life carry names and roles with them, and as we grow, we pass those down to the next generation and move up to the following phase of our lives. This all stems from those first four generations as the smayusta describes them." As the first generation of ancestors came down from the mountains, says Snxakila, they created new names that reflected the lands they came to settle. "They found their places and built their houses, their fish weirs, and they began to prosper. They intermarried. The women

The community of Bella Coola lies at the mouth of the Nuxalk (Bella Coola) River, which empties into the North Bentinck Arm of Burke Channel.

moved from their villages to go to their husbands' villages; it was as if they carried a rope, fastening each village to one another. That in time formed our borders as a Nation: four territories unified by our language and our land and our tradition."

When Snxakila goes out into Nuxalkulmc, the ancestral territory of the Nuxalk, he sees all of that history and feels it within himself. "When I am out there, I realize that I am part of that continuous connection. To be in that long line of ancestors going all the way back, to be part of my generation now as a working adult is something that only a Nuxalkmc—someone whose family has existed continuously for thousands of years—can truly understand; that connection we feel to our lands, our waters, our territory, and the responsibility that goes with it. There is a reason and a significance for us to be born Nuxalkmc. Walking that path with our traditions, our teachings, our world view, and our language allows us to understand what it means to have that full human experience, stl'mstaliwa: to be Nuxalkmc and what it means to walk in this world."

For a Nuxalkmc citizen like Snxakila, "walking in the world" is a phrase imbued with this history. However, it is also saturated with the more recent difficult story of the Nuxalk Nation. The Nuxalkmc, Talyuumc, Kw'alhnamc and Ista-Sutslhmc once comprised a population of as many as thirty-five thousand people, but smallpox and other diseases introduced by nineteenth-century settlers to the west coast of British Columbia devastated the Nuxalk. By the early twentieth century, just three hundred survivors remained. Those individuals were forced out of their homes by the Department of Indian Affairs and resettled on a small reserve in Bella Coola. They were not allowed to return to live in Nuxalkulmc. (Subsequently, most of the lands within Nuxalkmc were sold to settlers or otherwise privatized through the granting of forestry or mining tenures, making it challenging, if not impossible, to return.)

They were also prohibited from engaging in their customary governance practices through which stataltmc (hereditary Chiefs) took responsibility for the care of the territory and the sustainable management of its resources and relations with their neighbouring Nations. Instead, they were subjected to the constraints of the *Indian Act*, initially under the charge of a government-appointed Indian Agent and later required to hold elections for Chief and Council to manage their reserve. Nuxalkmc were arrested and imprisoned if they attempted to lhlm (potlatch) in accordance

with their traditional ways of conducting community affairs. They were forbidden access to lawyers to defend their legal and human rights. They were not allowed to vote in either provincial or federal elections. Stl'mstaliwa—that full, beautiful, human experience—could barely be dreamed of, let alone embraced, in those dark decades.

In 2011, Snxakila was recognized as an alkw (official speaker) for the Nuxalkmc stataltmc.

By the time Snxakila was born in 1987, some of these things had been reversed in Canadian law, but the imposition of the settler government continued to plague the Nuxalk Nation. It still does. Environmental degradation brought about by industrial activity and unsustainable resource extraction in the region, over which the Nation has had little or no control, deeply challenges Nuxalkmc wellbeing. Commercial logging, fishing, and mining threaten culturally important places and food sources that the Nuxalk have depended on for millennia, physically, spiritually, culturally, and economically. Trees, medicinal plants, sputc (eulachon fish), salmon, shellfish, and the myriad of other creatures with which Nuxalkmc people coexist in their territory have all suffered from the impacts of these activities. As a result, so have the Nuxalk.

Snxakila is determined to do whatever he can to help restore the wellbeing of Nuxalkulmc and to help his Nation regain self-determination, to regain their rights and their connection to their land in ancestral terms, free of non-Nuxalk interference and control, and to exercise original, ancient stewardship roles and responsibilities in Nuxalkulmc. He has been working with his community and his Elders toward that goal since he was a teenager; but the seeds of his beliefs and values were sown even earlier.

Snxakila was the firstborn grandchild of his maternal grandparents, Gloria and Roger Tallio. In accordance with custom he was raised by Gloria and Roger, whom he describes as "the biggest influence" in his life. "They are both descendants of high-ranking forebears. We had a really strong cultural family continuing our traditions and keeping our connection to the land. My grandparents were always out in the territory, fishing and hunting. They are approaching their eighties now," says Snxakila, "but are still out there maintaining trails and cutting firewood. They still go fishing. They are really hardworking people and a good inspiration. Despite all the hardships they experienced in their generation, they raised us really well, with strong values and a good sense of our responsibilities."

Snxakila's grandmother Gloria only speaks English to him, although he recalls she understood It7Nuxalkmc, having spoken it fluently as a small girl. Gloria had been taken from her family and sent by the government to residential school in Alert Bay when she was just five years old. She could not overcome the trauma of being punished at school for speaking her mother tongue. She has never spoken it again.

On his grandfather's side, Snxakila's great-great-grandfather also suffered at the hands of the government. He was a Japanese Canadian commercial fisherman who lost everything he owned when he was interned, along with thousands of other Canadians of Japanese descent, during the Second World War. The resilience of his family, evidenced in their strong, healthy lives despite such trauma, helped create a foundation for Snxakila's generation to be successful, he says. "They made sure we are proud of who we are and of the work we do, what we do for the community. They instilled that strength in us."

At the beginning of Grade 10, Snxakila moved to Victoria, where his mother was living. There he befriended a Bhutanese lama, a Buddhist spiritual leader. Buddhist teachings resonated strongly with the teenager, who in turn shared stories with the lama about his Nuxalkmc culture. The lama suggested that Snxakila explore his roots more deeply. "He explained that your karma determines where you are born and there is merit to be discovered there," recalls Snxakila. "He encouraged me to look into the traditions that I was born into. So I decided that for my graduating year I would go back to Bella Coola and follow an interest I had in learning my language."

Snxakila and Ts'xwiixw (Megan Moody) at the Bella Coola River.

Within two months of his return, however, the eager student had already exhausted all the It7Nuxalkmc language materials available at the provincial high school. Recognizing Snxakila's enthusiasm and wanting to encourage it, his teacher invited the sixteen-year-old to join the adult classes he regularly attended with Elders over the fall and winter. Snxakila accepted the invitation immediately and loved every minute of the experience. That winter he was offered an after-school job recording Elders speaking, a part-time role that would, if he wished, become full-time when summer rolled around.

As graduation loomed, Snxakila started thinking about leaving Bella Coola again to go to university. Then, yet another offer sparked a different and life-changing decision. "Ximaltwa (Clarence Elliot) and his wife Ilistays (Beatrice) were language teachers at our Nuxalk Acwsalcta (Band-operated) school for thirty years," explains Snxakila. "After they retired, Clarence started working more at the cultural centre doing community language. They both sat me down one day just before graduation and asked me if I would be willing to stay in Bella Coola instead of going away to university. If I stayed they would put me through a traditional training course in the It7Nuxalkmc language."

Clarence pointed out to Snxakila that in his thirty years as a language teacher in the non-Indigenous provincial school system, he had been unable to produce a fluent speaker using that system of learning. "He said now that he had the time to do it properly he would like to train me in the

Snxakila, Ts'xwiixw (Megan Moody), and the Nuxalk community herald the return of the sputc in 2014 at the first annual sputc ceremony.

traditional way and that he would get a group of Elders to work with me. It would take several years, just like a university degree. It was an incredible offer." Snxakila accepted immediately and began working intensively with Clarence and Beatrice and the other Elders. He learned not only his language but its history. He was taught ceremony and all the nuances of the lhlm. He learned song composition and the different dialects of his language. He soaked it all up like a sponge.

In 2011, when Snxakila completed his training, the Nuxalkmc Elders and hereditary leaders considered him ready for a new and immensely important role as a Nuxalkmc alkw. An alkw is an official speaker for a staltmc (hereditary house) holding authority to conduct ceremony, working on behalf of the staltmc. Recognizing his enormous and passionate commitment to the work, the hereditary Chiefs formally conferred the status of alkw on Snxakila, signing a document that recognized him in that role not only for the staltmc that he belonged to but for all of the Nuxalkmc stataltmc. As an alkw, Snxakila would conduct his future work on behalf of all of his leaders. It was an acknowledgement of his hard work and achievement and an immense honour.

Snxakila at work on a Nuxalk exhibit at the American Museum of Natural History in New York City, 2019.

Being in the role requires Snxakila's close and active involvement with the Nuxalk community on a day-to-day basis. "I work with Elders in Potlatch ceremony. Potlatch is one of the biggest works that I do, but I also have worked with funerals and memorials. That's right from ceremony with the person to burial to the feast, working with family through grief. It's important that our community has that solid cultural support and that I do this work as an alkw, restoring history and ceremony, our essence of who we are as Nuxalkmc, and support the hereditary leaders in doing so."

Snxakila is not shy of hard work. On top of his It7Nuxalkmc studies, he obtained his teaching qualifications and was an instructor at the Nuxalk community Acwsalcta school and Lip'alhayc College for several years. While performing his duties as an alkw, he also became involved in museum and repatriation projects as a visiting scholar at the University of British Columbia in Vancouver. He is working with the American Museum of Natural History in New York City, directing the renewal and redesign of the Nuxalk section in their exhibit of the culture of the people of the Northwest coast. He is building a strong relationship in order to investigate opportunities to bring Nuxalkmc treasures in the museum's collection home, initially on loan and eventually permanently.

Well before then, however, all of his work became a platform from which to embark upon the next phase of his experience: bringing his knowledge to bear in a collaborative project, working with Nuxalkmc fisheries biologist Ts'xwiixw (Megan Moody) and the Nuxalk leadership and community to gather the Nation's collective knowledge, laws, and practices relating to sputc or eulachon. "That's when I really started doing governance work," recalls Snxakila, "when Megan invited me to contribute to the Nuxalk law component of the sputc project."

Alhqulh Ti Sputc, which was completed in 2017, is a comprehensive community-owned book that incorporates It7Nuxalkmc vocabulary and smayusta about sputc. It describes ancestral Nuxalkmc governance roles and practices in relation to the small and highly prized anadromous smelt fish and all aspects of community and territorial wellbeing connected to its care, harvesting and use. "It has always been our right to take care of the sputc in our territory," explains Snxakila, "but also our responsibility. Sputc are part of our smayusta, our origins, and our heritage. That is an ancient relationship." Smsmayamk ti sputc, one of the Nuxalkmc smayusta of the sputc, describes how Qwaxw (Raven) first brought the fish to Bella Coola in ancient times. Sputc has ever since been food, medicine, and a tradeable commodity for the Nuxalk. It can be eaten fresh, dried, smoked or salted. Its sluq' (grease) is renowned for its nutritional value and greatly prized by Indigenous Peoples throughout the coast and interior of what is today known as British Columbia. The ancient trade routes over which it was carried were known as "grease trails" and were used by early non-Indigenous explorers to reach the west coast.

Sputc and sluq' have always been far more than a commodity or food to the Nuxalk. The fish, arriving annually in February and March each year, signalled that the end of winter was finally approaching. Each year, as the spring breezes blew over the river, Nuxalkmc people would gather in excited anticipation on its banks, watching for the first wave of sputc to arrive. It would be followed by surge after surge of fish, so thick in their numbers that the river would turn black as the tide brought them avalanching upstream. The screams of gulls and eagles mixed with the happy shouts of fishers getting to work and people rejoicing in the knowledge that the long, often lean winter months were over.

Fishing for sputc also involved governance protocols that were thousands of years old, and tried and tested tools and methods that helped maintain the wellbeing of the fish and guarantee their return the following year. The annual harvest embraced social connection, culture, and ceremony. People had different hereditary roles and responsibilities in managing the sputc fishery, from monitoring the river to managing the nets to making sluq'. Age-old rules were observed. The first wave would always be allowed to pass and spawn. The second would be harvested and distributed to the Elders and others in need. Only then would the harvest by individual groups begin in earnest and the making of sluq' get under way.

Families would gather on the riverbank and around the grease pits to share their stories and teach the children the smayusta as well as the practical skills needed to catch and process the fish. Every able-bodied person participated. Everyone worked, laughed, and enjoyed this social time, building and rebuilding bonds and friendships. This connection between sputc and Nuxalkmc was fundamental to their nationhood, health, and happiness, and to Nuxalkmc stl'mstaliwa. "Describing the importance to the Nuxalkmc of this rare and wondrous fish," wrote Megan in the Afterword to *Alhqulh Ti Sputc*, "is almost impossible."

Megan worked for the Nation as its fisheries manager from 2001 to 2004 and studied sputc for her 2008 master's degree in science, which she undertook at the University of British Columbia's Fisheries Centre. "Eulachon time was an occasion when the family—grandparents, parents,

The community gathered in 2014 for the first of what would become an annual sputc ceremony on the banks of the Nuxalk River.

children, et cetera—all gathered together and worked on a common activity," she wrote in her thesis. "This was the time when the younger generations would witness and learn, through hands on experience, the grease making process...The importance of sharing and working together was also something taught to younger generations during the eulachon season." The 1996 Bella Coola River sputc run, she learned from the community, was so abundant that one Elder described the wave of fish surfing upriver on the rising tide "so thick that that they were coming onto the beach...we were able to just put them in buckets and bring them home." Everyone feasted to their hearts' content.

Within just one year everything changed. The sputc runs in 1997 and 1998 were much smaller. By 1999, the Nuxalk were waiting in vain for any fish to return. Nuxalkmc woman Nuskmata (Jacinda Mack) described the scene she witnessed that spring to Megan: "[The] arrival of the eulachon is always a big event in the Nuxalk valley. In the days preceding their appearance, throngs of birds and people line the shores of the river watching and waiting for the eulachons to return. Families ready their smoke houses, inspect their nets and prepare the stink boxes. However, in the spring of 1999, after weeks of waiting, anticipation turned into anxiety and finally into confusion and despair."

The despair grew as year after year the fish failed to come back to the Nuxalk River. A decade passed. Community meetings and eulachon monitoring projects took place, but nothing changed. There was no help from government. After a decade, fear of what the vanishing of the sputc would mean spurred a call to action by the Nuxalk. The community decided in the mid-2010s to put back into active practice the laws, ceremony, roles, and stewardship regime that had always been the foundation of Nuxalkmc management and use of sputc, and in turn raise up the role of sputc in supporting Nuxalkmc social, cultural, and spiritual bonds. Everyone firmly believed that the sputc would return in their former glory one day. This work would be vital to ensure that people would be ready when they did. Demonstrating Nuxalkmc commitment to uphold ancient ways of relating to the sputc might even encourage the fish to come back to their ancestral river.

The creation of *Alhqulh Ti Sputc* would be vital to that outcome. From 2013 to 2017 Megan took on the role of director of the Nuxalk Stewardship Office, leading the work on the book. "It was my intention to help everyone

understand how, as the Nuxalk Nation, we have always made decisions on the land and on the waters in our territory," says Megan. "The work was a way to really look at and explain our ancestral governance roles and responsibilities through describing the eulachon fishery and its importance to us and how we always conducted it."

The mountains of the Bella Coola valley are a breathtaking view from the Bella Coola River in Tweedsmuir Park.

The process of creating the sputc book was momentous and empowering. *Alhqulh Ti Sputc*, explains Snxakila, was the first literary encapsulation of Nuxalk Oral Tradition undertaken by Nuxalkmc for Nuxalkmc. "For us everything has a story. When we began the work on the sputc we had to connect the smayusta and our history to the work. *Alhqulh Ti Sputc* is therefore a foundation for upholding Nuxalkmc stewardship authority, learning about sputc practices and applying Nuxalkmc knowledge to restore and protect sputc." The book also sets out management principles that the Nuxalkmc would follow when sputc return, says Snxakila, "to ensure they are not overharvested, that the spawning grounds are properly protected,

Thorsen Creek, flowing in the Thorsen Creek Conservancy, in Bella Coola valley, is a sacred place for Nuxalkmc with its valuable fish habitat and significant collection of petroglyphs.

and that they will be able to return for generations to come."

In tandem with developing the sputc book, the first of what would become an annual sputc ceremony took place in 2014 with the raising of a ceremonial pole and bringing back an ancient sputc welcoming ceremony to symbolize the presence of the sputc and herald its return. The event was far more than ceremonial. Although there were no sputc to harvest, it was an opportunity for Nuxalk individuals and families to resume and practise their hereditary roles and responsibilities, whether in relation to monitoring the river, setting nets, or regulating the distribution of fish according to strict protocols. It was also an opportunity to make sluq', which that year had to be done utilizing sputc acquired from the Nisga'a Nation, whose annual eulachon harvest takes place on K̲'alii-Aksim-Lisims, the Nass River, to the north of Nuxalkulmc.

Doing all of these things brought the Nuxalk together, strengthening social bonds that had been at risk of becoming frayed through the absence of that important time together each year. It brought back memories, language, and knowledge that might otherwise have been lost. It also brought back the feeling of lixsatimutilh, being medicine for each other, says Snxakila. "The ceremony now happens every year, and even though the sputc aren't with us physically for harvesting, the spirituality in the ceremony has reconnected us to our understanding of the importance of being good caretakers of our land." Megan reflects, "The return of the sputc ceremony, the carving of the sputc pole, the visiting of other eulachon Nations, all act as symbolic and ceremonial gestures which seek to balance our relationship with sputc and hold a place within the Nuxalkmc heart and mind of the memory and spirit of the sputc until their eventual return."

In 2018, the year after *Alhqulh Ti Sputc* was completed, the sputc rewarded the faith of the Nuxalkmc community by returning to the Bella Coola River for the first time in twenty years. "It wasn't enough for a harvest," recalls Snxakila. "But it was wonderful. Everyone knew what to do. The Nuxalk Guardians went to watch and monitor the size of the run. The Chiefs went down and stayed by the river, singing and welcoming, praying, thanking the sputc for returning. They spoke to the people, telling them we will not harvest this year, we will let them continue to return until they're at enough numbers to harvest. It was a really beautiful experience." The sputc returned again in 2019, 2020, and 2021, still in numbers too small to harvest but large enough to maintain hope that they will appear again one day in wave after wave of fish so thick that the river swells over its banks.

The year before the sputc returned for the first time, Snxakila and Megan had begun work on a new, broader governance project for the Nation. "When Megan invited me to be a part of the sputc project, we realized that Nuxalkmc law is referenced all the time, but we don't have it collected together in one place," recalls Snxakila. "So, at the request of the hereditary Chiefs we started our ancestral governance department. As part of that, we began to develop an ancestral governance handbook where we have all of the traditions organized in a way that we can use with our stataltmc, the hereditary leaders, to support them in using our laws."

The goal is to help the stataltmc use Nuxalkmc foundational teachings as they make decisions to protect and support the community and the Nuxalk Nation's territory. "That will also give more strength to all the work we want to do to regain our autonomy over our territory, and our sovereignty. It's a Nuxalkmc world view that works for us," says Snxakila. "In the same way Ximaltwa, my language teacher, wasn't able to produce fluent speakers using a western system, using western governance is not helping us reach the results we want. What we really need to survive and function as a community, as a Nation, is to be rooted in our traditions and our world views."

That world view is human based, explains Snxakila, "so the laws founded on it are very natural." Canadian law, by comparison, is "very unnatural and very forced. Nuxalkmc law is liveable. It is a way of encouraging the good things in life to appear and to be prepared for the bad things, to have preventative measures and awareness so that when we do have trouble we have a protocol to help us deal with it. It is a very natural way in which human beings work together." Nuxalkmc law also requires thinking of the next generation and what it will need. "Being good caretakers has always been our way of being, having a culture based on sustainable resource management practices. Embracing stl'mstaliwa means we must live with purpose. We must take care of ourselves and of our lands and waters and sustain them for the next generation. We call that work nuyalcalhlayc and putl'alt, which translates to 'clearing the path' and 'to think of those not yet born.' How do we as Nuxalkmc live with our traditions and by doing so clear the path and help support the next generation?"

The answer to that question requires, as much as anything, leading by example. "An Elder remarked to me that non-Indigenous people learn the three 'Rs,' but we learn by the three 'Ls'—looking, listening, and loving. Our younger generation are looking to us and our behaviour and listening to us. We must show them that there is so much to love in what we are doing, in embracing our traditions, taking care of ourselves, and living with purpose." In some ways, Snxakila thinks, after so many years of suffering from the consequences of colonization, the Nuxalk are once again a "first generation" of this era of their existence. It is an era in which they are relearning the smayusta and applying them to clearing the path for all the generations to come.

The opportunities, says Snxakila, are brilliant. His generation of working adults in the Nuxalk Nation is deeply invested in putl'alt. "We want to build a cultural centre and a museum to hold our Nation's treasures, for example, the ones we are trying to bring back home. There is a totem pole that we are working on having returned from the Royal British Columbia Museum in Victoria, for example. We want them held here in the community so that all Nuxalkmc can learn from them, so we can create new carvings based on what we have learned and bring them out at Potlatches, where they will be witnesses to our restoration of our culture."

The repatriation of Nuxalkmc treasures this way, he reflects, is representative of everything he is working toward. "It's a good example of the balance I talk about in speaking to stl'mstaliwa. Applying our traditional practices this way is part of reaching that balance as humans. It validates our collective ancestral rights as a people. It helps us understand our connections to the land and our culture and history and gives us the strength

to withstand all the other issues we still face as a result of colonization: the systemic poverty, the encroachment by industry on our sacred lands, and the healing we need to do. If we apply this kind of approach to everything we do, it will be the medicine that heals us."

Stener Creek, in the Saloompt Forest, flows into the Bella Coola River upstream from the Bella Coola community.

The sputc experience was also a fundamental part of putl'alt, says Snxakila. "This is all because of the resurgence of traditions sparked by the sputc project. Sputc was an amazing medicine to inspire that." Each new piece of the work, he adds, cleared the next part of the pathway. "The sputc project pulled us back together and focussed us on where we need to be. Losing the sputc really affected the health of our people once we did not have the grease and the fish. It woke us up that we need to fulfil our responsibility as the original stewards of our territory." Building on that, the next project that the Nation is working on is a lhk'uulh (Big House) to hold ceremonies and lhlm (Potlatch), and kusyut, the sacred winter dance ceremonies. "In the lhk'uulh, people will dance to their stories, sing their songs, and they will feel the spirit pulling them to the places of their ancestors wanting to care for them, and to build there once again. We are also planning to have an Elders' centre. The youth centre has already been completed," says Snxakila. "We are working on a radio station. We want to design everything consistent with the Nuxalkmc style, such as that of a tsaakwaluulh, or Longhouse, our traditional family housing unit."

Snxakila also remains focussed on It7Nuxalkmc and its restoration as a living language. With only four elderly speakers still living as of 2021, the importance of documenting their knowledge as well as the historical record of the language is greater than it has ever been. "We have formed a language team to record what we already know," says Snxakila. "There are hundreds of hours of video and audio clips, as well as historical records of anthropologists like Franz Boas, who came to the west coast after seeing Nuxalkmc dancers perform in Germany in 1885. It is a huge amount of work to bring it all together so it is accessible to our people, but we are lucky to have it." The work is made even more challenging by the fact that early linguists safeguarded the sensitivity of some terms in the language by recording their meanings in Latin, German, and even in Norwegian. "But at least we have it all to work with," says Snxakila.

In documenting It7Nuxalkmc this way, the language team is adding to the contemporary Nuxalkmc literary tradition that began with *Alhqulh Ti Sputc*, supporting the continuing oral transmission of knowledge, law, and ceremony. "We are working on a guidebook that will tell the story of the language in a series of chapters. It will break down the elements of the language and explain the structure of words and terms and their meanings. It will also talk about how the language is used. What terms may be used only by certain people, for example, and when various stories may be told and where."

The importance of this work cannot be overestimated. As anyone who has ever attempted to learn a second language knows, much can be lost in translation. When it comes to an Indigenous language like It7Nuxalkmc, the implications of that are far more fundamental than misunderstanding. Embedded in the language are meanings that govern ways of behaving and ancient knowledge, both vital to stl'mstaliwa, the rich and complete fulfilment of the human experience. Through the language, Nuxalkmc ways of living can be restored, says Snxakila. "We are now looking at doing more things our way again, like following our own seasonal calendar, for example, rather than being bound to a western system of weeks and months that simply don't apply to how we always conducted ourselves." Snxakila would love to see this as part of the everyday life of Nuxalkmc people. "It would work so much better for us, so it is really important to talk about this work. It is part of clearing the path, reincorporating our original way of life. We have always been responsible for our territory," he emphasizes. "This way we are undertaking the work we need to do to fulfil those responsibilities fully once again. We've got so many traditions and stories that help us understand how to apply the teachings to our daily practice. It is all part of stl'mstaliwa, that full human experience."

The journey has not been easy for the young Nuxalkmc alkw. To do his work and give everything he needs to serve his community, Snxakila has had to put aside his own personal struggles with health, with grief, with the day-to-day struggles of life. The last thing he seeks is sympathy. These challenges are all part of the experience, he says. They are what is required for him to be useful and a change maker for his Nation, someone who can make a real difference. "Snxakila is an incredibly important person to our Nation," reflects Megan. "He is an extraordinary treasure who was wisely recognized by our Elders for his intelligence and heart. Some say that he is an Elder in a young man's body. He has the rare ability to fluently speak our language and understand and interpret Nuxalk culture and history while also having the ability to carry out ceremonial practices and share his learnings with the community. Most importantly, he is an amazing spirit who has a great love for Nuxalkmc." What makes Snxakila's struggle worthwhile is working with a community who is eager for a promising future for Nuxalkmc, and for the mnmnts' (children), the slh7imts (grandchildren), and the putl'alt (children yet unborn).

"We are really trying to use our ancestral system to create a good path forward for our people and to be an example of how we can live in balance and harmony in our beautiful land and territory," concludes Snxakila. "That's where the teachings have brought me in my journey with stl'mstaliwa. I believe that is where we are all journeying together as Nuxalkmc."

The Sacred Connection

CHAPTER TWO

Accessible only by water, Takush Harbour, in remote Smith Inlet, lies sixty-odd kilometres northeast of Port Hardy and as the raven flies some 390 kilometres northwest of Vancouver. In 1950, Paddy Walkus was born in the tiny Gwa'sala village of T'a̱kus, nestled on the sheltered shores of Takush Harbour.

The baby's arrival was celebrated in T'a̱kus in the Bak̓wa̱mk̓ala dialect of Gwa'cala, the language of the Gwa'sala people. His first solid foods included a wholesome array of both fresh and cured fish and shellfish, deer meat, wild greens, berries, and other delicacies harvested from the ocean and islands surrounding the village. As a little boy, Paddy helped his family with the typical tasks assigned to youngsters, like fetching wood for the cookstove. He had plenty of time, all the same, to enjoy simple youthful adventures in the sublimely beautiful forests and waterways around T'a̱kus.

As he grew older, Paddy learned from his Elders about his heritage, his sacred connection to his Gwa'sala homelands and the beautiful ancestral way of life Gwa'sala people had enjoyed since time immemorial. He attended events in the much-loved community gukwdzi (Big House). His was a childhood, he recalls fondly nearly seven decades later, full of joy and surrounded by unbounded love. "We were always happy and so in tune with nature. When I look back to those years, I realize how fruitful and loving our lives were. Even as children we had jobs to do, but that was natural, too. We accepted that as part of our daily life. We

"Our values and teachings are based on our sacred connection to our lands and waters, those traditional lands that we were forcibly removed from. Now we are rebuilding our people's future upon those values and teachings and that sacred connection."

—Paddy Walkus, former Gwa'sala-'Nakwaxda'xw Chief Councillor, September 2020

Facing page: Near Blunden Harbour, 'Nakwaxda'xw territory.

packed water to the house. If my mother asked us to get some fish, we knew where to go and how many we were allowed to catch."

That was something the Elders had taught him and his young friends. "They educated us about what was important and our values as Gwa'sala people. They told us we must always take care of each other and the homelands. They taught us we must sustain our resources. My grandfather told me, you must recognize how important the fish, the animals, and the trees are to us all. He said we must acknowledge these gifts, not exploit them. I remember that so clearly. They knew you can't just take everything you want. This kind of teaching," reflects Paddy, "has kept us strong with the values that our old people passed on to us. It is part of our culture and our way of life and our laws. It is a system that has existed for thousands of years. We did our part, even as children, to carry those values within us in everything we did."

Former elected Chief of the Gwa'sala-'Nakwaxda'xw, Paddy Walkus

Not far from T'a̱kus was an equally remote village called Ba'as, in Smith Inlet's Blunden Harbour. The people of the 'Nakwaxda'xw Nation from Ba'as speak a different dialect of Bak̓wa̱mk̓ala, called Nak'wala. Although they practise similar cultural and social protocols, the 'Nakwaxda'xw and the Gwa'sala have always been two related but distinctly individual Indigenous Peoples.

What they have in common is that each Nation has followed those protocols with remarkable determination. They have remained strong despite the devastation wrought by the diseases settlers carried with them; despite the occupation and ravaging of their territories by commercial fishing, mining, and logging; despite the hijacking of their rights to govern their vast territories and being confined by the federal government to a handful of tiny Indian reserves; despite having so many of their human rights denied. Worst of all was the theft of their children, taken away forcibly to residential schools, where many were subjected to horrific abuse.

It's difficult to imagine the depth of hardship of that time for Gwa'sala and 'Nakwaxda'xw people. What Gwa'sala and 'Nakwaxda'xw people could not have imagined as the 1960s dawned was that things could get even worse. The Gwa'sala and 'Nakwaxda'xw were about to embark upon a grim journey in the course of which, on top of everything else they had already been through, they would suffer the loss of their ancestral homes and forced removal from their beloved homelands. Subsequent decades of despair, disease, and darkness would threaten to wipe them completely out of existence by the turn of the twenty-first century.

The Gwa'sala and 'Nakwaxda'xw people, however, give life and meaning to the word "resilience." Ultimately—because of Elders who tenaciously clung to the values that Paddy was taught as a child, of visionary leadership, and a community of people determined to reclaim what was always rightfully theirs—the journey would eventually become one of transformation and rebuilding. It would become a passage into a new era of cultural reconnection, optimism, prosperity and hope for the twenty-first-century descendants of the two Nations. Despite how impossible it once had seemed, the Gwa'sala and the Nakwaxda'xw are now on a firm pathway toward independence and wellbeing. They are once again becoming culturally whole, working toward control of their destiny, and exercising their age-old rights of self-governance in caring for their ancient homelands to sustain future generations.

This is a story of defiance of seemingly impossible odds and of overcoming the worst of human experiences. It is a story of courage, strength, resilience, and determination. Above all, it is a story of the triumph of culture over colonization, hope over great hardship, and love over immense loss.

By Paddy's tenth birthday, in 1960, the villages of T'a̱kus and Ba'as were both struggling with poor housing, sanitation and health services. Rather than upgrade the village systems, the Department of Indian Affairs (DIA) decided, without consulting the Gwa'sala and the 'Nakwaxda'xw, to relocate

'Nakwaxda'xw hereditary Chief Hiłamas (Thomas Henderson)

them to the Tsulquate Indian reserve near Port Hardy, sixty kilometres away on Vancouver Island. From the DIA's point of view, Tsulquate was much more accessible. The DIA could also kill two birds with one stone and for the government's administrative convenience amalgamate the two Nations into one Indian Band at the same time.

When the Gwa'sala and 'Nakwaxda'xw learned of the DIA's plans, both Nations balked. For a start, the artificial merger of their two Peoples into a single Indian Band would at best degrade ancient cultural inter-governmental protocols and relationships between them, and at worst, completely ruin them and cause lasting generational effects. On top of that, they were being told they had to move from the places they and their ancestors had lived since time immemorial to somewhere they didn't know, far from their traditional homes and ancient harvesting grounds, and where they had no relationship with either the local Kwa'gut people at Tsulquate nor the non-Indigenous community at Port Hardy. Their response to the DIA's plan was unsurprising: a polite but straightforward no.

In 1962, however, the DIA upped the ante. First the department tried bribery, painting an enticing picture of what was waiting at Tsulquate: good houses for everyone, power and running water, a medical centre, a school, and employment for all who wanted work. That was still a poor substitute for staying in their own homelands. So the DIA then cut off all health, education, and housing services to both villages. Paddy remembers sitting in his mother's kitchen as government officials spoke to her. "She didn't want to move. But they said she had no choice."

Powerless to do anything else, in 1964 people reluctantly succumbed to the DIA's demands. Paddy's mother packed what was most important into suitcases and boxes, and along with everyone else in T'a̱kus and Ba'as, took a boat across Hecate Strait to begin a new life at Tsulquate. They left behind everything they had ever known: their homes, most of their possessions, their memories and the burial sites of their ancestors, and a way of life that had sustained them and their ancestors for thousands of years.

On arrival they discovered that the DIA's promises had all been lies. Just three houses had been partially built for one hundred people. In the absence of any other shelter, families crowded together with as many as thirty people forced to share one dwelling. Some families resorted to living on their boats despite the lack of safe anchorage. At the first storm many of those boats were damaged or destroyed. Some people went back to Ba'as and T'a̱kus, but they were already too late. By the time they arrived, the government had destroyed their remaining possessions and burned down every building in the empty villages. In despair, they returned to Tsulquate.

To their dismay, the newcomers were also not welcome in Port Hardy. Gwa'sala and 'Nakwaxda'xw people in Tsulquate were beaten by gangs from the nearby town. Gunshots were fired through windows and reserve houses set on fire by angry locals who wanted the intruders gone. Doctors refused to treat them. Non-Indigenous teachers beat children for speaking their languages, even if they knew no English.

The consequences of all this were profound. As an initiative calculated to wipe out the cultural identities of two Indigenous Peoples in a single expedient blow, the federal government's relocation initiative was horrific but highly effective. "We were so alienated, not only physically but spiritually, from our lands and the teachings of our old people," mourns Paddy. "We completely lost our way of life."

Everything familiar had gone, said 'Nakwaxda'xw hereditary Chief Hiłamas (Thomas Henderson), who passed away in early July 2022. Hiłamas was a teenager during the relocation. The results, he recalled in 2021, spoke for themselves. "Our people were heartbroken. We were in a strange land where we didn't belong. We were no longer called by our names. We were called by English names we didn't care for… The people there kept telling us to go back where we came from, but we couldn't. Our homes had all been burned. Anyway, the DIA and the police told us if we tried to return to the homelands again, we would be put in jail…

"All we wanted was to go back home," continued Thomas. "In the homelands we had little need for money. We didn't have electricity or running water, but we also didn't have to go to a store to buy food. We lived off the land. We thrived on a diet of seafood. We were healthy. Then we came to Tsulquate and the government did not allow us to fish. We had nowhere we could go to harvest food. We survived on supermarket food. It was no good for us. Our people started to get sick with diabetes and with heart disease."

Many Gwa'sala and 'Nakwaxda'xw people died over the next few decades from disease, neglect, and suicide. Alcohol played its part, offering an escape into numbness from pain, grief, and hopelessness. Thomas, who as a child had been taken from Ba'as to residential school in Surrey, near Vancouver, left the school to attend his mother's funeral in Tsulquate. He recalled what happened to his mother in bleak terms: "She was one of the first that died after the move. She was drinking and bled to death after being cut by broken glass." Both Thomas and Paddy turned to drink, as did so many others. "We didn't care anymore," remembered Thomas. "We didn't know the meaning of being loved."

Paddy describes that time as a "decade of apathy," of years being lost in a wilderness of despair. "We almost didn't consider ourselves as people; it was that bad. We were drunk all the time. We didn't know who would be gone tomorrow. It could be us or it could be someone else. We just didn't care." Elders died at unprecedented rates. Children were taken from their families by social services, adopted out to strangers or sent, as Thomas had been, to residential school. Many of those children died, too. At one point it was brutally predicted that by the early 2000s there would be no Gwa'sala or 'Nakwaxda'xw people left alive.

It would have been easy for everyone to give up: the Elders, the hereditary Chiefs, younger people like Thomas and Paddy. But, says Paddy thoughtfully, "while we lost so much, we never abandoned the values our old people taught us as children. We never, ever forgot our sacred connection to our homelands. One thing we also never lost," he adds quietly, "was the ability to keep loving each other." In a way it was that love that was instrumental in reversing that terrible prediction of extinction: loving and taking care of each other; loving their children; an unshakable love for their collective ancestral strengths and ways of being as Gwa'sala and Nakwaxda'xw people; and, not least of all, Paddy's own immense capacity as a natural leader for loving his community and his people.

For Paddy, a tragic accident that took the life of his five-year-old son changed everything. It could have utterly destroyed him and his wife, Nellie, but instead it did the opposite. The need for their love had not gone away; if anything, it had become more urgent. "The Chief of the day came to us not long afterwards," says Paddy, "and asked us to become house parents for foster children. We ended up with seventeen children in our home to nurture and protect. We had no time to think about anything else."

Paddy stopped drinking. With a clear head, he became more aware of what was happening in the community. His interest did not go unnoticed and in 1976 he was urged to run for Chief Councillor of the Gwa'sala-'Nakwaxda'xw Band. To his surprise, he won. The twenty-six-year-old was immediately confronted with what might have seemed like an insurmountable challenge. "The Tsulquate community was so high in incarceration and hospitalisation rates. All our statistics were negative. We had school dropouts at Grade 4. Grade 8 was our highest level of achievement for education. We had no Grade 12 graduates. It was a sad, sad picture. To try to turn that around—it felt very hopeless trying to achieve even day-to-day survival. It was very dismal," he says.

Despite the difficulties he faced in his new leadership role, Paddy was determined to achieve change as quickly as possible. He took off running, only to quickly learn that even with the best of intentions, any transformation of the Tsulquate community could not be pulled off quickly or singlehandedly. "One evening, an Elder came to my door. He said to me, 'Paddy, slow down. Stop running, just walk. Let us walk with you.' Those simple words meant so much," recalls Paddy. "I couldn't move faster than the community. I had to keep pace with them." The Elder's advice to the new Chief Councillor was invaluable. A different and better future for his people, Paddy realized, required nothing less than "a total community effort."

Mentors from some of his neighbouring First Nations took Paddy under their wing, as did his Elders. "Those people of wisdom guided me on what we needed to do," he recalls with profound gratitude. The Nations had also recently hired a manager, a non-Indigenous man named Cliff Emery who had been teaching in the Tsulquate school. Emery devoted himself passionately and with great integrity to his new job, helping the community to turn things around. There were other people in Tsulquate trying to improve social conditions in various ways as well. These individuals were instrumental in what Paddy calls “an awakening of the soul” that was crucial to success. “All of these people were so important to the rebuilding work. What everyone gave was so immense.”

It started with the old people, says Paddy. “They wanted us all to reconnect with our culture, our identity. Our uncle, Harry Walkus, for example, he started potlatching to remind us of our traditional values. The Elders helped us start to relearn our languages. They worked so hard for us.” The process was slow and difficult. People do not recover from decades of what Paddy described bluntly as “attempted cultural genocide” in one generation. “It took a long time to grasp it all. It was painful in the beginning even to practise our traditions because we had been so forcibly distanced from them, spiritually and physically. We didn’t necessarily know what we were doing. But we were also blessed to have teachers like Harry.”

In the 1980s a new elementary school was built in Tsulquate. “Our younger teachers started bringing our matriarchs into the classroom and to integrate their teachings into the children’s education, educating them about who they are and their cultural heritage. That was a key turning point,” recalls Paddy. “The kids started grasping onto those cultural learnings with such hunger. We had found the missing link they so desperately needed.” Graduation rates, unsurprisingly, slowly started to improve.

The Gwa’sala and ‘Nakwaxda’xw also began to undertake extensive research into their past and started relearning their traditional songs and practising their original laws. They examined their sacred connection to their lands and what it meant to embrace their ancient values. They brought those values not only into their school but into their homes and their community centre and every community event. Gwa’sala people started visiting T’a̲kus. ‘Nakwaxda’xw citizens went to Ba’as. By 2005—the year it had once been predicted they would all be gone—a growing population of Gwa’sala and ‘Nakwaxda’xw people were instead daring to dream of a promising future.

Then, in 2008, the federal government paid a multimillion-dollar settlement to the Gwa’sala and ‘Nakwaxda’xw in reparation for the relocation. It was nowhere near enough to compensate for what had happened, but for the first time the Nations had an independent means to improve their lives in real, concrete terms. They had a chance to reclaim their wellbeing as Indigenous Peoples, their rights, and their rightful place in the homelands.

Tlali'ila'ogwala (Jessie Hemphill)

The first step was to bring the community together to discuss what that future should look like and to make a plan. Tlali'ila'ogwala, Jessie Hemphill, a young 'Nakwaxda'xw woman, took on the job of planning coordinator. Jessie had just graduated with a degree in Linguistics and Indigenous Studies from the University of Victoria and knew little, if anything, about community planning. She instinctively understood its importance, however. "When I reached the end of my degree, I wanted to work with language revitalisation. But I realized that was not going to be successful in the absence of economic development, health reform, education, or housing. All these other barriers to language had to be dealt with first."

Over the next two years, Jessie and her planning team held dozens of community meetings asking what people wanted to see happen, not merely in the next five to ten years, but over the next seven generations; a question that reflects a worldview shared by many Indigenous people that decisions should result in a sustainable world seven generations into the future. The room at the Elders' centre where the meetings were typically held would fill up with Elders, with young parents, and with children running around and playing while the grown-ups talked. Jessie recalls, "When we started, we asked them, what do you want for these kids? What is your vision, what are your goals? What do you want to see happen in every area of our community in the next one hundred years: culture, education, economy, housing, infrastructure, lands and resources, the social realm, governance, administration?"

Sometimes, however, people need to clear the table of the past before they can look to the future. "It took us a long time to get to the visioning because we had a lot of work to do telling the pain of history," recalls Jessie. "At the beginning, there were many Elders who couldn't talk about what the future looked like. They had to talk about these very traumatic things that had happened to them and tell stories they had never shared before. It was really hard, but it felt like we were healing these areas in the community that had been ignored for too long."

When people were ready at last to think about the future there was no stopping them, says Jessie. "It became a joyful process, to think about how anything could be possible. We covered the walls with sticky notes with everyone's ideas on them, even when they seemed outrageous. One man, Bob Swain, suggested that we should have a hotel of our own, with our own staff, our own food, our art and designs everywhere. Everyone laughed at the idea. It seemed so preposterous that we could ever have something like that. But that was part of the fun. This was a long-term vision, so why not? Let's put that down, too. Let's dream big." The plan, when completed, contained thirty-seven goals identified by the community. They ranged from grassroots measures to improve daily life to big, ambitious, economic dreams, like owning a hotel.

At the time—regardless of whether those goals could or would be fulfilled—something priceless had taken place, observes Jessie. "The planning process reawakened something in all of us. It became the embodiment of practices we had all along that had just been dormant. It was a revitalization

Mahpahkum-Ahkwuna/Deserters-Walker Conservancy, in Gwa'sala-'Nakwaxda'xw territory, is comprised of reefs in the middle of the northern entrance to Queen Charlotte Strait.

of oral culture, and community gathering, and collective decision-making; all these things that were already in our culture long before a modern term like 'community planning' was coined. Talking about what we needed to do connected to people's intuition about the right way to make decisions about the future. That was what made it so powerful. It was truly ours."

Owning a hotel was not the only business goal in the plan. Among other things, the community identified economic development generally as a priority, to build the financial independence of the Nations and free them completely from the constraints of DIA funding. With money coming in from good business investments, the Gwa'sala and 'Nakwaxda'xw could build housing for their citizens, create job opportunities, and establish health and education programs. In other words, they could finally achieve everything for themselves that had been promised by the government when they were relocated to Tsulquate but had never happened. Perhaps most importantly, they could plan a return to their homelands.

Finally, everyone could start running fast—not just Paddy, but the community and all its leaders alongside him. An economic development adviser named Conrad Browne was hired to help implement the community plan. In 2014, the Nations established the k'awat'si Economic Development Corporation to integrate and manage their business activities. Something remarkable—almost magical—started to happen. "Within five years of finishing the plan," marvels Jessie, "we owned not just one, but two hotels!"

It was almost as if by dreaming so big the community had willed success into being. "In those first five years we created our marine services division, providing water transportation services for all kinds of activities. We acquired three floating barge camps that could be hired for business meetings or conferences. They have kitchens, gyms, TV rooms, and accommodation. We bought our hotels. We had k'awat'si Construction working on building houses, we had a logging company, and the beginnings of an aquaculture company and a fish-processing plant. It was incredible!"

All those businesses have now expanded into full operation. Although they are independent operations, they also complement each other for an even greater sense of wellbeing and achievement. The lumber company supplies the construction company; the construction company renovates the hotels; the marine transportation operation supports the flourishing tourism business that has been added to the portfolio; the cold storage operation services the commercial fisheries and aquaculture businesses.

In the same time frame, a community centre has been built, a new high school is under construction at Tsulquate, and a raft of social programs are in effect, including everything from mental health services to a community garden and food box program for Elders. The Gwa'sala-'Nakwaxda'xw Guardians celebrated the tenth year in operation of their environmental stewardship program in 2022. Docks and cabins have been built at both Ba'as and T'a̱kus and community members are staying in the cabins every summer to re-establish the Nations' presence in the homelands.

All of this has been done in a way that supports both the contemporary vision and the ancient values of the Gwa'sala and 'Nakwaxda'xw. It has been vitally important that the effort to reclaim their wellbeing, whether through economic, social, or cultural initiatives, be undertaken consistently with the history, values and traditions of the Nations, the inherent Indigenous principle of sustainability in the harvesting and use of resources, and above all, their sacred connection to their homelands. Paddy—who stepped down as Chief Councillor in January 2022 after more than forty years in the role—reflects at length on what mattered most to him personally in the Gwa'sala and 'Nakwaxda'xw journey of transformation:

"I cannot emphasize enough how important the voices of the old people have been and our hereditary leaders like Thomas. They kept the seeds of knowledge alive and have planted them in all of us to grow for future generations. It was their values and their teachings that have brought us here. I never forget that Elder who told me to slow down, to listen to the water lap on the shoreline, listen to the wind as it goes through the trees.

"Our old people gave us guidance in how to survive. They gave us the tools to work with. I believe it is so critical for our people that we go back to those values and teachings. Everything we do must be sustainable. We cannot just take and take. Everything must still be here one thousand years from now. That is a critical part of this whole picture, maintaining a sustained effort to ensure that there will always be something here for everyone. That is so important in how we move ahead in our economic growth.

"Prior to colonization, our gukwdzi, our Big House, was our parliament building. The hereditary Chiefs governed everything. Over these decades I have been an elected Chief, I have had to keep in tune with their wisdom and what is happening around us, sitting down and taking the time to sit with the Elders, sitting with the youth and hearing from them what makes

Looking out from the midden beach at Ba'as (Blunden Harbour), in 'Nakwaxda'xw territory.

their worlds go 'round. I have been so blessed to step back and realize how vital all of that has been to progress for our community.

"Now we also see our young people wanting to do things that are connected to our lands. Many of them want to pursue something that is connected to what we originally did but applying it in the contemporary world, adjusting some of the old teachings and creating a better direction for themselves. We have young people that go regularly to our remote locations, our original villages, our rivers, and other parts of our traditional territory and work there, focussing on rebuilding. They are looking at environmental initiatives that could help us and create a better future for our people and a better world for us to live in.

"That is really exciting for us old folks, when we can see that kind of determination from the younger generation. In a way, that acknowledges the efforts of the old people."

Jessie Hemphill is now a partner in her own planning company, Alderhill Planning Inc. She visits her homelands in Smith Inlet whenever she can. "I feel like I come into a part of myself that I'm detached from most of the time...your whole body connects with your soul and you remember what it means to feel human. In Kwak̓wala, in our language, it's literally a feature of the grammar that we acknowledge that the land is an extension of our body and both of those are an extension of the cosmos. I am the land and the land is me. It's not a metaphor, it's a reality."

Walter George, a 'Nakwaxda'xw artist and hereditary Chief, is an active member of the younger generation of which Paddy is so proud. Born in Port Hardy in 1991, Walter was part of the carving team that in 2021 completed four house posts for a new gukwdzi to be erected at Tsulquate. The gukwdzi would, as far as possible, replicate one of the original big houses from the homelands. It was designed to be used in the traditional manner,

Kent Island, Mahpahkum-Ahkwuna/ Deserters-Walker Conservancy near north Vancouver Island.

as a parliament building where the leaders take care of community business according to ancient protocols, and feasts, ceremonies and Potlatches could be held.

In his art practice, Walter says, he was taught always to undertake his work "with a good heart." His late grandfather William George Sr., also an artist, had passed away before he could pass on his teachings. Nonetheless, as Paddy had at the same age, Walter had good, wise mentors to set him on his path. "I make my living as an artist now, but I was taught to also always be a contributing artist to our traditional ceremonies, Potlatches and feasts. I carve ceremonial pieces for families who need certain masks, and I've carved a number of pieces for the Gwa'sala-'Nakwaxda'xw school. It balances things out to give back to the community that way. That's the way we are as a Nation—we help each other out."

As a hereditary leader, Walter embodies both spiritually and physically those values and concepts that Paddy describes. "When I received my chieftainship from my uncle, four older Chiefs came to talk to me about our role. It's to look after our people, our family, and our community; to be there for our people in any way, shape, or form that we can be. We used to have an ancient village and a location down on a beach that we called the Awakwis. The hereditary Chiefs would go to meet there and talk about things happening within the community, how to do things in a good and healthy way."

Those meetings were still practised, says Walter, even after the global pandemic that began in 2020. "We started having conference calls weekly so that we could continue to think about how we can look after our people during a tough time and continue making progress in a good way. There are still challenges facing us," he continues. "Many people are still on the journey to recovery from the past. But our forefathers fought so hard to keep our traditions alive. As today's generation we have that same drive, to keep clearing the way the best that we can for the generations to come. I hope they will understand what it is that our old people fought so hard to keep alive for us. That's what people of my generation are doing right now—we're trying to reawaken the spirit fully amongst our people."

Until his final days, Thomas was also helping young people recover from the legacy of the past and dreaming of moving back to the homelands to live in freedom again. He was content to see the changes that have occurred, and proud. "It is so different now," he said earlier that year. "Our

Artist and ‘Nakwaxda’xw hereditary Chief Walter George with the team who carved the Sisiyul cross beam for the new Gwa’sala-‘Nakwaxda’xw gukwdzi(Big House) in Tsulquate.

Artist and 'Nakwaxda'xw hereditary Chief Walter George

kids are a lot happier. Our school's doing really well. We're teaching our language, bringing that back. I have a little group of youth that are bringing our songs back that we danced to in our homelands, a lot of those good things, and we're looking forward to our Big House being completed."

Thomas wanted to bring as many of the children and youth with him to the homelands as possible, so that they too could experience what he and Paddy and their ancestors had enjoyed. "When we are there, every day you work and feel good about yourself. You can learn to live off the lands, where you hunt and what food you get from season to season, how you prepare it. We have ceremony. I can see how it will be," he said. His vision was beautiful and inspiring. "Every morning, first thing, we'll report to a Big House and all the Chiefs and matriarchs will speak about what's important in day-to-day life. You will sit and listen to what you need to do. You're not being asked; this is what you need to do in order to survive. You go out and hunt, go out and gather seafood, go out and fish halibut. These things you share with your community. You look after the elderly first, you looked after the widowers, the widows, and those who have families with lots of kids. You help provide for their needs. That's what we did before, that's how happy we were as a people with our connections to the lands, to all living creatures, to one another. We stood proud that we could do these things every day. We will do all of this freely when we return to our homelands."

At seventy-two years of age, Paddy is enjoying having let go the reins of leadership (although he still sits on Council). The future of his people, he

View toward Ba'as (Blunden Harbour).

feels, is in excellent hands. "Today we have a young Band Council. I said to them recently that I am really thankful and appreciative of their efforts. They speak very strongly for the rights of our people and understand the importance of acknowledging traditional protocol. I feel a lot of comfort that we are in a better position and have a better understanding of where we are going, and how we hope to achieve good, meaningful direction, economic growth, and social and cultural wellbeing, than ever before."

Paddy takes immense pride in the ability of Gwa'sala and 'Nakwaxda'xw people to have survived in the face of so much adversity over the generations. "It has been a tough journey but we are reconnecting to our homelands, rebuilding that sacred connection for all time. I believe where we are headed will benefit not only today's generation, but all the generations to come."

The Work of Tx̱eemsim

CHAPTER THREE

For Nicole Morven, a Nisg̱a'a woman from the small village of Gitwinksihlkw, in the remote Nass Valley wilderness of northern British Columbia, there is nothing better in life than to be out fishing on K̲'alii-Aksim Lisims, the Nass River.

It's been that way almost as long as Nicole can remember. Some of her happiest early childhood memories are of being on K̲'alii-Aksim Lisims with her beloved father, Perry Azak, fishing for salmon. "We'd go after school or after dinner and on weekends," she recalls. "We were always out on the water, rain or shine, even in the snow."

Sometimes Perry would take his young daughter to Ts'im K̲'olh̓l Da oots'ip (Fishery Bay), a seasonal Saak fishing camp located a few kilometres downriver from the village of Lax̱galts'ap (Greenville). Nisg̱a'a families have harvested Saak at Ts'im K̲'olh̓l Da oots'ip (often simply called Da oots'ip) every spring since time beyond memory, feasting on their fresh catch and making rich grease from the small, oily fish. The process of making Saak grease is slow and laborious, taking days, sometimes even weeks, before the thick, golden fat is ready to be put in jars for storing. Saak grease is used to flavour food and as medicine. It is traded with other communities and is valued as much in the making as it is in the eating. Families and friends spend days with each other out at Da oots'ip, observing age-old rituals in the preparation of the fish and sharing stories, history, and laughter as they work together over the steaming grease pots.

"Nisg̱a'a people in ancient times studied the movement of the heavens so that they could predict when different fish harvesting seasons would begin...Here in the Nass, we celebrate Hoobiyee, the Nisg̱a'a New Year, upon the rising of the February crescent moon. We know that when it comes up over the mountains, the Saak, our eulachon fish, have arrived in the river. And you know, the moon calls not only the eulachon; it also calls the salmon."

—ẃahlin[11] Sim'oogit Hleek̲, Dr. Joseph Gosnell, Nisg̱a'a Nation, 2011[12]

Facing page: Ts'im K̲'olh̓l Da oots'ip (Fishery Bay) during the annual Saak (eulachon) run.

Nisg̱a'a fisheries monitoring coordinator Nicole Morven at Ts'im Ḵ'oíhl Da oots'ip (Fishery Bay) monitoring the annual Saak (eulachon) harvest.

Nicole's childhood education in Nisg̱a'a history, culture, and relationships that came with these experiences was priceless. As an adult—whether out in the slushy late February snow at Da oots'ip, watching clouds of seagulls and eagles scream and windmill over the river as they fight for their share of the bounty or standing in the quiet shallows of the river in the steaming heat of the Nass Valley summer—for Nicole, being on the river is also profoundly existential. "The river and the fish are in my bones," she reflects.

On the water, the outside world and all her troubles disappear and she feels at one with nature in a way she cannot in any other place. Sometimes, she says, it feels as if the earth is almost speaking to her. "There might be eagles soaring above me, calling, or grizzlies growling down from the hills. I might look up from my line and there's a moose only a few metres away. I become totally lost in those moments of pure connection to these creatures and this place."

Nicole's job as a fisheries harvest monitoring coordinator for the Nisg̱a'a Nation's Fisheries and Wildlife Directorate suits her well, involving far more time on the river than sitting behind a desk. In the course of her duties, she collects information on the annual run sizes, productivity, and harvests of various fisheries in the Nass region, all critical information needed to assess the health of those fisheries (which include, among other species, wild salmon, steelhead, Saak, and halibut, as well as crabs and shellfish).

The data she gathers also supports the Nisg̱a'a Lisims Government (NLG) in determining annual harvest entitlements for their citizens under their post-2000 treaty with the Government of Canada, setting annual spawning targets for the different Nass stocks and managing the Nation's fisheries for long-term sustainability. That latter objective is particularly important when it comes to the five species of wild salmon that frequent Nisg̱a'a traditional fishing waters. Annual returns of several Nass salmon stock have been in decline for the past decade, under duress from the impacts of climate change. The potential for wild salmon in the Nass to vanish completely and the cultural catastrophe that would follow is both real and terrifying.

Nicole Morven fishing for coho salmon on the Cranberry River, in the northeastern region of Nisg̱a'a lands.

Nicole and her colleagues in the Nisg̱a'a Fisheries team play a profoundly important role in this regard. They manage harvest numbers to ensure sufficient numbers of fish can spawn each year, to help their precious salmon stocks rebuild and ensure there will always be enough fish for future generations to harvest and enjoy, both for cultural and commercial purposes. It is work that requires hard skills in boat operation, digital data collection and fish-tagging, as well as an appreciation for the rigours of scientific and environmental analysis. But as Nicole carries out her daily tasks on the river—dealing with Nisg̱a'a fishermen whose livelihoods, as well as their physical and cultural wellbeing, depend on the fish they catch—she draws as much upon her understanding of Nisg̱a'a history and the ancient relationship of Nisg̱a'a people with their river and the fish as she does upon her technical skills. It is a relationship fundamental to the contemporary wellbeing of both people and place, to Nisg̱a'a identity, embedded in the beginning of time.

According to Nisg̱a'a creation history, a very long time ago K̠'am Ligii Hahlhaahl, a supreme being from the Great Beyond, sent his grandson Tx̱eemsim[13] to help the Nisg̱a'a who were struggling in hardship and darkness. Tx̱eemsim brought sunlight to the earth, made the tides, the river, and the mountains, and bestowed on the Nisg̱a'a abundant fish, like Saak and salmon, as well as other animals, trees and plants. "As Tx̱eemsim created the Nass River, which at first was called Ksi Tx̱eemsim and later became known as K̠'alii-Aksim Lisims, he journeyed down from Mag̱oonhl Lisims to Saxwhl Lisims," explains Nita Morven, who has worked for many years for the Ayuukhl Nisg̱a'a (Cultural Department) as the cultural researcher. "Magoonhl Lisims means 'from where Lisims (waters) starts flowing,' or the headwaters, and Saxwhl Lisims, 'to where Lisims goes out (and joins the ocean),' or the estuary. The people then were called Git Tx̱eemsim (people of Tx̱eemsim)."

In the Nisg̱a'a *Feast Book*, which Nita worked on in close consultation with and under direction from Nisg̱a'a Elders and leaders, Nita describes the story of Tx̱eemsim, and the societal relationship of the Nisg̱a'a that has evolved over the millennia, since Tx̱eemsim was first born in the Nass. It is a structured relationship that embraces adaawak̠ (Nisg̱a'a oral history and knowledge) and ayuuk̠ (laws expressed through customs and traditional practices based on that history and knowledge). Also embedded in the structure are the principles of kwhlix̱hoosa'anskw (respectful behaviour) and hagwin-yuuwo'oskw and amnigwootkw, which comprise a permission system relating to the use of natural resources like fish and other wildlife on Nisg̱a'a traditional lands.

In researching the *Feast Book*, says Nita, the Elders highlighted the ancient values that underpin Nisg̱a'a society. "Those values ensure social order and purpose to our way of life. For example, that includes the principle of 'taking only what you need,' keeping in mind future generations, and the principle of reciprocity—sharing, trusting the belief that in one way or another your kindness will come back to you—and in being respectful of the resource, always giving thanks to the creature giving up its life for your sustenance."

This, Nita believes, is a way of thinking entirely consistent with the essence of Tx̱eemsim, whose spirit and values are as present and relevant in the twenty-first century as they have been since the beginning of time. When she was much younger, Nita asked her father whether Tx̱eemsim could still be alive. "He didn't answer straight away, but then he turned to me and said, 'Yes, he is. Tx̱eemsim is alive in you and he is alive in me.'" In other words, contemporary Nisg̱a'a ways of being and behaving, and the values of sustainability, respect and reciprocity imbued in the spirit of Tx̱eemsim, remain deeply intertwined, embracing principles that are as practical as they are mystical, and which are integral not only in Nisg̱a'a governance and fisheries management, but in every aspect of Nisg̱a'a life.

For Nicole, this way of behaving is vital in her work for practical reasons. In the course of her weekly routine, she collects data from the local

Saak drying at Ts'im K̲'olhl Da oots'ip (Fishery Bay).

fishermen she monitors on the river, such as how many fish they have caught, what type, the health of the fish, what kind of nets they are using, and so on. Anecdotal information these fishermen provide about the fish and what they see happening out on the river can be equally valuable. This information enables better predictions of future run sizes based on the age of the fish they are catching, for example, and contributes significantly to accurate assessments of the return numbers each season.

"Sometimes our scientists come across data that doesn't look normal. They can tell when there's a difference or an anomaly but won't always know why. That's because the raw data we collect doesn't include things like weather conditions on any given day or natural events like a rockfall or an ice barrier or human activities that might affect the numbers," explains Nicole. "The fishermen are out on the river every day, so when something doesn't add up, they may be able to provide us with the answers.

Nisga'a Director of Lands and Resources Mansell Griffin

By including that knowledge in the data assessment, that helps us and our scientists to understand better what is really happening with the fish."

Other useful information, says scientist Richard Alexander, whose company LGL Limited Environmental Research Associates has worked with Nisg̱a'a Fisheries since 1992, are the observations the fishermen make of injuries or unusual physical features of the fish they are catching. "They may see fish that have been affected by growing up in warm water conditions, for example, with unusual body or head shapes as a result." In the years immediately following the 2011 earthquake near Fukushima, in Japan, says Richard, a number of fish showed up in the Nass in poor health, with yellowing that indicated jaundice. "Things like that may translate into poorer survival when these fish reach the spawning grounds, and lower forecast projections for their offspring. Warmer conditions are also causing fish to not grow as large and females returning having fewer eggs. So the size and injury observations the fishers provide help immensely in our assessments."

In other words, saving the fishery is a team effort. "In a sense, the fishermen are our co-workers because we really depend on them for that information and knowledge," agrees Nicole. That requires treating the fishermen in her monitoring role with respect and care, the way she would like to be treated. "I always make it clear that I am not just there to count their fish or check their nets, but to learn from them, and how important what they do and what they have to tell me is. I always pay respect to their knowledge and experience."

When final reports on the season's returns are completed each year, Nicole and the Nisg̱a'a Fisheries team hold community meetings so everyone can share in the results. "When we tell them what we're finding, as we always do, everyone who contributed their knowledge to the findings will be there and know they've had a really important part to play. I can tell them the numbers that you see in those reports are from you, and I remind them of the importance of their participation. I try to make sure that they feel appreciated for helping us to protect our resources." After all, as Nita points out, this work is to ensure that Tx̲eemsim can live on in future generations of Git-Tx̱eemsim. "What they are contributing is for our Nation," agrees Nicole, "to help us protect our precious fish for those future generations."

Nisga'a Fisheries and Wildlife Director Harry Nyce, Sr.

Nicole also likes to spend time every February and March down at Da oots'ip working with the Saak harvesters. Saak is sometimes called the "saviour fish" because of its timely return to the Nass each year after what is often a long, lean winter. The first glimpse of the treasured fish running upriver each spring is always a cause of celebration for the Nisg̱a'a, and its impending arrival is celebrated each year at Hoobiyee.

The word "Hoobiyee" is related directly to the shape of the crescent moon, whose rising each February signals the start of the new year and the new harvesting season, says Nisg̱a'a Director of Lands and Resources Mansell Griffin. The moon's slender curve resembles a ladle, or hoobix (spoon), says Mansell. "Hee[14] means cheer, so when we celebrate Hoobiyee, we literally cheer for Spoon, saying 'Hlaa ksigwantkwhl hlok̲sis dee! Hoobiyee!'" Nita adds, "Elders have explained that when the points of the crescent moon aim upward and resemble the bowl of the wooden spoon, hoobix, this signifies an abundant season of Saak and subsequent seasons of food resources. Naturally, when winter food supplies are depleting and the Guxw-hlok̲sit[15] yells out for all to hear, 'Hoobixis hee-eey!' Nisg̱a'a know what this means, and they are exuberant. Everyone yells, 'Hoobiyee! Hoobiyee!'"

After Mansell completed his university education in First Nation studies and environmental management in the mid-1990s he returned to the Nass, where he was born and raised, to work for his Nation. A passionate fisherman, he was more than happy to come home. "It took me travelling and living elsewhere to appreciate this place is a piece of heaven," he says. As it is for Nicole, for Mansell, the inseparability of the fish, the river, and his own wellbeing—and by implication that of all Nisg̱a'a people—is foundational to his existence. "We are not apart from nature; we are a part *of* it," he explains. "We are part of the same ecosystem and what's better for the ecosystem is better for everything in it, ourselves included."

It is a way of being infused with spirituality and the principles of kwhlix̱hoosa'anskw. Mansell grew up being taught to respect everything around him as a living being. "We were animists, believing that everything has spirit, and that everything has its own perspective and role to fulfil as it lives its life." To him, a tree is considered to be more than just alive. "It has emotions, perspective and agency and the ability to make choices. While those choices may seem limited from our perspective, something else might look at us and see how limited our choices are. Even the stones," believes Mansell, "can feel our weight on their backs."

When it comes to fish, he adds, the same principle applies. Creatures with agency must be given the choice to give themselves to humans, to fulfil their needs. "We look at salmon as coming up the river to give us, from their perspective, the blankets on their backs, which for us is the meat on their bones." To make sure that salmon feel they are respected in doing so, it is important to maintain certain traditions. "When you are fishing and a fish hits your net, I say 'G̱al hee, hadiks!'[16] That translates as a cheerful welcome to the salmon to 'come here, brother' or 'come here, swimmer,' cheering that it came to visit with you and gifted itself to you. That," Mansell observes, "is the relationship we have always had with animals and other living things, treating them as beings with their own agency rather than just taking what we want."

It is hard sometimes to balance that perspective with the way people live in the twenty-first century, says Mansell. "But it is something that I try to practise. I still talk to the salmon whenever I am fishing." It is also a perspective that is an important environmental lens through which to consider diminishing wild salmon stocks. "It is important never to disrespect that self-giving for fear that the fish would choose not to return in future. Our ancestors could regard the shrinking runs of salmon right now, for example, as proof of our lack of fitness to receive their gifts. Given that more and more fish are choosing not to come back, we must be doing something wrong. Why have we lost their faith?"

The loss of their salmon was a matter that by the dawn of the 1990s was becoming increasingly concerning for the Nisg̱a'a; something had to be done and quickly. The Nation had been in formal treaty negotiations with the federal government since 1976 and discussions about fisheries had initially centred on Nisg̱a'a harvesting rights and guaranteed annual allocations of fish for food, social and ceremonial purposes, and commercial use. As their precious stock continued to dwindle year after year, however, the Nisg̱a'a negotiators refocussed their discussions with Ottawa on the governance and management of the Nass fisheries. "We looked at what was happening everywhere on the coast of British Columbia," says former

The Nass River at the suspension bridge at Gitwinksihlkw.

commercial fisherman and Nisga'a Fisheries Director Harry Nyce, Sr., who led many of the negotiations with the federal Department of Fisheries and Oceans (DFO). "As the stocks decreased, everyone had started fighting over them. In 1990 we started saying to DFO instead of arguing over who gets to fish and how much they get to catch, let's talk about how we can work together to improve the scientific data available and rebuild the salmon stocks so that everyone can keep fishing. Let's partner in that goal through our treaty arrangements."

Protection of what fish remained could not wait until completion of the treaty talks as they were still far from being complete (the Nisga'a Final Agreement would not come into effect until 2000). But without accurate data on the size and timing of various runs of different species, explains Harry, as well as harvest numbers and other relevant information like habitat health, it would be impossible to manage the stocks effectively in the meantime, let alone put in place measures to rebuild them. The available data at that point was woefully inadequate. "With the support of our

Lava beds at Anhluut'ukwsim Lax̲mihl Angwinga'asanskwhl Nisg̲a'a (Nisg̲a'a Memorial Lava Bed Park).

leadership, that's when we established the Nisg̲a'a Fisheries department, with a mandate to accurately assess the status of fish stocks in the Nass so that we could determine what needed to be done."

Nisg̲a'a Fisheries' first steps in 1992 were to employ LGL's contemporary scientific expertise to assess the data on their behalf and to install a fishwheel at Gitwinksihlkw, on the Nass River, in order to count the numbers of salmon returning to spawn. More commonly used to harvest fish, a fishwheel is also a highly accurate counting mechanism that operates a little like a waterwheel. Baskets turned by the current capture fish long enough to be counted and tagged before the unharmed fish are released into the river to continue their journey to their spawning grounds.

The results of the first year's research were staggering, recalls Harry. Until that point, the Nisg̲a'a had relied on estimates of fish numbers provided by DFO from annual gillnet test fisheries undertaken during early salmon runs. Fish caught in these gillnet fisheries, unlike the fishwheels, do not survive (and frequently other types of fish are inadvertently caught and killed). In the test fisheries, total run size numbers are extrapolated from sample catches. "DFO thought it was a good tool, but when we ran that first fishwheel, we found that their numbers were out by more than fifty per cent."[17] The discrepancy was shocking and eye-opening. "A light bulb went on for us. This was how inaccurate DFO's test fishery data collection was compared to our little fishwheel on the river."[18]

Of equal importance to the scientific data in the approach to saving the Nass salmon stocks was the incorporation of Nisg̱a'a worldviews and traditional law, applying the principles learned through their adaawaḵ, ayuuḵ, and ankw'ihlwil to the implementation of their contemporary methodology, and embracing kwhlix̱hoosa'anskw in every aspect of the work. These two complementary sides of the Nisg̱a'a fisheries coin, old and new, would each lend the other immense strength.

Nisg̱a'a leaders also wanted to encourage and train their own citizens to become scientists, laboratory technicians, and harvest monitors rather than have to rely on non- Nisg̱a'a expertise on an ongoing basis. That meant bringing young Nisg̱a'a into the Fisheries team right from the beginning, including people like biology student Cheryl (Stephens) Moore, who began work with the brand-new organization in the early 1990s, although still only partway through her undergraduate degree. After finishing her studies and obtaining her degree, Cheryl joined Nisg̱a'a Fisheries fulltime as a field technician (the same role in which Nicole would later begin her career with Nisg̱a'a Fisheries), subsequently completing a master's in business administration and moving into management. As it was for Nicole, the job was a good fit for a young woman who had grown up watching her father, uncles and cousins harvesting fish and who learned how to process the catch from her aunts and mother. "Working with Nisg̱a'a Fisheries was a natural extension of both my formal education and my childhood experience," reflects Cheryl. In total, she spent twenty-one years with the Fisheries team before leaving in 2013 to take on the role of executive director for NLG, assisting the chief executive officer.

It was when the Nisg̱a'a treaty finally came into effect in 2000, recalls Cheryl, that the "real work" began. Nisg̱a'a Fisheries continued operating seamlessly through the transition into the post-treaty world. With stocks still steadily declining it was more important than ever to have good

Ts'im K̲'olhl Da oots'ip (Fishery Bay)

information about everything that was affecting the fish. The Nation had been working with DFO since Nisga'a Fisheries was first established, but the provisions of the new treaty formalized the relationship and the way in which NLG and the federal government would work together in the future to support the salmon fishery.[19] "We agreed that there would be a formal joint fisheries management committee (JFMC) established," says Cheryl, "and that going forward the committee would guide the work in our river, gathering the best information possible to stabilize the fisheries together."

Whereas those arrangements realized the goal of collaboration to protect the fish that the Nisga'a had been working toward for ten years and more, agreeing to joint management was nonetheless a significant concession on their part, reflects Harry, given the Nation's original stewardship role and fisheries rights (rights which, he points out, were recognized in Canadian law in 1973).[20] But, he adds, the interests of the salmon as well as other Nass fish species of importance to the Nisg̱a'a came first. "We accepted that the ongoing administration of the fishery would be shared through the JFMC." Using its treaty funding, the newly established NLG also set up the Lisims Fisheries Conservation Trust Fund to support the ongoing important work of Nisg̱a'a Fisheries and to promote Nisg̱a'a stewardship through making bursary funds available to Nisg̱a'a biology students.

Cheryl Moore, executive director of Nisg̱a'a Lisims Government

The next step for NLG was to enact contemporary laws to govern the exercise of their Treaty Rights by their people and the sustainable harvest from K̲'alii-Aksim-Lisims of salmon and other fish species. "The treaty required us to pass our own laws," explains Cheryl. "We had to develop our own *Fish and Wildlife Act* and our own fisheries and wildlife regulations." That required consideration, among other things, of seasons and openings. "Our starting point was to establish when we would traditionally harvest. We went to our Elders and the harvesters and asked them when the right time is to harvest these species."

Salmon was easy. "It is always harvested from May to October, when the fish are running upriver to spawn." For other fish species and shellfish, says Cheryl, there are also certain times of the year to harvest and others when no harvesting takes place. "There were good reasons for that, all of which make sense in terms of the biology of the species. We don't harvest Dungeness crabs when they're moulting. People knew that the crabs would be creating a new shell and there wouldn't be a lot of meat inside, so from a food perspective, it's not worth harvesting them during that time. They provided similar advice about shellfish based on their knowledge. We don't harvest clams and cockles in the warmer months when there might be toxic algae blooms. Modern science supports that, too, of course."

That longstanding wisdom became the baseline for establishing harvesting seasons. The Nation had to decide when to harvest and how much. "We had to ask ourselves two questions," says Cheryl. "What is good for the people? And what is good for the resource?" Nisg̱a'a people have always

The idea that wild salmon might one day not return to the Nass River is inconceivable, says Nisg̱a'a Lisims Government executive director Cheryl Moore: "We must ensure that doesn't ever happen."

needed fish to live on but have also always been taught to only take what is needed. "That's one of the reasons why it still remains so important to get accurate numbers through Nisg̱a'a Fisheries' stock assessment and monitoring programs each year. Only based on those numbers can we really answer the question of how many salmon we can take to satisfy the need, because if you over-exploit the fishery then of course you won't have any fish left."

Cheryl recalls that not long after the Nisg̱a'a treaty came into effect, a Lisims Fisheries Conservation Trust Fund trustee asked her, "What will you do if the salmon *don't* return?" She replied, "I can't even fathom that. This is why we are here, to ensure that doesn't happen, to ensure that the salmon do always return." By using the information Nisg̱a'a Fisheries continues to collect and the science tracking run sizes to achieve annual spawning targets, says Harry, NLG can now make decisions quickly and efficiently from year-to-year to support that outcome. "You can allow more opportunities to harvest in years when there is a really good return but act to reduce the take in lean years to ensure enough fish can reach the spawning grounds and maintain the sustainability of the fishery."

That, he adds sombrely, is exactly what NLG had to do in 2020 and again in 2021, when salmon runs were so poor that no commercial fishery could take place. "In July 2020 we realized that the numbers were not adding up at the fishwheel. Salmon returns were not on track to reach our spawning targets for the year, so we decided we had to close any kind of fishing on the Nass River for nearly three weeks. That had never happened before, but it was the right thing to do. While it was difficult for the fishermen and the community, people accepted that decision, which allowed us to meet the spawning targets."

Nisg̲a'a science student and avid fisher James Griffin is a recipient of a bursary from the Conservation Trust Fund.

In the face of an ongoing decline of salmon stocks, closing the fishery may be a decision that NLG will have to repeat in future years to achieve sufficient numbers of fish spawning and safeguard later returns, says Harry. But dedicated efforts are being made by Nisg̲a'a Fisheries to rebuild wild Nass salmon stocks, as well as steelhead, in partnership with DFO and the provincial government. Given the level of commitment by Nisg̲a'a people to protect their prized fish, he is hopeful that the tide will eventually turn again and that Nisg̲a'a people will enjoy abundant wild salmon on their tables once more.

In 2022, Nisg̲a'a Fisheries celebrated its thirtieth birthday. Data collected through the fishwheels and other assessment programs continues to be combined with ancient Nisg̲a'a knowledge and conventional science to produce consistently accurate and useful results. A year earlier, Richard Alexander posted on Facebook that he considered Nisg̲a'a Fishery's fishwheel program on the Nass to be "the best test fishery in the world to manage salmon and steelhead returns to a river."

By then more than forty Nisg̲a'a staff were employed by the department. Among them were Nisg̲a'a biologist Niva Percival, who was the first recipient of the Lisims Fisheries Conservation Trust Fund bursary to support her university education. More and more young Nisg̲a'a, says Harry, like Mansell Griffin's nineteen-year-old son James—an avid fisherman and also a recipient of a bursary from the Conservation Trust Fund—are choosing to study biology in order to come back home to the Nass and work for Nisg̲a'a Fisheries.

ẃahlin Sim'oogit Hleek̲,
Dr. Joseph Gosnell

James, says Nicole, is always a joy to observe on the river. When she sees him out there working hard and loving every minute of what he is doing, she is not only reminded of her younger self but of why she, too, does what she does. Like his father, James is always happiest out on the water. Becoming a scientist and coming back to work for the Nation to help protect their fisheries is a pathway that is simply beyond question. "Ten years from now," says James firmly, "I don't want to have any regrets, and I believe if I continue down this road I won't have any."

In a short video produced by Nisg̲a'a Fisheries in 1998, ẃahlin Sim'oogit Hleek̲, Dr. Joseph Gosnell, spoke about why the fisheries program was so important to the Nation. Anticipating future generations of Nisg̲a'a youth wanting to fish and revel in the same bounty their forebears had always enjoyed, Dr. Gosnell said, "We are looking at people that have yet to be born, twenty, thirty, one hundred years from now. Will they have salmon? That is our ultimate goal, to make absolutely certain that the answer to that is yes."

Inherent in that goal is not only the sustenance of the people but of their pride and joy in a way of life and a food source that their ancestors enjoyed for millennia. Despite the challenges, this gives people like Harry every reason to be hopeful. "To watch the engagement of the people with the fishery now is so exciting," he observes. "They understand what we are doing and why we have to work together to save our salmon, the best food in the world. Everyone is part of that. People's chests are way out, their heads are up, and the laughter and the camaraderie of everyone out there harvesting is really, really indescribable. It's true all the way up and down the Nass River. It's so vast, it's such a beautiful area to be in and to experience. It's wonderful to see the joy of the people."

Nicole, who was only a teenager when Nisg̱a'a Fisheries was first established, agrees wholeheartedly. "I love the places that working with our fish takes me," she reflects, "to the land, to the people. There is so much joy and excitement in the beauty of the Nass, in going to Da oots'ip to see people who have always harvested Saak still doing so together in their camps each spring. I feel incredibly blessed to be part of such steeped tradition and the community that this work brings me into, their hard work and dedication, their values of sustainability. I can't imagine not having that in my life—not having the river to go to and remind me of where I come from and what I'm doing for our people through my work. I love being in all of these places with all of these people doing what I do."

"When I look at Nicole," observes Nita quietly, "and all of the generations coming up behind us, and at the work of the Fisheries team—as one of the Elders in our Nation now, I can't help thinking, 'There's that Tx̱eemsim at work again,' up to the challenge and not giving in to any fear or ever giving up." Nita feels the future is in good hands. "I can't help smiling and thinking, 'Japs Tx̱eemsim.' This is the work of Tx̱eemsim."

Haíłzaqv Unfettered

CHAPTER FOUR

Every day during the spring of 2020 four-year-old Noen Ḣáusṫl would run eagerly outside to check on the growth of the new, tender green tips emerging on the spruce trees in his parents' yard in Wágḷísḷa (Bella Bella). Each afternoon when his mother Jess arrived home from work, Noen would greet her with an enthusiastic report on their progress.

Her little boy was engrossed with spruce tips, says Jess, because one year earlier, when his grandfather was injured in a fall, she had shown Noen how to harvest the tender tips as medicine for his papa. "They are high in chlorophyll, so good for tissue healing," she explains. Noen's memories of the harvesting process had imprinted themselves indelibly on his young and highly receptive consciousness. "Twelve months later he still remembered that spruce tips are an important medicine, so he was watching for them to appear. He also remembered that you don't harvest them until they are a certain size," says Jess. "He went out daily to pick any tips that were ready. He would show them to me when I got home and talk about the people that he wanted to give them to as medicine."

That Noen had so thoroughly absorbed that learning was phenomenal, reflects Jess. "It's so magical to know that's embedded in his little identity already. This year again I didn't have to remind him when the spruce trees started budding. He went out there by himself and called to me, 'Mommy, the medicine's coming.'" It was a gift of both identity and Haíłzaqv culture that was immensely important to Jess. "It's what I want for my kids as they grow up

"Noen (five) to Magnus (three): 'Why are you mad?' Magnus: 'NOT mad.' Noen: 'Okay… Are you haíl̓álá? That's like mad, but in Haíłzaqvḷa.' Magnus: 'I…haíl̓álá.' Noen: 'Sometimes it's easier to have feelings in Haíłzaqvḷa.'"

—*Twitter post, 'Cúagilákv, Jess Ḣáusṫl (Housty), Haíłzaqv Nation, October 2020*

Facing page: Haíłzaqv people have lived in their territory for at least fourteen thousand years.

to be Haíłzaqv adults, that they are grateful and excited about the fact that they can take care of the places and things and people that matter to them in a way that's so reciprocal and generous."

An extremely busy working parent, Jess is also mother to Noen's younger brother, Magnus. She recently completed two terms on Haíłzaqv Tribal Council, participating on several regional boards and committees on behalf of her Nation. She is on the board of Nature United, a national conservation organization, as well as on the board of the West Coast Environmental Law Foundation, acting as an adviser to Level (an initiative of the Vancouver Foundation) and to the Resilient Indigenous Leaders' Network, both of which work with Indigenous youth, and a member of the Governing Circle on Philanthropy and Aboriginal Peoples in Canada.

She is the executive director of the Qqs Projects Society, a Haíłzaqv charitable non-profit organization supporting youth and families, and an active volunteer in the Haíłzaqv community. When the global pandemic began in early 2020, Jess initiated a "Granny Gardens" project along the lines of the Victory Gardens of the first and second world wars, created to encourage people to learn to grow food and to provide fresh produce to the community. She also co-founded a much-needed on-reserve pet rescue service and initiated a drive for new contributions to the community library she had founded several years previously. In between fulfilling all of these commitments, Jess writes powerful, compelling essays for a range of provincial and national publications. Articulate and thoughtful, with extensive experience in environmental protection, youth programs and human rights, she is in high demand to speak on panels and at conferences.

Despite her hectic schedule, Jess is also doing her best to immerse Noen and Magnus in their language and cultural traditions. That is more challenging than it should be. For centuries, colonization has relentlessly assaulted the Haíłzaqv Nation, with ruinous effects on not only the retention of their language but of their cultural traditions and laws, and of their territory, their identity, and their wellbeing. By the time Jess was born, in the mid-1980s, Haíłzaqvḷa had become critically endangered. Few people were still proficient in the language and most of them were over seventy. Although it was taught in school, the language was not typically spoken at home, and as a result neither Jess nor most of her peers retained much of their mother tongue as adults.

Cúagilákv (Jess H̓áustl̓) standing in front of Gvúkva'áus Haíłzaqv, which took eighteen months to build and is made entirely of red and yellow cedar from the territory.

Jess is determined that Noen and Magnus will never experience that kind of limitation on their ability to celebrate their mother tongue or their identity as Haíłzaqv citizens. "I'm still just baby steps into my own Haíłzaqvla language journey, but I try to make a habit of using our words with the kids," she says. She also wants them to learn and understand why that is so important. "We remind the kids about the history all the time. I am from the first generation of Haíłzaqv who did not get taken away to residential school. I did not learn the language when I was their age but they can. They are able to be Haíłzaqv unfettered in a way that has never been true for any previous generation of our community since contact, including mine. They can be Haíłzaqv in every sense of the word without any fear. I want them to be conscious of that privilege and grateful for it."

To be Haíłzaqv is to have a deep and inseverable connection to the place that you are from. Both Haíłzaqv núyṃ́ (Oral Tradition) and archaeological evidence tell a formidable story in that regard. By the time Noen and Magnus were born the Haíłzaqv had inhabited their territory for at least fourteen thousand years; in human terms, effectively since time began. Some seven hundred generations later, the Haíłzaqv Nation comprises 2,500 people, all descended from five Haíłzaqvla-speaking tribes:

the Ẃúyalitx̌v (Seaward Tribe), Q̓vúqvaỷáitx̌v (Calm Water Tribe), Ẃúíƛ̓itx̌v (Roscoe Inlet Tribe), Ỷísdáitx̌v (Ỷísda Tribe), and the X̌íx̌ís (Northern/Downriver Tribe). More than one thousand Haíłzaqv live in Wáglísla, in the heart of Haíłzaqv territory, which encompasses the southern tip of Calvert Island, Dean and Burke Channels as far as Kimsquit and the head of Dean Inlet, and Matheson and Finlayson Channels to the north. It is a territory composed half of land, half of ocean.

This bears repeating: Noen, Magnus, and Jess, and all of their fellow Haíłzaqv citizens, are directly connected in an unbroken fourteen-thousand-year continuum of history to the first of their ancestors who walked and paddled the territory. The remarkable longevity of their DNA bears compelling and incontrovertible witness to the resilience of a people over multiple millennia, and the sophistication of their strategies for sustainable stewardship of the place to which their wellbeing is so inextricably linked. While other ancient civilizations rose and fell around the world, these people thrived until European explorers arrived on their doorstep.

The onslaught of colonization—the theft of their lands, the residential school system, the *Indian Act*, the Potlatch ban, among so many other colonial efforts to destroy Indigenous culture—exacted a horrific human and environmental toll on the Haíłzaqv, both collectively and individually. The Haíłzaqv have resolutely defended themselves and their territory against settler occupation of their unceded lands, but it has been a difficult and traumatic battle with the odds overwhelmingly stacked against them. The Haíłzaqv, however, have their history on their side and all of the knowledge, experience, wisdom and determination that comes with that history. Although the battle is still far from over, the tide has started to turn, and the Haíłzaqv have begun to reclaim a position of considerable strength in their homelands; albeit one that requires constant vigilance on their part to protect.

In the early 2010s, for example, the Nation was confronted by a significant environmental threat in the form of Canadian oil company Enbridge Inc.'s proposed Northern Gateway pipeline. The risk of oil spills in Haíłzaqv territory, either from the pipeline itself or ships carrying the heavy diluted bitumen to export markets overseas, was massive. Haíłzaqv yím̓ás (hereditary leaders) and the elected Chief and members of the Haíłzaqv Tribal Council were determined that the pipeline would never be built, and issued a proclamation reaffirming the Nation's sovereign Title and their rights

Haíłzaqv Tribal Council Chief K̓áwáził (Marilyn Slett) at the opening of Haíłzaqv ƛiác̓i (the Big House) during X̱aayda-Haíłzaqv Day in October 2019.

to exercise governance and stewardship authority over Haíłzaqv territory according to their traditional ğv̓iḷás (laws).

Haíłzaqv Tribal Council Chief K̓áwáził (Marilyn Slett) reinforced the message with an unequivocal shot over Enbridge's bow, declaring that the Nation would take "whatever action is necessary to stop this risky project." Enbridge offered money and jobs but the Haíłzaqv refused them; nothing was worth the risk. After a long and difficult campaign opposing the proposed pipeline, in which Jess and many other Haíłzaqv citizens devoted years to protest campaigns[21], Enbridge was eventually defeated.

Tragically, just as it should have been celebrating that outcome, the Nation's worst environmental and cultural fears were realized when on the night of October 13, 2016, the *Nathan E. Stewart*, an articulated barge carrying 100,000 litres of diesel fuel and oil, sank at Q̓vúqvái (Gale Pass), an important Haíłzaqv food harvesting and cultural site. The trauma and fear triggered in the Haíłzaqv community by the catastrophic spill is difficult to describe. Years later, Jess, who led the Haíłzaqv emergency spill response team, still succumbs to tears of anger and sadness recalling the effect on the community. "In the context of any threat to land and ocean and food security, the impact went so much deeper than the loss of a resource that was precious to us. It was about everything we are and everything that

Above and facing page: The objective of the Haíłzaqv Oceans Act, also known as Haíłzaqv H̓aíkilaxsi c̓íslá w̓áw̓áx̌tusa gáyáqḷa qṇts dṃxsax̌v (Haíłzaqv respecting and taking care of our ocean relatives) is to safeguard the marine life in Haíłzaqv territory. That includes everything from humpback whales to herring roe, which is both an important commercial and cultural fishery.

we've been taught our whole lives we can trust and rely on suddenly being taken away from us and from our children."

At a community meeting in the midst of the crisis, an Elder took Jess aside. "He shared with me that he had grown up in poverty and that in his childhood, if he hadn't had access to ancestral and traditional resources like those available at Q̓vúqvái, he felt that his family would have starved," she says. "He'd always been able to trust that the territory would provide for him. But what happens if you can't trust the territory anymore? What happens if the thing that at the seat of your soul has always given you a sense of comfort and security and nourishment and love and protection has suddenly gone?"

It was a pivotal moment in Jess's comprehension of the scale of healing required from the impacts of colonization. "That was an incredibly important lesson for me," she reflects. "I realized that you can't separate the really difficult and traumatic parts of our history as a people, the ways in which we've been regulated off our own territory since contact, the removal of children to residential school systems and the ways that social and cultural systems have been fragmented by colonization, from the way we respond to situations like that happening."

Frustrated by a vacuum of government action following the disaster, the Haíłzaqv Integrated Resource Management Department (HIRMD) undertook an environmental assessment of the damage to Q̓vúqvái so that it could implement remedial measures to the best of its ability. The Nation also proposed new processes be put in place to reduce the risk of a repeat incident and that an Indigenous marine response centre be created to increase the capacity of coastal Indigenous communities to respond to future spills and similar environmental crises. In 2017, HIRMD worked with the West Coast Environmental Law Association to initiate a project to enact new Haíłzaqv oceans legislation that would provide greater protection to their territory than the federal *Oceans Act*. The *Haíłzaqv Oceans Act*, also known as Haíłzaqv H̓aíkilaxsi c̓ísḷá w̓áw̓áx̌tusa gáyáqḷa qṇts dṃxsax̌v (Haíłzaqv respecting and taking care of our ocean relatives) would be a living and adaptable set of ǧv̓iḷás giving effect to Haíłzaqv ways of protecting the environment.

After finally settling a longstanding court case defending the right of the Nation to a commercial herring roe fishery, the Haíłzaqv also entered into Haíłcístut reconciliation talks with the federal and provincial governments. Haíłcístut translates to something like "turning things around

Kelly Brown, former director of the Haíłzaqv Integrated Resource Management Department, at the opening of Haíłzaqv ƛíáci̓ (the Big House) during X̱aayda-Haíłzaqv Day in October 2019.

and making them right again," a principle that the three governments agreed would form the basis for a new relationship between them. The Haíłzaqv are determined that Haíłcístut will be a platform to give full effect to the Nation's self-government rights, their ancient rights of stewardship and management of their territory, and their laws.

None of these initiatives or decisions were easy to undertake for a Nation still encumbered by unhealed trauma. The strength of the Haíłzaqv to do so, reflects HIRMD former director Kelly Brown, comes from many sources but two of them are fundamental. "Despite everything done to us, we have never let go of our ways of life, our culture, and our relationship not only to ourselves as people but to the territory," he says. "We have always taken responsibility to keep our Nation and our territory healthy. That is something we have always taught our children and still do today so that they will continue to uphold that responsibility."

The second source of Haíłzaqv strength, says Kelly, comes from the Haíłzaqv matriarchs: "Women are the backbone of our community and our people, and always have been. Our long line of matriarchs through the ages have continuously passed their wisdom and strength down to their descendants. Through the worst times, they saved our culture, they saved our songs and our stories. They kept us alive and held up our identity. They are still doing that. I am so grateful to have all these amazing women leading us and working for us. That speaks to our way of life and who we are."

Among these women is Haíłzaqv Tribal Council Chief Marilyn Slett. In her fourth term as Chief Councillor in 2021, Marilyn attributes much of her success as a leader to what she learned from her maternal grandmother Florence Humchitt. As a child, Marilyn spent most of her summers with Florence and her grandfather Wesley Humchitt, and particularly remembers the warmth, laughter and love shared among the older women who surrounded her grandmother. "She had a circle of friends, Peggy Housty, Emma Humchitt, Grace Humchitt, and Catherine Goudswaard, who would spend many afternoons together drinking tea and knitting and doing community work."

The sense of camaraderie, social interaction and community purpose that bound the women left a lasting impression on the young child who learned much about what it means to be a Haíłzaqv matriarch from listening to their conversations. "Their wisdom was immense," recalls Marilyn. "Their strength of connection and purpose and their commitment to the community helped me in forming my own leadership principles, based on our values as Haíłzaqv people."

Marilyn Slett's beloved grandmother Florence (middle) with her dear friends Caroline Hall (left) and Grace Humchitt.

Like Marilyn, Jess has acquired many of her values and skills as an adult from Haíłzaqv matriarchs who enriched her thinking and her approach to life. Her aunt Hílístis, Pauline Waterfall, has been particularly influential. She is an artist, author, and educator who has dedicated her adult life to working not only for her community but for access to education for all Indigenous people. Pauline has, in her own way, shown the younger woman the true meaning and importance of being "Haíłzaqv unfettered."

Hílístis, the ancestral name that Pauline inherited from her maternal grandmother, means something like "starting out on a journey and staying on course until it is completed in full circle by returning home." Her dedication to education and cultural revitalization, including of Indigenous languages, has been driven in part by her own childhood experience. Sent away to residential school at the age of twelve, Pauline returned to Wáglísla many years later as an adult to reclaim the Haíłzaqv cultural self that had been stolen from her and, as Jess would also later do, to work for a better life for Haíłzaqv youth.

Jess learned a great deal from her beloved aunt, both as a child at her kitchen table and as an adult working alongside her. "I sat with her on Tribal Council for a term. I've also had the opportunity to work with her on different community projects. I've always had this consciousness that with anything I'm doing there's something to learn from her and some wisdom that she can share about it. Even now I never start something without thinking that it almost certainly ties back to something Auntie Pauli taught me or

Hílístis (Pauline Waterfall)

initiated herself. That level of community service and work on behalf of the people that you love is how I've tried to live my life and do my work, and something that I learned, among other people, from her."

Jess' upbringing was also formative, especially summers spent camping and exploring the territory with her parents. "That was a hugely influential part of my education. My parents both cared deeply about territorial stewardship and protecting species and resources in key places from industrial impacts and that was built into the fabric of how I was raised." As a child, having those experiences made her feel immensely rich. "I knew we were deeply rooted and resilient. I felt that way because I knew who I was and where I came from. I understood myself and who I was entirely in relation to the places around me, the ways that I interacted with them, the ways that they nourished me, and the ways that I could take care of them." As an adult, says Jess, all of these things are inseparable from who she is. "The deep collective values and teaching, customs and laws that are embedded in me come from these lands. They give me strength and power that is so deeply rooted in my identity that I carry them with me everywhere like a second skin."

Jess' father Larry Jorgenson was one of the people behind the establishment of Qqs in 1999. Qqs (eyes) was created as a vehicle to attract philanthropic support for land-based education and wellness for Haíłzaqv youth. It is a natural home for Jess, who has worked for the organization since its inception. "The mandate of Qqs is to open the eyes of our young people to their responsibilities as stewards of our land, culture, and resources, and to empower them to be strong leaders," she explains. Qqs evolved over the years to take on a broad range of community projects, but Haíłzaqv youth remained its central focus. "Our responsibility as an organization is to show our kids a world where they're valued and loved and powerful, where their Haíłzaqv identity and culture is a point of strength, and where they are active contributors to the work that's happening and a key part of the fabric of who we are."

The Koeye River, location of Haíłzaqv's camp, cabins and ƛáƛiχsístala ("completing the circle of knowledge"), the camp Big House at Koeye.

Qqs' founding project is a youth camp established at the mouth of the Koeye[22] River, some fifty kilometres south of Wágḷísḷa. The ecologically rich Koeye watershed was designated as a provincial conservancy area in 2007. The cultural value of the area and the Haíłzaqv's spiritual connection to it are profound. Haíłzaqv history speaks of Koeye's occupation since time immemorial. Seven villages once existed along the river, from its mouth up into the lake country near its headwaters. Culturally modified trees along ancient riverside trails tell a story of ancestral Haíłzaqv activity taking place between the villages.

The establishment of the camp in that particular spot has re-established a physical link for Haíłzaqv youth to that history. The past footprints of their forebears at Koeye continue to sustain and nourish their descendants in the present. "You can see how this place has been looked after for thousands of years, since the time of creation by our ancestors," observes Jess. "I have seen that for myself when I've been out harvesting with my kids. Maybe it's a root garden in a meadow, at a place where I've been told my great-grandmothers went to harvest medicine. The medicine

‘Cúagilákv (Jess H̓áust̓l) with her sons Noen and Magnus.

is still there because they harvested it sustainably and cared for it, passing down the knowledge of how to do that to their children and grandchildren.” That continuity of wisdom is, she hopes, something her children will in turn pass on to their own descendants someday. “They will be able to teach their grandkids what to do and tell them that this is where their mom taught them to harvest medicine. It will give them a tangible sense of connection to their ancestors. That’s another gift I can give to my kids.”

Over the course of six camps held at Koeye each summer, Haíłzaqv children and youth spend their days exploring the area on foot and in a canoe and learn to harvest traditional foods and medicines. They are taught practical skills, science, and Haíłzaqv environmental and resource management principles and techniques. “In the evenings, they have language lessons in the camp Big House, hear stories, and learn songs and dances and ceremonies,” says Jess. “Every kid can pick a role that they want to really do a deep dive on learning about. Some kids want to drum or learn songs, others want to be in the back learning which regalia goes with which dance and how to prepare dancers. Some of them want to dance, some of them want to be on the floor attending, some of them want to learn the public-speaking roles. Our staff coach them through all those roles. On the last full day of camp we invite the community to come down for what we call feast day and gather in the Big House. They get to watch the kids put on a feast where they are singing and dancing and drumming and taking everybody through all the ceremonies. It is a wonderful experience for everyone involved.”

Jess attended Koeye camp in its early days when the routine was more basic. “When I was a kid there it was really a simple agenda: get us out on the land, build our sense of connection to it, and give us some useful skills that will grow our feelings of independence. But as the years went on, the kids expressed an appetite to learn about culture and language, and that became the core of the camp program.” Everyone from the community got involved. One man, Ed Martin, or Pops as most people knew him, taught

Haiłzaqv territory is immense, and diverse in its ocean, land, and riverscapes.

language to the children every summer. "We were really blessed to have Pops. He moved down to Koeye every year for the season and lived in a little cabin we built for him," recalls Jess.

Pops, she says, was an amazing man. "He suffered the absolute worst horror stories of residential school. He struggled with alcoholism. He suffered from all the symptoms of poverty and violence and oppression and trauma. He had the language literally beaten out of him as a child." At some point, however, Ed decided he did not want to let that experience define who he was as a Haíłzaqv person. "When he committed to using the language again, he found that it was embedded deep inside him and he had not lost it. By the time I was born, Pops was one of our primary language teachers in the community," says Jess.

Ed was also the instigator for building the camp Big House at Koeye, naming it λáλix̌sístala (completing the circle of knowledge). "He insisted the children deserved to learn about our laws and customs in an appropriate

Language teacher Ǧvúí (Rory Ḣáustl or Housty)

context like a Big House. We've been incredibly fortunate," emphasizes Jess, "that there have been people like Pops and Aunt Pauli, who retained their knowledge deep down and who found the courage to push through all of the pain and trauma associated with the loss of that cultural knowledge through residential schools and reclaimed and gifted it to younger generations in ways that have enriched our lives so much."

Jess is constantly overwhelmed to see the results of the Koeye program embodied in Haíɫzaqv youth. "It is so amazing to see how the kids continue to blossom beyond our programs into cultural leaders in their own right in the community, performing various roles in our Big House, teaching language, you name it. If you look at our staff at Qqs in any given year, it's almost all kids who grew up as Koeye program participants. We found they want to continue doing that kind of work in a leadership capacity, whether as interns or staff members or even the camp director, so they come back year after year and ask to work there."

The phenomenon didn't stop at Koeye or Qqs. "Koeye graduates and alumni are doing everything. You can look everywhere in the community and see young people in leadership roles where they're bringing technical expertise related to their field to the position, but also their deep Haíɫzaqv world views and values to inform and empower what they're doing. We have Haíɫzaqv nurses, for example, who of course are fully qualified and licensed, but their practice is so much deeper because it is in their community with all of their teachings and their identity and their values behind them. We have amazing Haíɫzaqv teachers. Any industry, any job here, you can look around and see people who have been to Koeye and who enhance their contemporary roles with the depth of their Haíɫzaqv identity," says Jess.

Ǧvu̓í (Rory Ḣáusṫl or Housty), a young Haíłzaqv language teacher, worked at the Haíłzaqv College in Wágḷísḷa in 2021, teaching community members and children to Haíłzaqvḷa.[23] "After that, I started that year in a new position with the Haíłzaqvḷa Language Revitalization program, under one of the house posts of Haíłcístut, team-teaching Haíłzaqvḷa language immersion courses with Brett Waterfall." The program partnered with Vancouver's Simon Fraser University to successfully deliver the Haíłzaqvḷa Language Immersion program. "Our first cohort included ten community members that completed the courses and received their Certificate in Haíłzaqv Language Proficiency," says Ǧvu̓í. "In September 2021 we started with a second cohort of fifteen students. Once the second cohort completes the first year of the program, the two cohorts will combine to go into the second-year diploma program."

Ǧvu̓í, a Koeye camp graduate, is in his early thirties. "I started going to Koeye when I was about six or seven, with my grandfather, Pops. He was a beautiful storyteller, and whenever he would tell us stories, he would incorporate our language, Haízaqvḷa. It always captivated me, listening to him and spending time out on the land with him." Ǧvu̓í later worked at the camp as a teenager and during university holidays. "I was drawn back there to teach the younger generations our ways in the Big House, the singing and dancing and our stories." After graduating from Vancouver Island University with a BA in anthropology and First Nations Studies in 2012, Ǧvu̓í still wanted nothing more than to return home and teach. "It was very important to me to give back to a program that opened my eyes as a child to my sense of being a Haíłzaqv person and teach the younger generation something of what I was taught out there by my Elders," he says.

Like Jess, Ǧvu̓í wants the youth to understand and appreciate what their Elders had experienced. "My great granny, who is ninety-three, wasn't allowed to Potlatch. That is only a couple of generations away from me. She had to go underground, to hide what she was doing. We are so lucky some of them were able to hold onto the culture and the language. It is so important that our young ones today never experience that or have to hide what they do in the Big House."

Jaimie Teagle, who turned thirty in 2022, worked at Koeye as a teenager. Of the same generation of strong female leaders as Jess, Jaimie is also a very busy woman. With a degree in business administration from Capilano University, Jaimie was elected to Haíłzaqv Tribal Council in 2016

Following spread: Haíłzaqv citizens and guests gather to celebrate the opening of Haíłzaqv ƛiác̓i (the Big House) during X̱aayda-Haiłzaqv Day in October 2019.

Haíłzaqv councillor and business administrator Jaimie Teagle

and was given the education, youth, lands, housing and economic development portfolios. While managing the Nation's carbon credit committee, its business education and carpentry programs, the Haíłzaqv tiny homes project, and the Haíłzaqv heat pump project, she also joined the boards of Qqs, HIRMD, the First Nations Mid-Coast Training Society and the Bella Bella Community School Society.

At a personal level Jaimie believes she was fortunate to have been connected to her culture from an early age. "I was born and raised in Bella Bella. Right from the start, I was exposed to everything; our cultural teachings, our structured Haíłzaqv language classes and songs and dances. I would go to Potlatches here and there, depending on whether my mom and dad were available to go. If not, I was either out on the boat with my dad or on the land with my mom, doing something else," she recalls. "Through my everyday life I learned our Haíłzaqv values. I would not trade that childhood for the world."

As an adult, Jaimie brings those immensely important Haíłzaqv values into her various roles. In her economic development and housing portfolios, she prioritizes ancient Haíłzaqv environmental principles. "We have always been taught that we don't take more than we need and that we have to take care of our territory. If we build that thinking into our modern world of development we can accomplish so much without hurting the environment or destroying the world. We just have to rethink our values into our business practices. We can have contemporary economic development that is sustainable." The environmental values children are taught at Koeye, adds Jaimie, are a fundamental stepping-stone to that outcome. "Koeye is not just a camp, it's not just a job, it's not just a project. It truly is rebuilding our Nation to be stronger, to be more successful, and to be sustainable through our youth."

As to the next generation of matriarchs, says Chief Marilyn Slett proudly, they are already spreading their wings. In August 2021 an impressive group of teenagers, aged thirteen to eighteen, spoke in front of a

Haíɫzaqv matriarchs (from left): Haíɫzaqv Tribal Council Chief Ḱáwáziɫ (Marilyn Slett) with niece Tracy Carpenter, mother Bessie Carpenter, and sister Nicole Carpenter.

Council meeting. "These young women were strong and fierce and full of courage," recalls Marilyn. "Their names were Astrid Wilson-Sandy, Illiona Brown, Aria Reid, Natalia Windsor, Chailynn Windsor, Elle Brown, Analia Humchitt, Latoya Windsor, Shaylin Windsor, and Yaya Humchitt. They talked to us about systemic racism and the missing and murdered Indigenous women and girls, threats to Indigenous womanhood that are on a regional and national scale."

The young Haíɫzaqv women also spoke of the importance of the resurgence of the Haíɫzaqv language and learning about their culture. "It was amazing to hear their stories," says Marilyn. "These young ladies are the embodiment of our ancestors' resilience, reclaiming our voices and our roles of women in our community, and they make us so proud. They are the embodiment of what it means to be 'Haíɫzaqv unfettered.' They fill the hearts of our generation with hope for the future."

In early 2021, Jess wrote on Twitter, "My five-year-old just crawled into my arms and said: 'H̓íkúx̌vs ẇiúɫ, mommy.'[24] I think my heart just exploded." The significance of that simple but fundamental exchange in Haíɫzaqvḷa between mother and son could not be overstated. "Noen and Magnus," says Jess, "are part of a generation that will truly be, for the first time, Haíɫzaqv unfettered in every sense of the word."

The future is shining brightly for young Haíɫzaqv people, says Jess. "It is really magical that our kids are able to understand themselves as part of that long, deep continuum of Haíɫzaqv history in which people have carried on and practised and lived this knowledge and identity, and that they have a vital role to play in helping that continue to thrive. When I think about the future for my kids," she concludes quietly, "I am so unbelievably happy. It is such a gift to be Haíɫzaqv, in all the ways that manifests in their lives."

Our Homelands Build Us Up and Make Us Strong

CHAPTER FIVE

"T'áalan Stl'áng is always in my heart wherever I go. The landscape there sang to me and my soul sang whenever I was there; it made me feel fully who I am. Leaving at the end of each summer was like being torn away from your identity."

—Gwaliga Hart, X̱aaydaga Gwaay.yaay/X̱aayda Gwaay (Haida Gwaii),[25] April 24, 2020

X̱aayda Elder Xiihliik̲ingang (April Churchill) is a highly skilled traditional weaver. Born in 1951, she comes from a talented family of X̱aayda practitioners in that ancient art; her mother Dolores is a weaver, as was her naan (grandmother).

It was her naan who taught April how to weave and the fundamental X̱aayda values embedded in every aspect of the practice. It was important to April's naan that her granddaughter understand that the roots, bark, plants, and other materials she gathered for her weaving from the forests on X̱aaydaga Gwaay.yaay/X̱aayda Gwaay had to be treated with the utmost yahguudang (respect). After all, the trees that these materials are harvested from grow in a landscape that is the foundation of X̱aayda existence. "We are the land," says April, "and the land is us."

To April, the trees are sentient beings with agency and the ability to choose whether to make a gift of their bark or their roots for her to weave. "As someone who is X̱aayda, I respect the trees. I sing when I go among them to let them know I am there and I am their sister. I spend time sitting quietly listening to them to learn which ones have a gift for me, and I always thank them for that gift." This way of showing yahguudang, says April, the respect for all living things, "is at the core of everything we are and do as X̱aayda."[26] It is a relationship to the land and waters of X̱aaydaga Gwaay.yaay/X̱aayda Gwaay and a way of being that X̱aayda like April, and all the generations before her, have embraced for millennia in this unique and magnificent place.

Facing page: Agate Beach, at the base of Taaw (Tow Hill), looking toward Massett, on X̱aaydaga Gwaay.yaay/X̱aayda Gwaay (Haida Gwaii). In HlG̱aagilda X̱aayda kil agates are named hlG̱aa k̲'aats'ii (hard rock).

X̱aayda Elder Xiihliik̲ingang (April Churchill)

An archipelago comprised of more than two hundred islands, X̱aaydaga Gwaay.yaay/X̱aayda Gwaay is separated from the northwest coast of British Columbia by the one-hundred-kilometre storm-tossed breadth of Hecate Strait. It is a region blessed with abundant rainfall; even on a sunny day, the coastal air is infused with salt spray blown inshore from the west by the ever-present wind off Tang.G̲wan, the wild Pacific Ocean. Pristine sand beaches stretch along windswept coasts and curve into sheltered coves. Deep within the ancient forests that blanket the archipelago dim green light bathes rocky clefts coated in moss, the fallen trunks of decaying trees and, in some places, impenetrable undergrowth. The beauty of these islands, illuminated by the clear northern sun or awash in winter rain, is unsurpassable.

The salt-laden air, the thick ancient forests, the wild coasts and safe harbours are all embedded in X̱aayda DNA. The ocean water runs through their veins like blood. The trees, centuries old, witnessed their forebears raising totem poles. They were still there when those poles fell and began decaying into the landscape. Every beach, every forest clearing, has a story of the supernatural and of the kuuniisii (the ancestors); of villages that have come and gone; families harvesting together; traces of ancient traditions that echo down through the years to the twenty-first-century descendants of those who have lived and prospered on these islands since time beyond memory.

For X̱aayda hereditary Chief 7idansuu, James Hart, an internationally renowned artist, man and place are simply inseparable. “We have physical evidence that we have been here for more than fourteen thousand years and our oral stories are even older than that. We have always farmed the seas. We have always had names and stories for all of the places here and passed that knowledge on. So we know these lands. We know these waters. We know everything about the weather, the mountains, the rocks, every part of this place.”

7idansuu was born in 1952 in the town of Masset, just south of G̲aw Tlagee (Old Massett) in Delkatla, at the north end of Kiis Gwaay (Graham Island). Like most children on the archipelago at the time, he was born at home. His great-aunt Vesta (Edenshaw) Hageman was his mother's midwife. There was no hospital at the time in the north, only one nurse to tend to the needs of the villages and only one flight weekly to the mainland.

It was a difficult time to be "an Indian," recalls 7idansuu. It was an era in which the consequences of colonization were only worsening. "It was a tough time. There had been the introduced smallpox epidemic for one thing, and there were so few survivors from that. We were sent to residential schools, that was part of such an evil plan to destroy children, families, culture, all across the country. The abuse that happened at those schools, all the deaths—that happened to all of us, all of our kids. We were abused in so many ways. We were forced to live on reserves. You had to get permission from the government to do anything on our own land. We were experimented on in the medical system. The list goes on and on." Even in a place as remote as X̱aaydaga Gwaay.yaay/X̱aayda Gwaay, inhabited by a people famous for their resistance to settler governments, the typical effects were as hard felt as anywhere else. "We lost our sense of purpose. A lot of drinking was going on. We really had our wings clipped pretty heavy for a while."

7idansuu (Chief James Hart)

Despite all that, 7idansuu says firmly, "We are still here today. We understand now all the traps that were set for us, what was done to us." The X̱aayda are also determined to recover fully from what was done to them, he says. "So many people are working really hard to heal and to reconnect to our old ways and this place. That is happening at every level and in so many ways, for Elders, adults, families, and of course for the children." Of the X̱aayda Rediscovery youth culture camps, 7idansuu says, "Rediscovery, especially for the children, is a big part of that healing and recovery and reconnection. It is one of the jewels on this earth, such good medicine for the children and for all the adults who go there."

The Rediscovery camps are the result of decades of commitment, passion, and hard work on the part of many people, both X̱aayda and non-X̱aayda. X̱aayda K̲'aay.yas (Elders) and people like Gidansda Guujaaw, Michael Nicol, Ethel Jones, Gaadgaas Nora Bellis, K'iis Gwaay Naan, Mary Swanson, John Yeltatzie, and many others who would become Elders and

The first Rediscovery camp was established at T'áalan Stl'áng.

leaders of the X̱aayda one day, were all involved. "It was a young American man called Thom Henley, though, who really spearheaded it all and got the program going," says 7idansuu. "Thom worked so hard with us for years and years to make Rediscovery happen."

Henley, from Michigan, arrived on the archipelago in the mid-1970s. With the permission of the G̱aw Tlagee leadership of the day, he built a cabin on a remote but beautiful beach on the northeast coast of Kiis Gwaay. "Thom understood what had happened to us and he wanted to work with us to do something about it," says 7idansuu. Everyone agreed that revitalization of X̱aayda wellbeing would best begin with their children, through cultural reconnection to their lands and waters, their stories and heritage, and their X̱aayda values and practices. Everyone wanted the youth to overcome the legacy and the typical impacts of colonization and to thrive and to be healthy and proud of who they were.

They also wanted them to be strong, capable stewards of their sovereign lands and waters, taking care of them for future generations. To achieve those goals, X̱aayda children and youth needed to understand where they came from, the language that defined those places, and their ancient stories and values. They needed to learn how to not only take care of X̱aaydaga Gwaay.yaay/X̱aayda Gwaay, but to allow it to take care of them in turn. These wise, loving leaders and Elders also simply wanted their children to enjoy laughter, friendship, and adventure together, learn practical skills that would serve them well in life, and enjoy increased confidence to take on the world and what it could offer them—whether as environmental stewards, community leaders, teachers, artists, entrepreneurs, or in any other way they chose.

The first Rediscovery camp was established in 1978 at the site of Thom Henley's small cabin at T'áalan Stl'áng (the beach that has everything), a remote sheltered cove deep within in the Duu Guusd Heritage Site at the northern end of X̱aaydaga Gwaay.yaay/X̱aayda Gwaay. Henley subsequently worked as the camp's director in collaboration with the X̱aayda leadership for more than a decade, eventually earning himself the X̱aayda name Yaahl Hlaagaay Gwii Kaas (Raven Walks Around the World) and later writing a book about his experiences.[27]

Ancient forests blanket the archipelago of X̱aaydaga Gwaay.yaay/X̱aayda Gwaay.

The second Rediscovery culture camp at 'Laanas Dagang.a began operating in 2003 on Kiis Gwaay (Burnaby Island), in Gwaii Haanas, a five-thousand-square-kilometre protected area in the southern part of the archipelago that is co-managed by the Council of the Haida Nation and Parks Canada. Every year since, over the short northern summer in the islands, small groups of X̱aayda children aged ten and up have gone to T'áalan Stl'áng or to 'Laanas Dagang.a for multi-day trips in which they experience a reconnection to X̱aayda culture and ways of being made immensely rich by being in these places. By 2022, more than two thousand children and youth had experienced Rediscovery, which had become a model for dozens of similar culture camps worldwide.

The difference that Rediscovery makes to youth, particularly youth at risk, is phenomenal, says April, who managed the 'Laanas Dagang.a operation for a few years. "Rediscovery is nothing less than life-changing." She remains deeply emotional about what Rediscovery does for X̱aayda children. "I remember going to the dock the first time to help out with a delivery of gear that needed to be loaded into the boat. Here were a bunch of high school kids standing around so cool, half-heartedly helping, hoodies pulled down low over their faces so you couldn't really see them, barely talking." When April went down to meet the same kids returning a week later, she could not believe her eyes. "Even now my tears start falling, remembering. Those young people who came off that boat were not the same kids who had gotten onto it. Their hoods were thrown back. They were smiling. They

Following spread: 'Laanas Daganag.a (Swan Bay) Rediscovery Camp.

were cheerful, saying haawa (thank you) to everybody. They were loving with each other and hugging the staff. Their whole attitude had changed in just those few days."

For April that day, for the first time in a long time, Rediscovery spelled hope. "We had so many kids at real risk, and in one week I could see this is what it did for them. If we could just get them to come even once, then we would have a young person who was looking toward a productive life, who was changing himself. We've had kids who we really thought we were going to lose," she says, her voice choked with emotion. "One kid, he had been running drugs, he had all kinds of problems. Then he came to Rediscovery. Now he's at university. He's completely turned about. Rediscovery," she concludes simply, "doesn't just change lives, it saves them."

Sandlanee Gid (Raven Ann Potschka), who has been a director of the T'áalan Stl'áng camp, has experienced the same phenomenon. "You can see it in their eyes. They are completely different from when they arrive at camp. They are bright-eyed, they are beautiful, they're thankful, they're in the light. It is so beautiful to see."

A X̱aayda woman by birth, Raven Ann was adopted by a non-X̱aayda family when she was two years old and did not grow up on the islands or attend the culture camps as a child. Her work with Rediscovery was as much a personal reconnection as a job. In many ways, at least at the beginning, she was learning as much as the children in her charge. In its own way, Rediscovery was also lifesaving for Raven Ann, returning her confidence in being a X̱aayda woman. "People that have been displaced, people that have been either taken away or given up for adoption, all of the people that went to residential school, we all have so much healing to do. This program wouldn't exist if it wasn't for the history of trauma placed on our people, all the children in foster care, kids that were part of the Sixties Scoop,[28] kids that were taken away to residential school and endured horrific treatment. Personally, I don't think I would be anywhere near where I am in my own wellness journey without Rediscovery. That place," she says emphatically, "has saved my life again and again and again."

Being out on their ancestral land is what makes the difference for X̱aayda of any age, believes April. "When you are at 'Laanas Dagang.a, for example, it just tells you that you are part of the earth and the earth loves you. You are part of something big and powerful. Every child is born with knowledge and purpose. Everybody is born beautiful," she says firmly.

"Rediscovery helps children learn just how beautiful and precious they are, and how much they have to give to the world and teaches them how to overcome obstacles that as adults the world will put in front of them. You can see the results of that on X̱aaydag̱a Gwaay.yaay/X̱aayda Gwaay today. Many of our leaders are graduates of Rediscovery. They came away knowing that they could accomplish anything they wanted to accomplish because they were born beautiful and with purpose, and now they are fulfilling that purpose."

Edward Davis, from the village of G̱aw Tlagee, is one of those Rediscovery graduates, now a cultural leader and a thirty-year veteran of the local volunteer fire brigade. Born in 1976, Edward did grow up on X̱aaydag̱a Gwaay.yaay/X̱aayda Gwaay and learned about his culture as a young child. "I was introduced to drumming and singing at an early age by my late nanaay Ethel Jones, my grandmother." The little boy took to his traditions immediately, loving every aspect of it. "Just to hear the singing and drumming, that was so beautiful." Edward had his share of tough times

East Beach at Tlell, looking toward Naikoon.

Sandlanee Gid (Raven Ann Potschka)

growing up and the cultural practice was also healing for him. "It could turn a person's bad day into a really good day just by doing those two things." Encouraged by his grandmother, he also joined a dancing group, quickly excelling as he became more and more practised in it.

In 1986, Edward went to Rediscovery at T'áalan Stl'áng for the first time. That, too, he found immensely rewarding, and he returned year after year. In 1988, at the age of twelve, he won recognition from his peers in the coveted G̱uudang X̱yuuwid (Stone Ribs) award. G̱uudang X̱yuuwid was a supernatural being who had fought off a threatening sea monster. The Stone Ribs award named for him is given to the camp youth, male or female, who everyone thinks best embodies X̱aayda values. Edward subsequently returned to T'áalan Stl'áng as a junior guide and then as a Guardian Watchman. Inspired by the sense of community responsibility he had experienced at camp, he volunteered for G̱aw Tlagee's fire department when he was just fourteen years old.

Edward credits Rediscovery with giving him ways to better himself. "I wanted to be a really good singer. I wanted to be a good dancer. It gave me the tools I needed to work toward that and be able to go and talk to people. I was a quiet kid. I didn't like speaking in public. But now here I am. I'm leading our fifty-strong clan dance group." Rediscovery also taught him empathy and kindness. "I learned to respect what's around me and to take responsibility for what's up with me, and not put a person down but pick them up and help them out." Not least of all, Rediscovery opened doors to opportunities he would never have otherwise dreamed possible.

Edward was still a teenager when his talents were harnessed in 1994 to play the role of an assistant to a sshagu (holy man) in the Disney movie *White Fang 2: Myth of the White Wolf* being filmed in Vancouver. "That's when everything just really started rolling for me," he recalls. Edward was subsequently invited to the Canadian embassy in Washington, D.C., to support the installation of X̱aayda artist Bill Reid's Black Canoe. Other similar opportunities started coming his way, but his first love remained his work on X̱aaydaga Gwaay.yaay/X̱aayda Gwaay. "It's home," he says simply. "It's where I belong, where I am most comfortable. Everything around me here makes me feel warm and safe."

Cultural leader and volunteer firefighter Edward Davis

After becoming a full-time Guardian, Edward remains involved with Rediscovery. He unfailingly attends the last night of each program, helping the youth celebrate their experience in a final ceremony where guests are invited to witness what the participants have learned. “It is so cool to watch these kids and see the transformation in them after just one week,” says Edward. The camps help the youth understand that if they are capable of being part of Rediscovery, they are capable of anything. “Rediscovery tells you that if you put your mind to it, you can achieve anything. What it taught me is never to give up. When I won Stone Ribs, which is pretty hard to do, it showed me that I could take on a role of leadership. Now I am a cultural leader in my community, which I would never have imagined as a child.”

When their children were younger, 7idansuu and his wife Rosemary worked in Vancouver, migrating home with the family to X̱aaydaga Gwaay.yaay/X̱a̱aydа̱ G̱wa̱ay every summer. The Hart children, who attended school in Vancouver, all went to T’áalan Stl’áng, something the couple felt was fundamental, as X̱aayda, to understanding the place that they were from. “My dad took my sister and I out to T’áalan Stl’áng the first time on our boat,” recalls Gwaliga, who was nine years old in 1997. “We landed at this old village site, K’yuust’aa, and hiked a trail over a cliff because the tide was up. I had never been there before and no idea what to expect. I will never forget Dad saying, ‘There it is,’ and pointing out a beach in the distance. I could see a cabin or longhouse. I didn’t know what it was. Dad said, ‘That’s Rediscovery.’ When we got there, it was the coolest thing. It was the most amazing experience.”

Gwaliga returned to T’áalan Stl’áng several times. The last year he attended as a participant he was asked if he wanted to work at the camp. The answer was easy. “I just jumped at it. I said, ‘Yes!’ That was one of the best yesses I have ever said.” The teenager spent five seasons as a guide at T’áalan Stl’áng, always finding it difficult to leave at the end of the summer and return to school in Vancouver. “It was the hardest thing to leave, even as a guide, because you felt like you were being uprooted from everything. Not just the place, but the language, the culture, even yourself. All

7idansuu and Rosemary Hart with their son Gwaliga

these experiences I had at camp were so fascinating, living in longhouses, singing, dancing, hearing all these stories of Elders, learning the language. It was all right there." At Rediscovery, says Gwaliga, participants live in the full context of their identity. "It is magical. It just doesn't get more powerful than that. We are shown our culture and way of life and how absolutely brilliant and fascinating the inner workings of spiritualism and magic are and how all the things that our stories have always talked about were true. These things weren't myths, they were histories and realities. It was the most eye-opening experience for me."

"Why," he started wondering as a young adult, "were we not still living this way?" Gwaliga initially sought the answer through his studies. "I wanted to understand why we are who we are now in the twenty-first century, so I ended up getting into cultural anthropology and archaeology at the University of British Columbia." By 2021 he had returned home to work. He was studying X̱aad kil, the northern dialect of the X̱aayda language, and following in his father's footsteps, working on developing his skills as an artist. He was also building a house for himself near the windswept northern beaches on which he loved to surf. The latter activity felt as natural to the then thirty-three-year-old as paddling a canoe would have been to his ancestors. Indeed, says Gwaliga, many terms in the X̱aad kil dialect of the X̱aayda language are water-related. "If you think about everything we do out on the water, fishing, in canoes, we have a huge plethora of language that relates to water-based activities. It isn't difficult to apply that to something modern like surfing, which is really great. It is a cool way to connect to our culture."

There are two recognized language dialects in use on X̱aaydaga Gwaay.yaay/X̱aayda Gwaay: X̱aad kil in the north and X̱aayda kil in the south. There are now few fluent speakers of either dialect remaining, but determined efforts to revitalize the language are well under way. The importance to wellbeing and to yahguudang of X̱aayda language competency cannot be overestimated, wrote language teacher and Elder GwaaG̱anad (Diane Brown) in the 2011 book *That Which Makes Us Haida*.[29] "Our connection to the land, when you hear it in Haida, it's much more direct and clear; you can understand our relationship better...Everything feels more real; trees, grass, the ocean. X̱aayda kil gives us the ability to feel and understand our relationship to the earth, sky and ocean. If you were to ask what my first lesson was in X̱aayda, it was respect for all things, for all beings."

Gwaliga Hart

Language is a key part of the Rediscovery experience for participants. "If you think about Rediscovery as being all about our identity as X̱aayda," says Gwaliga, "and about our values here as a culture, how we interact with the place and how we look at the world—the language holds knowledge and values that help us understand the landscape and what it needs. You see the land in the way it is meant to be seen. Everything is in the language: humour, philosophy, all the intricacies and interconnectedness of our art and how that is woven into our everyday lives. It is unique, just as we are. It is the most wonderfully woven fabric of the most incredible blanket of our identity and our existence."

X̱aayda language teacher Jasḵwaan Bedard worked at Rediscovery for two years as a senior guide and was also a camp director at T'áalan Stl'áng for three years. For Jasḵwaan and the children she teaches, like every part of X̱aaydaga Gwaay.yaay/X̱aayda Gwaay, the land and ocean at T'áalan Stl'áng are natural cradles of X̱aayda culture and language. "That place has a beautiful space in my heart," reflects Jasḵwaan. "The teachings that the land inherently gives you when you are out there are really beautiful."

The work she is doing in language, says Jasḵwaan, is a direct result of her time at Rediscovery. Speaking the language results in better quality of life, she emphasizes, and improves mental and spiritual health, better outcomes in education and career goals, and even longer life expectancy. But language was a prime target of the residential school system, where Indigenous children were violently and sometimes fatally punished for speaking their language or in any way acknowledging their culture. "Colonial policy focussed on dismantling our children's ability to live as

X̱aayda language teacher Jask̲waan Bedard

Indigenous people, that was the aim of the residential schools," observes Jask̲waan. "Indigenous children were taught that they were less than capable or even less than human because of who they were, essentially that their identity was worthless. That toxic and erroneous notion still recycles itself in the Canadian system, through education, through media, and through socialization of Canadians."

This deliberate theft of language and pride in identity is the reason why so many Indigenous children are still under the authority and so-called "care" of the Canadian state. Jask̲waan adds, "So it's everything. To teach an Indigenous child that they are capable, they are loved, they can be anything that they want to be. That they are special because of who they are, the language they speak, and where they come from. Being out at Rediscovery does that." Jask̲waan, too, has seen the difference being at the camp makes to youth. The look on children's faces when they return from camp, she says, is amazing. "They're coming back almost from another world. Their smiles say it all. They are healthy, happy, grounded X̱aayda children who feel confident and proud of themselves and that, as X̱aayda, they can be anything they want to be."

The first film ever made in the X̱aayda language was released in 2020 at the Toronto Film Festival. *SG̱aawaay K̲'uuna* (*Edge of the Knife*) recounted a story from the nineteenth century about a man who carelessly causes the death of a young boy, played by young actor Guustlas (Trey Rorick) from HlG̱aagilda. Guustlas was a participant at 'Laanas Dagang.a for several years and in 2021 worked his second season as a junior guide at the camp. He credits his success in the film to his close connection to his X̱aayda culture and that connection to his time at Rediscovery. "I learned there how much I love being on the land and being in my culture," says Guustlas. "Going to the camps at such a young age opened up my eyes to what my people do, what we have done for so many years. That's when I started singing and dancing and hearing old stories, absorbing them and retelling them, basking in my culture and learning my language. 'Laanas Dagang.a

Facing page: The connection of X̱aayda people to their ancestors remains evident today in the forests of X̱aaydaga̱ Gwaay. yaay/X̱aayda Gwaay.

Guustlas (Trey Rorick) acted in the first film ever made in the X̱aayda language, *SG̱aawaay K̲'uuna* (*Edge of the Knife*), released in 2020.

really helped me start off on that journey to becoming who I am today. Maybe if I didn't go there, I wouldn't have been in *Edge of the Knife*, I wouldn't have been so interested in the culture."

When the teenager is out on the land or out in his people's old villages, he feels immensely grateful. "I have sadness that we've lost so much culture, but now after being to Rediscovery, I want to learn what it means to be X̱aayda and what it meant to gather all of your own food and live off the land back in the old days." One of the key aspects of the culture camps is that everyone relies on each other doing their part to have a good experience. "That is how it used to be back in the olden days in a village, when everyone needed each other." Traditionally, says Guustlas, someone might fish, someone else might gather seaweed or gather berries. "Someone would go get wood, someone would be making art, all kinds of different things to help out the village. Everyone had a role and everyone was dependent on each other. 'Laanas Dagang.a really encapsulates what it used to be like because we also assign jobs to everyone so it feels like they're really contributing to being out there. At camp, people have to fetch water from the creek, clean the longhouse and the cookhouse, and help make meals. Someone might have to go out on the boat to help harvest food. It's really a sense of a family and dependency on each other to keep the whole camp going."

His goal is to become an artist, following in the footsteps of great masters like 7idansuu. Guustlas learned basketry and weaving from his naan, a master spruce root weaver, and is apprenticing with an uncle who is also an artist. "Learning the artform here is a really big part of learning about my culture, because art was such a big everyday part of life back in the day," he explains. "Totem poles said whose Clan lived in this longhouse." If you were going into a village, you would be able to tell what house you were heading to by reading the carving on the totem poles. "It was like a family name or a signature. It was a part of every single day life for X̱aayda. Even something little on your spoon, there'd be beautiful art on it to say whose family this spoon belongs to. Art is just such an important thing to us. Being able to practise that myself is connecting me so much more to my culture."

Children at 'Laanas Daganag.a (Swan Bay) Rediscovery Camp.

Stories like his, and those of others whose lives have been changed so fundamentally by Rediscovery, are immensely gratifying to Ginn wad-luu un uula isdaa ayaagang (Trevor Russ), vice-president of the Council of the Haida Nation. Trevor was brought up by his great-grandparents on X̱aaydaga̱ Gwaay.yaay/X̱aayda Gwaay. Through them he is strongly connected to his home and culture and well-versed in how to live sustainably off the land. He did not attend Rediscovery as a child but vividly recalls taking his young daughter to T'áalan Stl'áng the first time and the feeling when he arrived with her at the beautiful beach that is home to the camp. "When you come out of that trail at K'yuust'aa through the forest that first time and you see what's there, you know you're coming to a great place. Your heart becomes light," remembers Trevor. Even as an adult just visiting the camp, he remarks, "everything about it brings you that sense of community everybody needs to feel, being connected to being X̱aayda."

Every child is different, he says, but what Rediscovery gives all of them is an unshakeable sense of belonging. "It's helped many in identifying their roles within community with the experiences they've had out there," Trevor observes. "It's that sense of being valued for your contribution. It's so important for young people. Rediscovery instils in them that responsibility

Ginn wadluu un uula isdaa ayaagang (Trevor Russ)

going forward that it's part of their duty growing up to provide for others within the community." Like April, Trevor firmly believes that every child is born with purpose. "The camps help youth find that sense of purpose within themselves." In 2021, Trevor's daughter turned twenty-one. "T'áalan Stl'áng, and the connection that she built to the land, really helped her in her path. Now she's pursuing a degree in science so she can come back and take on a role in natural resource conservation management."

Marine biologist Niisii Guujaaw, daughter of Rediscovery co-founder Gidansda Guujaaw, was born in 1994 and raised in the X̱aayda village of HlG̱aagilda. Like Trevor's daughter, Niisii pursued her love of science, and in 2013 she took a job as a resource conservation technician working for her Nation. When Niisii was a child, her parents took her and her siblings by boat to many different parts of X̱aaydag̱a Gwaay.yaay/X̱aayda Gwaay, telling them the old stories as well as the more recent history of the fight to protect Gwaii Haanas from resource exploitation. "All of us grew up hearing these stories, especially from Lyell Island,"[30] says Niisii. "I don't think it's lost on any X̱aayda that goes to Gwaii Haanas that we're there because a generation before us protected that place so that we could experience it in the same way. It was certainly important for me, growing up, to hear my dad's love for the land that was so deep and why he stood for the land."

When she was a little older, Niisii went to both T'áalan Stl'áng and 'Laanas Dagang.a as a participant and later worked at 'Laanas Dagang.a as a guide. As it had been for Gwaliga, leaving to take on her current role was, she recalls, heart-breaking. Growing up on the land, she believes, is something all X̱aayda children deserve to experience. "X̱aaydag̱a Gwaay.yaay/X̱aayda Gwaii is so rich. Everywhere here there has been a X̱aayda presence for a long time. We can go onto a beach we've never been to before knowing stories about that place and imagine the village that was there. It's a good feeling. We all need to be on the land and experience that connection so that we will all grow up loving it and wanting to take care of it." That is what Rediscovery gives children, she says. "The kids just come alive there."

Some children may not have left their villages before or have much idea of their X̱aayda traditions or history. To go to a camp in the wilderness could be a completely new and sometimes uncomfortable experience for

Marine biologist Niisii Guujaaw

them. "To see these youth, in just one week, become so relaxed and contented, to know they are being their best selves out there and take such pride in what they have learnt—it really is lifesaving for some of them," agrees Niisii. "Those kids stand out in my heart, they always will. A lot of them don't want to go home at the end, but when they do they go knowing they can do this, they are X̱aayda and they belong to X̱aaydaga Gwaay.yaay/X̱aayda Gwaay. That has such big benefits not just for them but for our people as a whole, for these young X̱aayda to know that and feel it inside themselves."

K̲ii'iljuus (Barbara Wilson) has spent much of her life residing away from X̱aaydaga Gwaay.yaay/X̱aayda Gwaay. Now eighty years old, Barbara is living back home once again. An elected member of the Council of the Haida Nation in 2019, she also graduated that year with a master of arts degree in education from Simon Fraser University, defending her thesis on her home turf at HlG̲aagilda. She is on multiple boards both at home and internationally, a teacher, a cultural advisor, a published author, and a photographer. She speaks French. Over the course of her career, she worked for Expo '67, the National Film Board, and Parks Canada, the latter for twenty-three years. She has written extensively about climate change and conservation, co-designed a training program for the X̱aayda Guardian Watchmen, and studied law as well as education. In her spare time Barbara likes to surf, especially on X̱aaydaga Gwaay.yaay/X̱aayda Gwaay. Back home now, she is studying her own language, something she has yearned to do for a long time.

Barbara has also put a great deal of thought into her history of who the X̱aayda are and what that means in the context not just of Rediscovery, but conservation and the wellbeing of planet as well as people. "It's all interconnected," she says. "Our bottom line is to be made whole again, for our land and waters to be made whole again. Our land deserves to be treated respectfully. It's looked after us for thousands of years." Thinking this way is simply part of being X̱aayda, says Barbara. "You don't think of the ocean just as water by itself, for example; you think of it as it pertains to food, to travel, separation or bringing you together. That's true of conservation

K̲ii'iljuus (Barbara Wilson)

as well. It's not about conservation, it's about living holistically, about looking after our food sources properly. You make all your decisions based on how you make the least impact but get the most out of it."

This, she adds, is what children learn at Rediscovery, amongst other things, and one of the reasons why the program is so important. "I'm a great-grandmother now, and I want my great-grandchildren and their children to know the things that I knew as a little girl. My grandfather died when I was two. Some of the women who were alive when I was much younger used to smile and say, 'We'd see you and your chinG̲a, he'd be carrying you on his shoulder and then he'd put you down and he'd kneel beside you. We'd see him picking up things and explaining them to you.' I grew up knowing that that was very much a part of my life and taking it for granted," says Barbara. "That's how it should be for them. In becoming whole, we have to embrace our history. We have to retrieve the parts of it that are in a deep sleep and awaken them so that our kids heal more than we have. Imagine what it would be like if everybody was whole again and could have the confidence and the knowing that anything was possible? That's what I want for our kids."

When 7idansuu was the same age as Guustlas, he felt much the same way as Guustlas about becoming an artist. 7idansuu had discovered X̱aayda art for the first time at high school and everything changed for him at that moment. "All of a sudden, I realized that as a people, we had our own art form," he recalls. "I looked closer and realized it was a great art form and that we had a culture embodied in it. I was on a natural high for the next three days, I was so happy." Still only a teenager at the time, 7idansuu launched himself into learning about his people's art, voraciously reading whatever he could in order to absorb its meaning and the skills embodied in it, travelling to museums and galleries to study the ancient pieces in their collections. "We come from where they came from," he explains. "Our people, our ancestors, created these wonderful things that tell us who we are. You start feeling it from the pieces after a while, what they really mean. You start realizing that was our written word. They speak to us."

The young man never looked back. Making the art of his people would become his life's work. "Every totem I raised on X̱aaydaga̱ Gwaay.yaay/

X̱aayda Gwaay," he says quietly, "proved we were still here." 7idansuu worked for many years in Vancouver but, he reflects, "creating art comes easier at home on X̱aaydaga Gwaay.yaay/X̱aayda Gwaay because it's where it all comes from, with depth and meaning behind it. We're still so connected here, so I want that in my work. I can work in the city, but if I touch our homelands, they build me up and make me strong."

Learning traditional weaving at 'Laanas Daganag.a (Swan Bay) Rediscovery Camp.

That connection to the homelands is what he and Rosemary want for their children and grandchildren, and the reason they both continue to volunteer as directors of the Rediscovery T'áalan Stl'áng non-profit society board. "Everyone has worked so hard to keep Rediscovery going over the years," reflects 7idansuu. "Every year we have to fundraise for it and deal with all of the logistics of getting people out there in boats and with weather and work out how we can keep making it even better. But we do it because everyone gets so much out of it, the children, our youth, and the Elders who go out there. It is so important we all have the chance to connect to our lands this way, to have them build us all up and make us all strong." Despite the impact of the pandemic, things are looking good, says 7idansuu. "We're in a really good place now. We're on a roll!"

The feeling of connection and strength for children and Elders alike is the essence of Rediscovery for people like Guustlas, Niisii, Jasḵwaan and Edward, Trevor and Raven Ann, April, Barbara, and all the thousands of X̱aayda children and youth, teachers, and Elders who have been part of the journey, the healing, and the joy for more than forty years. "The difference that Rediscovery makes is huge," says Gwaliga. "The children find their voice; they find the pride within themselves and who they are in their culture. It is empowering. It is amazing. They can be whatever and whoever they want to be."

That power, concludes Gwaliga, "reverberates so strongly. Not just for the youth, but around the world and into their future on X̱aaydaga Gwaay.yaay/X̱aayda Gwaay. They *are* the future for all of us here."

A Ligʷiłdaxʷ Bottom Line

CHAPTER SIX

The homelands and traditional waters of the Wei Wai Kum First Nation, to which Wei Wai Kum people have ancient physical, spiritual, and cultural connections, span the headwaters of Loughborough Inlet, north of ƛəmataxʷ (Tyee Spit) and the city of Campbell River, and stretch south to the Tsable River, west to the mountains that straddle the centre of Vancouver Island, and east to southern Johnstone Strait in the Salish Sea.

In the Liq̓ʷala language of the Wei Wai Kum, who are Ligʷiłdaxʷ people, "Ligʷiłdaxʷ" translates to an "unkillable thing." It is a reference to a story about a large sea worm that survives and keeps swimming, even when cut into pieces. It is an apt name for a people with a reputation for great strength and survival against difficult, sometimes almost impossible, odds. Christopher Roberts, who was elected as Chief Councillor of Wei Wai Kum in 2018 at the age of thirty-five, is proud of being a citizen of this strong, resilient Ligʷiłdaxʷ Nation and cherishes the heritage and values imbued in that citizenship. The newly elected young Chief had also, however, taken on the leadership of a people confronted by an overwhelming history of colonial assault on their physical, cultural, social, and economic wellbeing; a relentless onslaught that has done much to disconnect them from their homelands, their traditional laws, and sacred age-old community protocols.

In a sad story similar to that of every other coastal First Nation in British Columbia, the Wei Wai Kum had been deemed by the Canadian government of the nineteenth

"Reconciling who Wei Wai Kum are as Indigenous people requires us to be in tune not only with our physical world, but the supernatural world and related ways of thinking, and our belief that all things are connected. It requires an intergenerational investment in our cultural identity, knowledge and values, and the wellbeing of our lands and our resources. That is our wealth as Ligʷiłdaxʷ people, and I believe that has to be our bottom line."

—Chief Councillor Christopher Roberts, Wei Wai Kum First Nation, October 2020

Facing page: Forward Harbour/ƛəx̌əʷəyəm Conservancy, a sheltered bay on the central coast of BC, lies some seventy-five kilometres northwest of Campbell River.

Wei Wai Kum Chief Councillor Christopher Roberts at Knight Inlet Lodge.

century to be "Indians" under the *Indian Act* and forced onto a handful of small Indian reserves in and around Campbell River. The government renamed the Nation the "Campbell River Indian Band," imposing upon them a western-elected governance structure that purported to replace their traditional hereditary leadership framework. Over the course of the following decades, as more and more settlers arrived, the expansive, glorious territory in which Wei Wai Kum people had lived, prospered and exercised self-determination for millennia—a panoply of pristine waters, islands, forests, and mountains—became almost unrecognizable.

In 2018, Christopher ran for the leadership of Wei Wai Kum. By then, most of the community lived on a cramped reserve tucked into the waterfront skirts of a city of more than thirty-five thousand residents, in the heart of an industrialized and heavily polluted region saturated with mines, logging companies, and mills. A swath of open-net fish farms littered the Nation's front doorstep. The Wei Wai Kum had little choice in any of this. For much of the nineteenth and twentieth centuries, Wei Wai Kum citizens were systematically excluded from participation in the industrial resource economy in their territory. At the same time, their cultural livelihood was effectively extinguished as government officials removed or destroyed traditional weirs, traps, nets, and other fishing tools with which they had managed to harvest, consume, and trade with other First Nations in a wide range of sustainable fisheries.

Wei Wai Kum people were also deeply affected by the well-documented crimes of the residential school system, the theft of their children, and unceasing depredations on their culture, language, and traditions. Greatly impoverished economically and socially, their small handful of reserves and federal government program funding were poor substitutes for a once-thriving and environmentally sustainable economy, homelands abundant in thriving resources, healthy, happy, culturally rich people, and independent Nationhood.

By the time Christopher was elected, it was impossible to turn the clock back on the sprawling commercial and industrial development that had grown around Campbell River. Previous leaders of the Nation, going as far back as Christopher's great-grandfather William Roberts, had nonetheless worked tirelessly to rebuild Wei Wai Kum's financial and cultural wellbeing within their present-day setting. The First Nation had become an integral part of the modern Campbell River economy. They owned a number of thriving businesses on their lands downtown, held several forestry tenures, and operated a busy marina on the waterfront. The revenues derived from those commercial activities enabled the Nation to develop environmental stewardship and research programs, partner with the federal and provincial government in marine and terrestrial planning initiatives, expand its database of archaeological sites, and, not least of all, deliver various social and cultural programs to its citizens, as well as undertake language revitalization efforts.

All the same, some stark realities still faced Christopher in his new role. "Nothing could have prepared me for how challenging it is to sit in this seat," he recalls. Those challenges felt almost insurmountable at the beginning. "I started with this optimistic vision of a future in which we weave together community, cultural, environmental, and economic wellbeing, and we are working toward it, but almost straight away it was really hard to imagine it being achievable. Would it be possible to bring things back into balance, to a way that is consistent with our cultural identity of who we are as a community, as a people? The challenge for us is how we strike that balance of a strong cultural identity rooted in all those values that set us apart without it being all about commerce and being successful economically. Every Nation has this dilemma, but I think that being in such an intense urban setting adds another dynamic altogether."

It is also a dilemma that has to be negotiated with the utmost care for what Wei Wai Kum citizens, many of them still healing from the brutal impacts of colonization, might expect. Christopher is emphatic that the community must lead the direction Wei Wai Kum takes on his watch. However, like any small community, people are divided on what they want for the future. Do you lead the Nation further down the pathway of commercial development, with all the revenues that come with it, or invest in high-cost social housing and cultural space? If you are offered land that was once stolen from you to purchase at market price, do you accept and pay just to get it back? Do you cooperate with government to garner better environmental standards in the territory, even if they aren't as high as yours,

The Wei Wai Kum Campbell River reserve, on which many citizens of the Nation reside (centre-right in picture, with red roofs), is surrounded by large-scale commercial and industrial development.

to at least make some progress? These are the very real daily challenges that confront a young Chief Councillor desperate to improve the lives of Wei Wai Kum people.

On the one hand, Christopher feels that the Wei Wai Kum are fortunate in the economic advantage they hold as a community, owning land and businesses in a thriving commercial region. "Our reality is that we can't truly be self-determining unless we achieve economic independence from the federal government. But in our territory, every type of resource-related business has an environmental impact. Many of them have significant cultural impacts upon our values as Indigenous people. Our challenge is to find ways to incorporate our values that will help reduce or even remove those impacts, which is what we are trying to do in our marine planning efforts. That isn't easy."

Wei Wai Kum has chosen, for example, to work collaboratively with Transport Canada's Oceans Protection Plan, which was initiated in 2016 by the federal government to improve the country's marine safety systems in partnership with First Nations and other coastal communities.

"We are working with Transport Canada on things like emergency marine response to vessels in distress, which includes oil and gas tankers. We are co-designing marine spill response planning," explains Christopher. "That does not mean we support the amount of tanker traffic outside our front door increasing or approve of oil exports in the context of climate change impacts. These are the things that present us with such challenges here. We have to do what we can to protect our territory, but that is anything but simple. It sometimes requires difficult compromises."

How is he to work toward sustainable contemporary prosperity for Wei Wai Kum in a territory faced with such profound environmental challenges? How does he do so in a way that embraces Lig^{w}iłdax^{w} history, cultural values, and connection to their homeland? "The emphasis these days tends to be on profit and free enterprise, in the western capitalist world view of profit-driven material wealth and wellbeing that rule where and how we live. That does not always align nicely with our values of caring for our land and keeping it safe for future generations, or with putting our cultural history and the wellbeing of our people first. These values are

The connection of the Wei Wai Kum to their ancestral lands in Campbell River remains strong despite the heavy industrialization of the area. This installation on the waterfront was the result of a collaboration between Wei Wai Kum and the City of Campbell River. Christopher's great-grandfather Sam Henderson, a master carver, contributed his skills to the work.

not motivated by profit," Christopher emphasizes. "We want good revenues, but to achieve that we must focus on proper stewardship of our resources and the health of those resources, because if they are not healthy there will be no revenue and no profit. That," he concludes firmly, "should be what drives all of our economic decisions."

Christopher acknowledges that his views risk him sounding like a socialist, at least in the western way in which that term is typically defined. He begs to differ. He wants to see Wei Wai Kum thriving and doing well in business as much as anyone else. It is more a matter of recalibrating the approach to business to integrate principles of sustainability, a proper balance between use and conservation, and incorporating the values that Wei Wai Kum embraces of sufficiency over satiation and sharing before self-gratification.

"It was clear to me from the beginning," observes Christopher, "that reconciling who the Wei Wai Kum are as Indigenous people and our ambitions for prosperity, wellbeing and self-determination could not be focussed solely on our participation in the economy." In other words, the Nation's bottom line has to be defined in a markedly different way to contemporary business models that prioritize profit above all else, going far beyond standard double or even triple bottom lines and embracing nothing less than Wei Wai Kum's own cultural bottom line.

With an economics degree from the University of Victoria, Christopher is an economic development analyst by profession and has a formidable toolkit of business experience to draw upon as he considers the task before him. Immediately prior to becoming Chief Councillor, he worked for several years as regional economic development coordinator with the N̲anwak̲olas Council, an alliance of Kwakwa̱ka̱'wakw First Nations based in Campbell River. In that role, he worked on the development and implementation of a First Nations-led regional economic development strategy, community wellbeing and capacity strengthening initiatives, and coordination of a training and employment strategy. He had created business plans for the Ha-Ma-Yas Stewardship Network, an association of Indigenous land and water protectors known as Guardians, and worked on the N̲anwak̲olas acquisition of Knight Inlet Lodge, a high-end wildlife-viewing destination drawing tourists from around the world.

Of course, as Chief Councillor, Christopher's role is not focussed solely on the Nation's economic development opportunities. Indeed, the scope of any *Indian Act* Chief's responsibilities is massive. On the one hand, Christopher is expected to lead the Nation's defence of its constitutionally protected Indigenous Rights and Title, and its fight to regain its rights of self-determination and stewardship of its territory. As Chief Councillor, he has to guide the implementation of Wei Wai Kum's community plan, support regional environmental recovery, and engage with other First Nations and non-Indigenous community leaders in the region. He also has to work with his Council to make decisions on whether to support or oppose further commercial and industrial development proposals in Wei Wai Kum territory, including everything from open-net fish farms to forestry operations. All of this in itself is a huge job description, but on top of that, he is expected to oversee the day-to-day administration of Wei Wai Kum policy. He is also only ever one phone call away from someone expecting him to help with their problems, large or small.

Fortunately for Christopher, he also brings powerful leadership DNA with him into the role of Chief Councillor. His grandfather Aubrey Roberts,

Wei Wai Kum territory, near Campbell River.

Access to the traditional foods that Wei Wai Kum have always enjoyed is vitally important to the Nation.

a former elected Chief Councillor of the Nation and a highly respected man, was widely known and honoured in Indigenous circles for his quiet guidance and steady approach to taking care of his community. His grandmother Edith Wilcox, born in 1945 on the Wei Wai Kum reserve in Campbell River, is a Knowledge Keeper. His father, Bradley Roberts, has been on Council, and his uncle Tony Roberts, Sr. had also been Chief Councillor, succeeding Christopher's great-grandfather William Roberts, who was one of the first elected Chiefs of Wei Wai Kum under the *Indian Act*.

Christopher was raised by his family to understand the traditional and cultural responsibilities that kind of leadership entailed, and attended many Potlatch and other cultural events in the Wei Wai Kum Big House as a child. His mother, Janice Roberts, instilled his people's cultural values in him on a daily basis. "I particularly remember one day when I was still a teenager and she told me, 'Don't ever take anything that you haven't earned or worked for or that you don't deserve. Work hard. Take only what you need to live on and to support your family. You don't ever need more than that.'" Undertaking the role of Chief Councillor with all of these values and lessons thoroughly embedded in his character by then was a very personal journey.

As a child, Christopher spent many happy hours in Edith's home learning about his history and culture. Edith's views are important to him and her words weighed heavily on his mind when he became Chief Councillor. Both the reserve and the city are vastly different places than when Edith was a little girl, and as an Elder, she feels the loss of that way of life intensely. "When I was a child there were only a few houses here," she recalled in a conversation with Christopher in 2021. "There were no big box stores. We had a waterfront we could enjoy. We had a rowboat, and we grew up playing on the beach, digging clams, digging mussels. The ocean was our refrigerator. Now we have no beach. That is prosperity for you, though, isn't it? You don't get to have everything. I still cry about it because I miss it, but progress has done what it has done. You just try your best to continue with what you have."

Christopher's grandmother Edith Wilcox was born in 1945 on the Wei Wai Kum reserve in Campbell River.

At the same time, Edith told Christopher firmly that continued progress could not stand in the way of traditional values or the connection of Wei Wai Kum people to their lands and waters, a connection that is fundamental to their identity. "To understand where we come from is really important. To understand everything about our lands and how we got here, why we are here, our relationship to our territory and its relationship to our well-being," observed Edith. "Our waterways, our lands, we are eating from them. We make our traditional foods from them. These are the foods that keep us alive, so we must keep the land alive."

Christopher's great-grandfather William passed away before Christopher was born, but the stories he was told about William and his approach when he was Chief resonated equally strongly with him. William had fearlessly enlisted to fight in the First World War, despite being underage, and even managed to get as far as England. The authorities there gently stopped the determined youngster from going any farther. But they did not send him back to Canada, instead allowing him to complete his high school studies in London. "He was a very well-educated young man by the time he came back home," recalls Christopher. William was also generous by nature and kind. "He shared the benefit of his education freely and widely. He was a great supporter of other Nations in their struggles dealing with Indian agents and other federal government representatives and would always lend them a helping hand."

One of Christopher's much-respected mentors, former Chief Paddy Walkus of the Gwa'sala-'Nakwaxda'xw First Nations, told Christopher how

Wei Wai Kum Guardians work to protect their Nation's territorial waters for future generations.

fond he was of William, who he had met in the late 1970s. At the age of twenty-six, Paddy had been elected as a Chief himself for the first time. He had not been in the role for long when he had to meet with federal government officials to negotiate service agreements for the Gwa'sala-'Nakwaxda'xw in their new community in Port Hardy. Waiting nervously for the meeting to begin, the inexperienced young Chief was pacing anxiously in a hotel hallway outside the meeting room. William, who was in town for a meeting with the same government officials, walked over and introduced himself. He reassured Paddy that he had no reason to be scared. "He told Paddy that if he didn't know what to say in front of those government guys to say nothing at all. He said, 'It makes them nervous and they keep talking. They end up telling you everything you need to know.' Paddy told me that William was absolutely right. It was so great," reflects Christopher, "to have that wisdom transferred to me that way: from my great-grandfather, whom I never met, through Paddy, who I really look up to. I have used that advice myself since and it has been really helpful."

Christopher recalls another anecdote about his great-grandfather that a fellow councillor told him. "Back in the 1970s there was a grocery store looking to locate on our reserve lands. There was no Band office in those days. William ran the community from the basement of his house. This woman was just a teenager back then, walking home from school one day past his house," says Christopher. "He called her over and asked her to tell him what she thought of the proposal to put a grocery store over on the corner. She told him she thought that it was a place that had been important to their ancestors and that it would not be good to build a store there. He told her, 'I don't think I like the idea either.' That story has really stuck with me in terms of what it tells me about his values," reflects Christopher. "She was just a kid in high school at the time. My great-grandfather had this vision of what was needed to make the lives of our people better, including bringing in revenue from development, but first he wanted the opinion of a member, even one as young as that, because that mattered to him. He also cared a great deal about protecting our special places. That grocery store was never built."

Christopher treasures these anecdotes, keeping them in mind as he tackles what lies before him. He also takes to heart a piece of advice his father gave him when he was a teenager learning to drive. Christopher was at the wheel on the Vancouver Island Highway for the first time and his dad was in the passenger seat. "At that high speed the car was shaking from side to side," he recalls. "I could feel it and I was really nervous. Dad just said to me calmly, 'If you look farther down the road and through the corners, you will drive much more smoothly.' It worked straight away, of course. It was very practical advice, not just when it comes to driving. I try to take that long view in terms of how I work now for our future as a Nation, to help keep us stable and on a smooth course."

Christopher with his father, Bradley Roberts.

Although Wei Wai Kum values and principles will never change, the Nation may have to evolve in the ways in which they apply those values and principles down the road, says Christopher. "We do have to adapt to a changing world. We've already had to adapt, and there's no doubt we will have to keep doing so. The way things are going, for instance, it's possible in the future there may be no more wild salmon or no more cedar trees because of climate change. If we can't prevent that then how do we fill that space now in a balanced and sustainable way to ensure we will always have access to resources like these that are important physically and culturally to us? What's the best way to go? That is our fundamental challenge," observes Christopher. "How do we organize ourselves to evolve into the future? Can we position ourselves with a fundamentally different way of relating to and orienting ourselves to the land and resources than the capitalist system has taken to date?"

The answer, in one fundamental sense, is clear. "We could just keep making good business development investments that will have our members employed and be earning good revenues," muses Christopher. "We could certainly be successful at that. We already are, of course. But I feel right now that part of my role is to make sure that we are evolving in our approach and investing equally in our knowledge, and that our cultural

Christopher hopes that his children and grandchildren will enjoy their homelands, and the wildlife within them, in the same way that their ancestors have always done.

identity as Ligʷiłdaxʷ people is being upheld, nurtured, and cared for. That is the foundation of everything we do. It is what makes us distinctly unique. It needs to be there first and foremost as our criteria for all the decisions we make."

One day in 2021, three years into his first term as Chief Councillor, Christopher reminded his father about that practical guidance he had given his son so many years previously. They were once again driving down the Island Highway together. "I told him how much I had appreciated all of his advice over the years and compared the analogy with him—how I feel now about the importance of looking way down the road, fifty years ahead, one hundred years ahead, to where our Nation wants to be in the future."

At some point much further down the road, Christopher hopes that just as he has been inspired by William, in turn his great-grandchildren will be thinking of him as they embrace their lives as happy, healthy

Ligʷiłdaxʷ men and women. Perhaps they, too, will lead their Nation or they may become businesspeople, lawyers, language teachers, or scientists. Regardless of their chosen pathway, he hopes that they will be enjoying cultural, social, and economic wellbeing and independence, proud in their Indigenous identity and secure in their rights as Indigenous people. Not least of all, he hopes that they will be connected to their community and sustained by a thriving territory all around them. "That is what I am steering toward, to hold steady and remain focussed on achieving our people's long-term vision for our future. That's my bottom line."

His experiences, the stories he has been told, the insights and the wisdom of his forebears, the history and challenges he is dealing with, all of these things have interwoven into the person Christopher has become and the foundation for the pathway he has taken. In the end, he says, he is simply a Ligʷiłdaxʷ man, a Wei Wai Kum citizen, with everything that implies. "The values, the principles that I carry, are instilled in me. It is an innate way of being, because that is who we are. It is part of how we are raised. This community raised me as well as my family.

"These are the things that come to mind for me when trying to be a leader to the people in a way that is authentic to our cultural identity as Ligʷiłdaxʷ people," concludes Christopher. "We still have much work to do to overcome the impacts of colonization and the *Indian Act,* but I personally feel we can absolutely achieve what we want for our kids and our grandchildren if we come together as a Nation and hold true to our values. We can be a prosperous, self-sufficient Nation and a leader in our regional economy. We can have healthier, abundant homelands to enjoy. All of this is possible. The future is in our hands."

A Different Life

CHAPTER SEVEN

Crystal Smith jogs regularly through and around her home community of Kitamaat, or Tsee-Motsa as it is known in the Haisla Nation's Wakashan language.[31] As she traverses the small village of some six hundred people located near the head of Kitimat Arm on q̓ax̄ƛ̓álisela (the Douglas Channel) and thirteen kilometres south of the municipality of Kitimat, Crystal contemplates the challenging problems she is trying to solve and thinks about her endless to-do list. It is also her time to clear her head of both of those things and to absorb the beauty and the peace of the place that she—as generation upon generation of her Haisla ancestors have also done—calls home.

There are two spots on her route where Crystal always takes a pause. One is near her grandparents' old house on the waterfront where she, her mother and stepfather, two uncles, her twin sister, and her younger brother and sister all lived when she was growing up. Sometimes as a young girl she would go out with her grandfather in his boat to check his nets out front of the house. At other times she enjoyed sitting on the tiny dock that acted as a front doorstep to her home, listening to the waves. "It would calm me and allow me to think about things quietly and rationally, much as I do when I am running, so I always like to pause there and think about my childhood. My family was very close. I was always surrounded by love and support from all of them."

The other place that Crystal likes to stop is on a small rise overlooking the Douglas Channel, where she

"My stepdad, who was the coach of our junior girls basketball team, would always remind us that the effort we put into our sport and how we conducted ourselves playing, especially not quitting in the face of adversity—these were all things we had to apply in life in general if we wanted to succeed. If we did, that would always serve us well as adults and as future leaders."

—Crystal Smith, Chief Councillor, Haisla Nation, October 30, 2020

Facing page: North side of q̓ax̄ƛ̓álisela, the Douglas Channel, near the Haisla community of Kitamaat.

Haisla Chief Councillor Crystal Smith

takes a few moments to rest and to think about who she is as a Haisla woman. It is a vital daily reconnection to her ancestry, upbringing, and identity. "I think about my strengths and everything that my parents and grandparents taught me. It grounds me physically and emotionally every time." The runs, she says, are very therapeutic in that sense. "I am so grateful to be who and where I am. As I jog, it's an opportunity to just let all of that soak in. It rejuvenates and empowers me—it's enlightening, if that makes any sense. Seeing everything around me as I run literally helps me to reconnect every time to the strength I know I have inside me and motivates me to keep pushing forward."

It is basketball rather than running, however, that is Crystal's first love. Naturally athletic, she took up the sport as a young girl and never looked back. "As soon as I touched that ball the first time, from then on that is how I spent all of my time when I wasn't in school. The basketball court became my second home." On the court she bonded with other Haisla girls her age, developing friendships that have lasted into adulthood. The value of those friendships and the love and loyalty they represent cannot be overestimated, says Crystal. The relationship between the women is one of great strength and unwavering support, especially in difficult times.

The sport also instilled in Crystal many of the fundamental values that as an adult she applies not only to her leadership approach as Chief Councillor of the Haisla Nation but to life in general. Understand that about her and those values that she embraces, and you will understand much more about who Crystal is, both personally and as a leader of her people, and why she takes the approach that she does to her role as Chief Councillor.

For a start, basketball is all about community for Crystal. It has been that way since she began playing the sport. The satisfaction in winning tournaments as a Haisla team, especially against the odds, is always shared with everyone: family, friends, other youth and Elders alike. "Even when it was just the junior girls team, you could hear the pride in everyone's voices whenever we won a game," she recalls. "It was always such a great feeling and so satisfying to be giving that gift of feeling proud of ourselves to everyone in the community."

As she moved into her high school years, basketball also allowed her to believe in herself in a world where, as a young Indigenous woman, she was constantly fighting the odds. "I remember a couple of the coaches at the high school in Kitimat saying to me, 'You have the world against you. You're a woman and you're an Indian,'" says Crystal. "That was drilled into us back in elementary school, too, where we were always being told by the teachers that Indigenous rates of academic success are low and that pretty much we were destined to fail. In fact, they were setting us up to fail." Despite those predictions, Crystal did reasonably well at school. Her well-honed basketball skills also gave her the confidence to hold her head up amongst her non-Indigenous peers. "The other girls didn't know how to play, so they would just pass the ball to me and my twin sister and let us do the work."

Working hard was not a problem for Crystal. Her stepfather, who was also coach of the junior girls basketball team, had instilled deeply in her and her teammates a strong sense of accountability to each other as well as a culture of commitment and hard work. "His name was Albert Robinson, Sr. He would always remind us that the effort we put into our sport, and how we conducted ourselves playing, especially not quitting in the face of adversity— these were all things we had to apply in life in general if we wanted to succeed. If we did, that would always serve us well as adults and as future leaders. That work ethic, that determination not to quit and always wanting to improve myself is with me for life now."

These characteristics, principles, and values have served her well since first being elected Chief Councillor in 2017 at the age of thirty-eight. She expected the role to be challenging. As it is for most elected leaders of what are typically small communities, the demands on a Chief's time and energy are never-ending. As a young woman—even in the enlightened days of the twenty-first century—it can be even tougher. Throw a pandemic into the mix—a job description that already requires strong leadership, finely-honed political skills, knowledge of everything from Indigenous law to economic investment strategies, government and third-party relationship management to local waste management requirements, and, not least of all, an intimate and empathetic relationship with and understanding of your community—and the workload can be unbelievable.

But for Crystal, who was managing the second year of the pandemic for her community when she was re-elected in June 2021, there is nothing else she can imagine doing at this stage of her life. "It's a rollercoaster," she admits. "You have your good times and you have your bad times. But every day I get a reminder of why I love what I do. For me, ultimately, it is my opportunity to help change our story to one of success and prosperity for the Nation and for every Haisla citizen." It is a story, emphasizes Crystal, that has badly needed changing since the earliest days of colonization of Haisla territory.

Prior to the arrival of European explorers in the late eighteenth century, the Haisla enjoyed an enviable way of life in their homelands, in the heart of one of the most resource-rich parts of what is now coastal British Columbia. There were plentiful shellfish in Kitimat Arm and navigable access down the Douglas Channel to the ocean for fishing and trading. The wide, flat arable valley along the Kitimat River was abundant with plant life. Clean rivers throughout the territory embraced healthy annual runs of wild salmon and eulachon fish. The forests were plentiful and the mountains full of wildlife.

This is a stunningly beautiful part of the world. The Douglas Channel, a deep island-studded fiord that snakes its way northeast and inland for ninety kilometres before it peters out in shallow tidal waters at the mouth of the Kitimat River, acts as the Haisla Nation's front doorstep. Twenty kilometres to the south, the Gardner Canal doglegs away from the Douglas Channel, meandering southwards past the snow-packed peaks of the Kitimat Ranges, the mouth of the Kemano River, and through valleys punctuated by opaque glacial lakes and threaded with shallow rushing rivers braided in gravel washed down from sheer granite mountains. The canal ends its journey at the mouth of the Kitlope River, just west of the 322,020-hectare Huchsduwachsdu Nuyem Jees/Kitlope Heritage Conservancy, home to grizzly bears, moose, wolves and bald eagles, eulachon and salmon, and the largest remaining temporate coastal rainforest in the world.

Looking southwest up q̓ax̄ƛálisela, the Douglas Channel.

This wild, scenic place is also steeped in history and tradition. It encompasses the territory of not only the Haisla, whose homelands include the Douglas Channel and Kitamaat, but of the X̄enaksiala people of Xesdu'wäʷ, or Husduwachsdu, the Kitlope. X̄enaksiala Elder Wa'xaid, the late Cecil Paul, told author Briony Penn in *Stories from the Magic Canoe of Wa'xaid* that the name of the Kitlope in his language is Xesdu'wäxʷ, so called for its blue milky lakes and rivers.

It was the X̄enaksiala, led by people like Wa'xaid and Gagamguist (Gerald Amos), the Haisla Nation's Chief Councillor from 1980 until 1992, who fought an almost decade-long battle, from the late 1980s into the 1990s, to protect Xesdu'wäxʷ from encroaching logging operations. When they finally won, in 1996, said Wa'xaid, more than the land was saved; so too were all the X̄enaksiala stories embedded in the place; stories, Wa'xaid told Penn, that contained "all our wisdom for living." Gagamguist, a founding member of Ecotrust Canada,[32] co-authored and signed the 1991 *Kitlope Declaration of the Haisla Nation*,[33] in which he encapsulated the relationship of the X̄enaksiala and Haisla people with their territories this way: "We do not own this land so much as the land owns us...It is given to us to live within its boundaries in beauty and harmony, to nourish our bodies and our spirits with its gifts, and to protect it from harm."

But when Captain George Vancouver arrived on the west coast in 1793, everything changed for the X̄enaksiala and the Haisla. Settlers flooded into the Kitimat Valley and began to pre-empt large tracts of rich farming land bordering the river. X̄enaksiala and Haisla people who were used to fishing and gathering food along its banks were completely shut out. Instead, the Haisla were provided small and impoverished reserves along the coast.

Gagamguist (Gerald Amos), former Haisla Chief Councillor

The Bella Coola Indian agent at one point reported, "The [Indian] reserves of this band are the poorest reserves and of the smallest dimensions according to the size of the band than any other in the agency. They contain no farming land and no timber of any value."[34]

Coupled with the loss of their lands came the devastating loss of people. Hundreds of Haisla and X̄enaksiala died of settler-borne smallpox, and hundreds more were lost in the global influenza epidemic that began in 1918, lasting several years. The federal government, citing expediency, merged those who remained into a single Indian Band on the Haisla reserves, notwithstanding their distinct societies and homelands. Even then the assault on their culture did not end. As happened to other Indigenous Peoples in the country, their cultural practices were banned, their rights severely restricted, and, worst of all, their children were forced to attend residential schools a long way from home, where use of their language was actively discouraged and where many of the children, as is now widely understood, suffered horrific abuse.

Economically, over the same period of time, large-scale forestry and commercial fishing activity by non-Indigenous corporate entities and investors in the region boomed. But as with the restrictions on access to good land, the Haisla and X̄enaksiala were given no opportunity to participate. This pattern continued into the twentieth century. In 1948 construction began on a large hydroelectric generating station at Kemano, upriver from the Gardner Canal and roughly eighty kilometres in a straight line from Kitamaat. The project was being undertaken by the Aluminum Company of Canada (Alcan), now known as Rio Tinto, Ltd., to service its then brand-new aluminum smelter at the town of Kitimat, across the water from the Haisla community.

The pressure to complete the Alcan project was huge, given an unprecedented post-war demand for the metal. Environmental concerns were not a high priority under the circumstances. The destruction of formerly pristine wildlife habitat to clear the way for infrastructure, the damming of fish-bearing rivers for power generation, and carbon emissions from a smelter burning fuel twenty-four hours a day, were of little importance by comparison to the promise of economic bounty.

Over the same period, a new port was built in Kitimat Harbour to enable direct export by sea of the freshly smelted aluminum. In 1969 a pulp and paper mill began operations at the head of Kitimat Arm, releasing large volumes of chemical effluent into the Kitimat River. A factory producing 500,000 tonnes of methane gas and ammonia began operating on the Kitimat waterfront in 1982, also exporting its wares via the Port of Kitimat. By the time the methane plant finally closed, in 2005, Haisla territory around Kitamaat was suffering severely from the environmental impacts of all of this intense industrial development.

Water quality was poor. Eulachon in the Kitimat River, which the Nation's citizens depended on for sustenance and trade, became victims to the river's heavy pollution. Haisla fishers reported that the taste of the fish changed dramatically, making it inedible. Harvesters were forced to travel to the Kemano River, a far less accessible and convenient location. Important social bonds were disrupted. Those without boats could not travel to Kemano, and family groups who had once spent several weeks at a time together on the Kitimat River, catching fish, making grease, and passing their knowledge and skills down to the next generation, now spent that time apart. The chains of ancestral cultural knowledge were severely weakened as a result.

All of this took a heavy toll on the Haisla. By the early twenty-first century the loss of livelihoods and prosperity, of vibrant cultural connections and of language proficiency, and all of the other consequences of colonization, were showing in stark terms: a shockingly high suicide rate in Kitamaat, unemployment rates averaging seventy per cent, equally high rates of poverty, and widespread drug addiction and alcoholism. Federal government services were doing little to help alleviate this misery.

In her early twenties by then, Crystal was well aware of the troubled state of her community. But on top of her job working for the local school district, she was preoccupied with caring for her baby daughter, as well as her much younger sister and brother after their mother passed from cancer. Her sights were firmly set already, however, on working for her Nation. "I remember walking past the Band office when I was still at school and thinking, 'One day, I'm going to work there.' I had started studying business

Wild grizzlies still roam Haisla and X̌enaksiala territory, but their range has been severely impacted by the industrialization of the region.

administration after leaving school, and I really wanted to get into that kind of work as soon as I could on behalf of the people."

When the opportunity arose to take a job as an administrative assistant in the community childcare centre, she seized it as a first step in the right direction. It meant she was in the right place at the right time when in 2009 the newly elected Chief Councillor of the Nation, Dolores Pollard, came by Crystal's desk one day and asked her if she would come and work for her instead. "I said, 'Yes, of course!' Dolores was the first female Chief of the Haisla, and I became her executive assistant."

Ellis Ross, one of Crystal's former basketball coaches and a good friend, replaced Dolores as Chief Councillor two years later. Crystal stayed in the job to help him navigate his way through the challenging role. It was Ellis, says Crystal, and his vision for improving the wellbeing of the Haisla, who inspired her to take the next step and run for Council in 2013. "Ellis believed that our people and our territory needed to heal from the past. His goal was that our Nation would become independent and powerful and

that would fully test every aspect of Crystal's leadership.

In 2018 the Haisla, along with more than a dozen other First Nations, signed a partnership agreement with LNG Canada Development Inc., a multinational liquid natural gas (LNG) exporter, and with Coastal GasLink Pipeline Ltd., supporting the construction of a pipeline from northeast BC to a new export facility to be constructed at Kitimat. As the public face of that decision, Crystal immediately experienced a storm of powerful condemnation, not only from the environmental movement but from many of Haisla's neigh
First Nations. Many of those other Nations had fought ferociously f
to prevent any oil and gas development or expansion from affecti
territories and continue to actively resist it. The Haisla parted ways
controversy with the Coastal First Nations-Great Bear Initiative, a c
of coastal Indigenous communities working to create conservatic
omies in their territories. The resulting fractures in relationships b
these Nations have been painful for all concerned.

Despite bearing the brunt of the criticism, Crystal remains a
about her primary reason for taking the Haisla down that path. "M
mother taught me to do what I believe in. I believe in this. I beli
community deserves to heal and we deserve to have a quality of lif
equal in comparison to every other Canadian in this country. Gove
was doing nothing to help us. This was the way to do it."

This was not, Crystal emphasizes, an easy decision to make. R
industrial degradation of their territory had been part of the Nati
tory for decades. In 2012 Gagamguist had summarized that histo
lengthy editorial in the *Huffington Post* magazine, writing, "The Hai
been fighting to protect this region from ill-conceived industrial
ments for over thirty years. We have seen the magnificent forest
Kitimat Valley, and other coastal watersheds, obliterated in an orgy
and destruction driven by short-term economic interests instead

prosperous, as we were before colonization and all of its impacts on us and on the land. He said to me, 'We can't achieve that unless our people become independent and powerful and prosperous,'" recalls Crystal. "The way to get to that was to generate our own revenues, because government funding certainly wasn't doing anything to help us achieve improved quality of life or take care of our territory." She agreed with him. "I decided that I wanted to be part of contributing to achieving that goal, too. If being on Council was the way to do that, then that was what I was going to do."

A couple of years earlier, at a memorial service for a Haisla citizen who had taken their own life, Ellis had experienced an epiphany. "I had attended so many services like that. I looked back on all the people I knew who had committed suicide in my lifetime and it shocked me." The issue became personal for Ellis at that moment. "I made a decision right then that the next Haisla member that does that here, that's my fault because I did not offer that person an alternative to whatever they were experiencing. Everything crystallized in my head at that moment. I realized I had to make sure this generation is the first generation to break the cycle. If there's anything that describes what I was trying to do back then that encapsulates it."

Ellis decided that providing opportunities for Haisla people to gain meaningful, well-paid employment was the most likely pathway to improving quality of life for them and for building strength and resilience in the community. "At that time we were trying to fit people into job experience programs like internships and part-time work to give them a taste of the employment world," he says. "A few of them transitioned from that into full-time employment. When I talked to them later on, I noticed a change in them. They were happy. They were excited about buying a car. They were excited about the new boss that they were working for. They were learning new skills. They were even talking about saving up enough money to go on vacation. I realized, that's the way! We get them into meaningful jobs or vocations, we spark their passion in something and then just let the natural course take place. It doesn't have to be Council putting them in programs or telling them which course they should take. We needed to expose them to the world of independence through getting their own jobs and making their own money."

Haisla Council initiated opportunities for their citizens to get into full-time employment in the region, and things quickly started to snowball. "When you see good results that fast you get greedy for more," remarks Ellis.

The Kitamaat waterfront on q̓aχλálisela, the Douglas Channel.

That led to his next revelation: "It was pieceme
It was all one-off opportunities for individuals l
wanted was to affect an entire generation." That, fo
was the point at which he started to look at all tl
taking place in Haisla territory from a new pers
ively involved in development projects, he decid
only expand job opportunities on a huge scale f
to earn substantial independent revenues, settin
straints of limited and sometimes non-existent g
Nation could then commit its own money toward
infrastructure and invest in its own environmenta
grams tailored to their specific needs.

Shortly after Crystal successfully won a Ha
the desire for fundamental change also became
That year, the father of her two daughters commi
grief, Crystal's determination to help turn thing
became stronger than ever. By the time she bec
Ellis decided to stand down so he could run fo
building of the pathway was well under way. It

The Haisla Fisheries Commission has been actively monitoring and researching water quality in Haisla territory since 1993.

we asked for; long-term sustainable and science-driven resource planning." The biggest thing for him, repeated Gagamguist in 2021, "is that people understand that it is in everyone's interest to ensure that we look after properly the home that has been afforded us. This is our only home, and if we can't take care of it properly, it is all for nought. It will be destroyed."

For Crystal the vision was, and remains, clear. "As part of our pathway to restoring our wellbeing we wanted to put into place whatever measures we could to protect our lands and waters from any further degradation. In fact, we wanted to improve how they are treated. That was a condition of our partnership agreement. For me, that environmental rigour is critical. As the Nation's leader I would not and will not stand in front of my community and tell them we are willing to accept any greater impacts on our lands than there already have been for the sake of a dollar sign."

The coexistence of industrial development and the wellbeing of the environment remains an uneasy one. The contradictions between the ideal of achieving community wellbeing and environmental protection within a framework of industrial investment are realities Crystal continues to live with on a daily basis. "I don't want to sugar-coat any of this," she says. "It hasn't been pleasant. Moreover, despite the fact that we are the ones who have been here for hundreds of years and we know what is significant and what is acceptable, it can be difficult for us to get that knowledge and expertise accepted and applied even now. But we are doing it, and it is making a huge difference to us already."

These days, unemployment in Kitamaat is down to about ten per cent. The number of Haisla citizens enrolling in post-secondary education is unprecedented. Many Haisla and X̄enaksiala people are harvesting eulachon again—albeit still from the Kemano River rather than the Kitimat River—and making the rich grease that sustains them over long, hard winters. An Elders' centre has been built, delivering services to the Nations' seniors, including meals on wheels. The Na'na'kila Institute, created in 1998, is protecting and encouraging reconnection to Haisla culture, and a full-time culture coordinator has been employed. Language classes are being taught daily at the Haisla community school.

Candice Wilson, the Haisla Nation's environmental manager, with her daughter Zaylaa.

Born and raised in Kitamaat, Haisla Nation environmental manager Candice Wilson is engaged in research into acidification in the Kitimat River and working with the First Nations Climate Initiative, a collaborative forum focussed on climate change mitigation, to develop a policy framework for achieving net-zero gas emissions. With a bachelor's degree in environmental science, a certificate in traditional environmental knowledge from the University of Northern British Columbia, and a master's degree in environmental practice from Royal Roads University in Victoria, she is also monitoring riparian and saltmarsh habitat restoration by the Haisla's industrial partners in the Kitimat estuary, a condition of their investment agreement.

In the course of that work an exciting discovery was made in 2020, says Candice. "We discovered a huge fish weir complex in Minette Bay, which is between Kitamaat Village and Kitimat. Some of the wooden stakes are nearly two thousand years old." Fish weirs are an ancient but highly efficient technology used to anchor woven branches that trap fish in pools as the tide comes up and then recedes. In the twentieth century, the federal government banned the practice of using fish weirs, as they interfered with commercial fishing. The discovery was not only profoundly important in

In 2020, an ancient fish weir complex was discovered in Minette Bay, near Kitamaat, during the course of habitat restoration work in the estuary.

terms of Haisla's Aboriginal Rights and Title, but equally significant in cultural and emotional terms. "Knowing that we've been here that long and utilizing these resources," says Candice, "puts a whole different perspective on the way I think about who we are as Haisla people and how we use the resources today."

The Haisla Fisheries Commission, established in 1993, has broadened its role from a purely fisheries-related one to undertaking everything from water-quality research, salmon and eulachon monitoring and stock assessments, and dispersing herring roe on kelp to community members, to providing advance marine first-aid training and supporting culture camps for Haisla youth. Haisla youth camps are connecting children with their culture and providing them, as future environmental stewards for the Nation, with the opportunity to learn about sustaining resources and respecting the landscape and the creatures within it.

The latter initiative in particular is dear to Crystal's heart. As a teenager she had been part of a Haisla youth program that took young people on camping trips into the Kitlope, introducing them to the landscape, their cultural heritage, and the gathering and preparation of traditional foods such as eulachon grease. "I was nineteen. That was the first time I had ever been out on the Douglas Channel and into the Kitlope. We harvested halibut, black cod, and other fish. It was a wonderful experience, very empowering and grounding for me."

From left: Haisla Chief Councillor Crystal Smith with former Chiefs Ellis Ross and Dolores Pollard at a September 2021 reconciliation event in Kitamaat.

She had not been eager to go, Crystal recalls, because of the lack of showers and other inconveniences she would face in two weeks of camping. "But then I didn't want to leave. The connection I felt to the territory was amazing, even though I am Haisla rather than X̄enaksiala. Those two weeks were a huge part of making me who I am today. I want our youth to be able to have those same experiences. I like to tell our young people today, who are the same age I was then, that they are going to be the generation that brings back the strength of our people and that being connected to the land and our history is such an important part of that."

Crystal has little spare time to visit the Kitlope or any other parts of the territory these days. She also isn't playing much basketball. Even without a pandemic to consider and a torn knee ligament that still needs healing, her free time is almost non-existent. She continues to set her sights on a future for Haisla people that is prosperous and healthy, applying all of her leadership skills, everything she has learned from her predecessors, her forebears, and even—or perhaps especially—her basketball coaches and teammates over the years toward that goal.

It is a goal that is becoming increasingly tangible. "The transformation of our community to what it is today felt unimaginable a few years ago," marvels Crystal. "I have two daughters now and a grandson. I believe that their future is just going to be amazing."

A Voice for the Bears

CHAPTER EIGHT

On April 12, 2012, a typically rainy spring day on British Columbia's central coast, the community hall in Klemdulxk was packed with citizens of the Kitasoo/Xai'xais Nation.

The weather may have been cool, but the atmosphere inside the building was noticeably heated. The National Energy Board's Joint Review Panel for Enbridge Inc.'s Northern Gateway pipeline was in Klemdulxk to hear Kitasoo/Xai'xais people's views about the proposed project, the construction of an oil pipeline from Alberta to Kitimat Harbour, 165 kilometres north of the small Kitasoo/Xai'xais community. The pipeline would bring with it a significant increase in oil tanker traffic steaming south through the stormy waters of Hecate Strait and past the Kitasoo/Xai'xais' territorial front doorstep. The community was united in adamant opposition to the proposal. As the three members of the panel took their seats, the hall rumbled and echoed with apprehensive conversation.

Everyone fell silent, however, when Mercedes Neasloss walked up to the microphone and prepared to speak. Mercedes' voice was calm and clear as she introduced herself. "My traditional name is Hbuk'vas'tam-hyu, which was passed to me from my great-grandmother, Elizabeth Neasloss. The meaning of my name is 'mother,' the one who holds the family together. I belong to the Salmon Clan. My childhood name is 'lalag°de,' which means 'butterfly' in the Haisla language. I carry these names with

"The biggest lessons in my life so far are to always respect the territory and to protect the land and the bears, because we have so much to learn from them, and so that future generations will always have the opportunity to enjoy what we have."

—Hbuk'vas'tam-hyu Mercedes Robinson Neasloss, Klemdulxk (Klemtu), April 22, 2021

Facing page: Kitasoo/Xai'xais homelands boast steep, wild mountains and deep inlets, and are home to Moksgm'ol, the famous spirit bear.

Hbuk'vas'tam-hyu, (Mercedes Robinson Neasloss), 2021

great pride and honour. My English name is Mercedes Neasloss," she said, "and I am ten years old.

"I am here to speak for my generation and the next generations to come. I also speak for the ocean, and the animals that can't speak, like the whales, sea otters, fish, and seals, who all call the ocean home. The ocean," she emphasized to the panel, "is Klemtu's way of life. We are a remote coastal community and our livelihood depends on the resources the ocean provides. I have grown up here helping my parents and grandparents harvest and preserve our traditional foods, such as cleaning and drying miya (salmon), peeling herring eggs, cleaning chuwali (cockles), jeeka, clams and prawns. These are traditions I want to preserve and pass on to my children and grandchildren. Please consider my opinion," she concluded, "and the opinion of my Nation, in making your decision on the pipeline."[36]

Mercedes' mother, Roxanne Robinson, was watching with immense pride as her daughter spoke. Roxanne believes that it was significant for the panel to hear about the potential effect of the pipeline on the Kitasoo/Xai'xais through the voice of a child like Mercedes. "You could see the impact on them immediately, to realize this was a little girl who was already so connected to her culture through the land and the ocean and the wildlife in her territory," recalls Roxanne. "The fact she stood up to speak gave them real pause. They understood for the first time that their decision would not just affect some past way of life, but the future of children like her. It was very emotional and empowering to have Mercedes stand up that day and use her voice that way for our Nation."

A young Mercedes on the beach at Disju, on Princess Royal Island, a traditional gathering place for Kitasoo Chiefs to meet and discuss governance. Mercedes tells a traditional story that she has learned by hearing it from her Elders and teachers, and repeating it, in accordance with her oral tradition.

The Nation to which Mercedes and Roxanne belong comprises, as its name suggests, two distinct tribes: the Kitasoo, from the western outer islands of the territory, and the Xai'xais, from the mainland. Each speaks different languages: the Kitasoo speak the Ts'msyen language of Sgüüx̱s, while Xai'xais is part of the Wakashan language group. After each experienced massive losses from settler-borne diseases, the two tribes joined forces in the 1860s to settle together in what has become the twenty-first century seat of the Nation, the tiny community of Klemdulxk (as it is known by its Sgüüx̱s name) or łm̓du (its Wakashan name). Klemtu, as it is more commonly called, lies tucked into the sheltered waters of Trout Bay, on the east side of Swindle Island, five hundred kilometres north of Vancouver. It is a remote and peaceful village on the ocean, inhabited by some four hundred and twenty people and surrounded by stunningly beautiful wilderness in a region dense with wildlife, not only marine mammals and fish, but wolves, deer, and bears, among many other species.

The people of Klemtu have a particularly close connection, both contemporary and ancient, to the bears that roam their territory. Their relationship with the white bear, also known as the spirit bear, is especially intimate. Author Anthony Carter recounts in his 1967 work, *Somewhere Between*, that as one Ts'msyen story goes, Wee'get, the Raven, who created both the Kitasoo and the Xai'xais, wanted to ensure they would never forget that at one time the land had been covered with ice and snow. Wee'get first made an island for the white bear people, then went among the black bears, making one in ten of them white. Wee'get then decreed that the spirit bear, whose Ts'msyen name is Moksgm'ol, should never leave the island,

for there these extraordinary white bears could live in peace forever.

When Mercedes spoke to the Joint Review Panel, she emphasized the fundamental urgency of protecting the home of these precious white bears from the environmental threat of the proposed pipeline. So did incumbent Kitasoo/Xai'xais Chief Councillor Douglas Neasloss, who rose to speak after Mercedes. Doug, whose other name is Muq'vas Glaw, or "white bear" in the Xai'xais language, likewise urged the members of the panel to protect his territory. "We live in a unique part of the world," he told them. "This is the only place you will see a spirit bear, in the last remaining intact rainforest ecosystem on the planet."

Nearly ten years earlier, when Mercedes was still an infant, a different but equally pivotal gathering had taken place in the Kitasoo/Xai'xais community hall. The unemployment level in Klemtu at the time, recalls Doug, amounted to more than eighty per cent of the adult population, and the community was considering tourism as a way to create more jobs in Klemtu. Bear-watching tours seemed an obvious opportunity to kickstart a tourism economy in the village, and Doug, still barely in his twenties, enthusiastically supported the idea. "A few years earlier, I had taken a Japanese film crew out to show them bears. That was the first trip of that kind I had done and the first time I ever saw a spirit bear. I was seventeen years old and I absolutely fell in love," he recalls. Doug also loved the concept of trying to create a viable economy through wildlife tourism. "I thought it was a

The spirit bear is also known by its Ts'msyen name, Moksgm'ol, and as Muq'vas Glaw, or "white bear," in the Xai'xais language.

perfect fit for us at every level—in terms of our conservation work, sustainability, and our culture."

Muq'vas Glaw, Kitasoo/Xai'xais Chief Councillor Douglas (Doug) Neasloss

The bear-viewing operation in Klemtu at the time was basic, says Doug. In the early 2000s it consisted of "a three-man gig operating day tours out of a two-room float shack. We relied on once-a-week ferry passenger traffic and operated on a shoestring budget." Doug was pitching a much bigger dream to the community at the meeting. Wildlife tours were just one part of it. The real vision was to open a full-service luxury lodge catering to both foreign and domestic tourist markets, offering long-term, high-quality employment to community members and contributing meaningfully to the cultural, environmental, and economic life of everyone in Klemtu and the Nation as a whole.

The community, however, had doubts about the idea at the time. They had legitimate concerns about visitors using up limited community resources, for example—there are no roads to Klemtu and the village depends on boat and floatplane deliveries for most of its supplies. They were also worried about whether Kitasoo/Xai'xais culture might be negatively affected by tourism development. "There were a lot of questions especially about whether we would, effectively, be selling our culture," Doug says.

At the meeting being held to consider whether to support the tourism vision or not, the young man advocated passionately for the dream. "I showed them photos I had taken of grizzly bears and spirit bears. I talked about how connected we are as a Nation to the bears and how the future of Klemtu depended on protecting them by raising awareness through tourism and generating revenue to support our conservation work." Doug also reminded everyone of the economic realities facing the Kitasoo/Xai'xais in the early 2000s. Klemtu was, after all, a small village challenged by the interlinked threats of climate change, resource depletion, and diminishing work opportunities in remote locations.

"I remember saying that the era of commercial fishing is over," recalls Doug. "It died back in the sixties, and it hasn't ever recovered. We were burned by being a one-horse town—the cannery here shut down one day in 1966 and left the community almost totally unemployed." As things stood, there seemed to be few reasons for the young people to stay in Klemtu. The Nation had to diversify, he believed. "We needed to carve out a new path. To me, tourism was the way to create a long-term sustainable economy in Klemtu, especially as we were also working, as we have always done and continue to do, to protect as much of our territory as possible. We had to pivot to conservation and to non-extractive activities. There really was no other option."

The community still wasn't convinced. But as they teetered on the brink of rejecting the idea, Violet Neasloss slowly stood up. "Violet was Mercedes' other great-grandmother," says Doug. "She was in her nineties back then, the oldest lady in our community." Elders command a great deal of respect from Kitasoo/Xai'xais people, notes Doug, and everyone listened quietly as Violet echoed Doug's words about the importance of protecting the bears, and the special connection between these wild animals and Kitasoo/Xai'xais people. She emphasized another vital point: the pressing need to offer hope to the community's youth and to give them opportunities to reconnect to their culture that, at the time, were almost non-existent.

Doug recalls, "She said to us all, 'Listen. Our young people are becoming very disconnected. They are not learning their songs, their stories, their dances, their language. They're not learning their territory. If tourism is going to be the vehicle that's going to help change that we should entertain it.' Everybody voted in favour after she had spoken. She essentially saved the future of tourism in Klemtu that night."

At the end of the meeting the relieved young man expressed his gratitude to Violet for her intervention. Violet, in turn, had a message for Doug. She had a very clear vision of what she wanted the future to offer her great-granddaughter as an adult, and to all future generations of Kitasoo/Xai'xais youth, and responded to him unequivocally. "She said, 'Doug, if you're going to do tourism, you must not only protect the bears, but you must also take the youth with you in that work.' So that was our mandate. We had to make sure we took the youth with us on the journey."

That journey began when the Kitasoo/Xai'xais proudly opened the doors of their Spirit Bear Lodge in 2006. The Lodge offered high-end accommodation, wildlife tours, and cultural experiences to a tourist market eager not only to see bears in the wilderness of coastal BC, but to learn about

their Indigenous hosts, their culture, and their history. The curiosity was mutual, at least on the part of the village's young people. As tourists started to arrive that first season, the Lodge's managers noticed that youngsters from the community were dropping by in the evenings and chatting with some of the guests. They also noticed that the guests seemed to be enjoying the conversations.

Thus was born the concept of Súa, a Kitasoo/Xai'xais youth cultural program sponsored by the Lodge. Through Súa, Kitasoo/Xai'xais children learn about important sites in their territory, are given language lessons, and are taught their traditional songs, stories, and dances. "Súa" is a Xai'xais word meaning "thunder" and the children who participate in the program are encouraged to be "loud and proud" in celebrating their identity and culture, staging performances of their songs and dances for guests of the Lodge. When she was old enough to participate, Mercedes joined the Súa program, loving every moment of the experience and the role Súa plays in

Vernon Brown, who works with the Kitasoo/Xai'xais Stewardship Authority (KXSA), explains that these bears are like teachers: "The interactions the youth have with them gives them such a good sense of their connection to these animals and to the territory."

Kitasoo/Xai'xais Councillor Isaiah Robinson

educating outsiders about Kitasoo/Xai'xais culture. "I think it's really important for our children to be 'loud and proud,'" she reflects, "so that people know how important our area and our culture is. It's good the kids are helping educate tourists about these things. People should know that we're proud of who we are and where we come from."

One of the important goals of the Lodge was to provide job opportunities for Klemtu community members as originally envisioned. The management team designed a professional training program for Kitasoo/Xai'xais citizens with the objective of employing everyone who successfully completed the program. It was a highly successful strategy, says Kitasoo/Xai'xais Councillor Isaiah Robinson. the Lodge is now employing community members in almost every aspect of its operations, not only as tour guides, but as front desk management, operational managers, restaurant servers, and even as trainee chefs.

Although Isaiah was born in Klemtu in the mid-1990s, he grew up in the small town of Hope, in BC's southern interior. Isaiah decided to return to Klemtu in the mid-2010s because he believed that it was vital to the future of the community that young people like him come home, bringing their education, experience, and passion for a prosperous, healthy future with them. "The Lodge has proved to do what people hoped it would," observes Isaiah, who holds the housing and infrastructure portfolios on Kitasoo/Xai'xais Council and is general manager of the Kitasoo Development Corporation. "It has greatly supported our human capacity in the Nation and built new skills among our people. That has opened more job opportunities for them as well." The Lodge should be able to draw on local talent in the future for all of its management roles, says Isaiah. "We already know that we have people gaining the necessary experience and those people may well be in a position to take those positions on when the time comes."

Cognizant that the Lodge is also highly reliant for its commercial success on the ongoing presence of a healthy bear population in the territory, the Kitasoo/Xai'xais also established the Spirit Bear Research Foundation in 2011, in collaboration with wildlife biologists and bear researchers. The foundation, to which Spirit Bear Lodge contributes financially out of annual profits, conducts research into the behaviour and health of both spirit and

Douglas Neasloss speaks to Kitasoo/Xai'xais Stewardship Authority staff at an ancient village site near Klemdulxk (Klemtu).

black bears, as well as grizzlies, and offers summer internships to local school students like Mercedes.

In tandem with the establishment of the foundation, the Nation created the new position of resource stewardship director, appointing Doug Neasloss to the role. "This was a brand-new concept at the time but was still building on the goal of creating a conservation-based economy for the Nation, this time focussing on stewardship and protection of our territory and wildlife in conjunction with our tourism efforts." Once again, Doug was under firm instructions to ensure he involved local youth in whatever he did in the new role. "Our Elders and leaders were very clear that what we were doing was not for us, it was for future generations. That had to be ingrained in all of our work."

One way to accommodate youth in the stewardship work was to integrate into the new conservation arm of the Nation a program called SEAS[37] (Supporting Emerging Aboriginal Stewards). SEAS provides stewardship work experience for Indigenous youth out in the field, enabling youngsters like Mercedes to learn about the kind of bear research techniques that scientists with Spirit Bear Research Foundation employ, for example, and about the extensive conservation work being undertaken by Kitasoo/Xai'xais in the territory to protect their precious wildlife and their habitat. Mercedes, who had spent much of her childhood exploring her Nation's territory with her parents and Elders, enthusiastically participated in SEAS, later working for the program as a summer intern in her teens.

She was already accustomed to bear encounters by then. "Growing up, I became very used to being around wildlife," Mercedes recalls. Those encounters were more than just magical moments in the presence of beautiful animals. As she became more familiar with the bears, Mercedes increasingly understood how closely connected she was through her ancestry to her environment and the creatures within it. "The bears are, in a sense, part of who we are," she reflects, "and we are also the bears—in how we live and in our culture." How the Kitasoo/Xai'xais behave toward their territory, the bears, and each other is founded on that age-old relationship with the environment, she says. "The more time I spent out in the territory with my family and with SEAS, the more I realized our ancestors would have had the same experiences I was having, which was beautiful to understand. It made me feel so connected to the land and to who I am in my Kitasoo/Xai'xais identity."

Mussel Inlet, in Kitasoo/Xai'xais territory, is where Spirit Bear Lodge operates its bear viewing and ecotourism business, and where SEAS programs are undertaken.

There is no more valuable classroom in which to teach their youth about the bears and their relationship with them than the forest itself, adds Vernon Brown. Vernon, who works with what is now called the Kitasoo/Xai'xais Stewardship Authority (KXSA), has spent a great deal of time out in the territory with youth like Mercedes, both as part of the SEAS program and employing them as summer interns with KXSA. The territory provides an education to Kitasoo/Xai'xais youth that is without compare. That's for a very simple reason, he says. "Out there, the bears are their teachers. The interactions the youth have with them gives them such a good sense of their connection to these animals and to the territory."

Vernon Brown shows off a sea urchin on his paddle.

These are lessons that their forebears have passed down since time immemorial, Vernon adds. "Our ancestors were learning the same things from bears from the very beginning of time. Bears instinctively know the right foods to eat, which roots, what kinds of berries, and salmon, of course. Their techniques and behaviour in doing so and how they behave amongst each other—we learned that is how best to conduct ourselves as well in the wilderness. That learning from the animals was the start of our connection to this place."

These practical and cultural lessons are ones that Mercedes also learned out in the wild classroom of the forest. "It was the bears who taught me how important it is to protect our territory and how to help do that by protecting them. Bears depend on salmon, for example, and so do we. When bears feed on salmon, they bring the carcasses up into the forest to eat, and the nutrients from the fish feed the trees. The bears also fertilize the soil and help disperse seeds and oxygenate surrounding plants when they dig for roots," observes Mercedes. "That helps keep the land healthy and productive as well. I learned all of this through studying them. My ancestors knew it, too. They understood that our actions affect everything around us and therefore that it's important to understand, to respect the bears and to take care of them and protect the landscape we all share."

This history and these teachings and where they come from, emphasizes Vernon, is something young Kitasoo/Xai'xais people like Mercedes must never forget. "We live on the land and from the sea, and that explains

Salmon are a vital part of the food web and ecology of the BC coast.

who we are. Whether it's a story, a place name, or just the way things were, we have to understand our background and our identity and our history. As members of the Kitasoo/Xai'xais community, in all the work we do, whatever it is, we have to make sure that our values are completely reflected in all of it."

That is particularly important in terms of the Nation's ancestral stewardship responsibilities, adds Vernon, and in understanding that the values and the laws that go with them have evolved through experience and wisdom garnered over thousands of years. "In the Xai'xais language, laws or rules are called ǧviḷás. Ayaawx is how you say law or practice in Sgüüxs, in the Kitasoo language." These are rules, or laws, that have been fine-tuned over thousands of years. He adds, "All the environmental and cultural laws that we have didn't come into existence overnight. We have stories of famine, of war, of hard lessons learned. We have had to adapt just like everybody else to this landscape and this ocean. Along the way there's been a lot of learning from observation or trial and error."

These laws are all about protecting resources and the territory, he explains, and how to conduct oneself. "If you look at First Nations and our behaviour, mostly it's about managing our territory with clear purpose. We're here to continue what our ancestors have done, to protect the resources and our territory and all the living creatures in it. In that respect, we're adaptive conservationists. All throughout these generations that have gone by, they've protected it in every which way they could, from raids, floods, climate change, and overuse. We have had no choice but to keep adapting."

All of this, reflects Vernon, emphasizes the importance of young people like Mercedes not only being involved in stewardship but knowing the stories and traditions of their culture. "You cannot have stewardship if you don't have your youth there with you. There are so many different ways they can be involved, too, whether it's doing research or other types of work on the land or the ocean or archaeology or habitat restoration and monitoring. Even guiding, because all of it comes back to taking care of the territory."

Vernon Brown setting a wildlife camera trap to record bear movements in the river system on Princess Royal Island.

As Mercedes entered her teens, she continued to work with Vernon and with Doug at KXSA and the Spirit Bear Research Foundation, applying each year for summer internships to keep expanding her stewardship skills and experience. She learned how to set up remote cameras to record digital footage of bear activity, collect hair samples for analysis, and catalogue important evidence of bear health and behaviour. In 2017, still only fifteen years old, she starred in an Imax movie,[38] in which she described her home and talked about her cultural upbringing and what being Kitasoo/Xai'xais meant to her. With the international attention she had attracted from her appearance at the Joint Review Panel, Mercedes also juggled frequent interview requests for magazines, newspapers and films in between school classes and all of her other work. None of it went to the teenager's head. Ultimately, says Roxanne, Mercedes simply continued to do what she had always done for her Nation: using her voice for something she strongly believes in.

As Roxanne's daughter, Mercedes comes by that voice naturally. She is descended from a long and powerful line of Kitasoo/Xai'xais matriarchs, Roxanne, Elizabeth, and Violet among them. Roxanne carries the name Hbuks qaaps. The first female elected Chief Councillor of Kitasoo/Xai'xais, a role she held from 2018 to 2021, she will also one day receive the hereditary chiefly name of Git-kon that belonged to her late father, Ross Neasloss, Sr.

Mercedes with her mother, Hbuks qaaps (Roxanne Robinson), the first female elected chief of Kitasoo/Xai'xais, in April 2022.

When Roxanne decided to stand for the position of Chief Councillor, she had seen an opportunity to fulfil her inherited matriarchal responsibilities and in doing so to become a role model for other young women in the community. "As matriarchs we are the heartbeats of the Nations, we are the warriors, and the first to run the lines to fight for the rights of our community,"[39] Roxanne says. She also feels that if there are challenges to face in the community, it is important to contribute to overcoming them. "I wanted to come to the table and lend my voice to that effort." Roxanne taught her daughter, in turn, the importance of working hard for her people and doing her part for the territory, the same way Roxanne's father, his father before him, and her other forebears had all done.

Mercedes has taken these lessons to heart. It was her choice to appear in front of the Joint Review Panel in 2012, despite her young age, and it was also no coincidence that in 2020—by then studying social sciences at the University of Victoria on Vancouver Island—she took part in an occupation of the provincial Legislature aimed at protecting First Nations lands from further depredation and loss. "As much as I worried about her safety," recalls Roxanne, "I was so proud to know that she was standing up and using her voice for what she believed in. That has been true from the time she gave a voice to the spirit bear when she was just ten years old. She also gave a voice to our Nation back then, speaking for everything that we believe in and for our ancestors who were silenced. It was just what she had to do."

In an online article in which Mercedes was interviewed about her Imax movie role,[40] she recounted an anecdote about bears and "stomp trails." The filmmakers were interested in the field work being done by Kitasoo/Xai'xais researchers, using remote cameras to film the movements of the bears and collecting their fur for DNA analysis that revealed information about the animals' diets, their health, and other aspects of their behaviour. At one point in the film, a bear walked into view of the camera,

pausing to rub its back on a tree. "Stomp trails and rub trees are ways that bears communicate with other bears in the area," Mercedes explained to the interviewer. "On the trails they stomp their paws into the ground and the glands in their paws give off a scent. Every bear that walks along that trail steps in the same spots, so hence the name 'stomp trails.'"

Village of Klemdulxk (Klemtu)

As a young adult, Mercedes is walking on her own version of a stomp trail, carefully following the pathways that her ancestors once walked and that her Elders have taught her to walk upon in turn. "It's important for us as young people to do that," reflects Mercedes. "It's important for us to learn and practise the teachings so that when we are older we know how to take care of everything and so that we can teach the next generation and build our knowledge, knowledge that will help us sustain everything for future generations."

The vital thing about involving the Nation's young people in its conservation efforts in all these ways, reflects Doug, who was re-elected as Chief Councillor in 2021, is that they gain an understanding not only of the importance of their territory and the special places within it, but of their own future role in stewardship of those places. "We tell them, 'You are the future leaders, the next generation. You are going to be sitting at the Band

Protecting the land and the bears is a lesson that Mercedes believes is one of the most important for Kitasoo/Xai'xais children to learn.

Council table, you are going to be sitting on the board of our economic development corporation. It will be your job to protect the territory and at the same time to ensure there are jobs in the community and to create revenue.' These kids," he observes, "are in a way better position than I was at their age. Many of them are looking at going on to college or university, and some of them, like Mercedes, are there now. My hope is that one day some of them come back and say to me, 'Doug, you're obsolete, we have way more education than you do and it's time for us to take over.' That's really the intent. That is what Violet wanted back in 2002 and what we all still really want now."

Mercedes, far away from Klemtu at school in Victoria, remains nonetheless as closely connected to her community and territory as she has ever been. Going back to school is a wrenching separation from home after every visit, but Mercedes knows she always has her homelands and the bears. "Coming back, it is always so good and so peaceful to be back in my own territory. Even though this place is so small and so isolated, I am grateful for where I live and where I come from."

As she enters her third decade, Mercedes is in turn encouraging younger Kitasoo/Xai'xais children to follow her along the stomp trails she walked in her childhood. During her first summer holiday from school, she took a job in Klemtu as a stewardship ambassador, inspiring local youth to spend more time out in the territory and to enjoy learning some of the things she has learned along the way. "It's easy for them to take where we live for granted, I think. Going out into the wilderness opens their eyes to how lucky they are to live somewhere like that and to feel a newfound gratitude for that," she says.

"The biggest lessons in my life so far have been to always respect the territory and to protect the land and the bears so that future generations will always have the opportunity to enjoy what we have. I can't think of anything more important for these children to learn than those same lessons."

The Children Are Our Reason for Breathing

CHAPTER NINE

"We have many beautiful words in our language. K̲'wa̲la'yu is 'my reason for living.' Hasda̲xa̲la'yu is 'my reason for breathing.' What would our purpose be without our children?"

—Dzawada̲'enux̲w hereditary Chief Maxwiyalidizi K'odi Nelson, May 2, 2020

AUTHOR'S NOTE: The following chapter is a celebration of leadership, vision, and collaboration on a scale measured in terms of resilience, love of generations yet unborn, and beautiful outcomes. As K̲wik̲wa̲sut̓inux̲w Hax̲wa'mis Chief Councillor Rick Johnson reflects on page 182, "The foundation of our culture is love and respect. I see Nawalakw as building that foundation again, to get us back out there in our traditional lands and start the healing."

Within the chapter, Dzawada̲'enux̲w hereditary Chief Maxwiyalidizi K'odi Nelson recounts a story about the money provided by a private family foundation toward the creation of Nawalakw, a Musgamakw Dzawada̲'enux̲w healing and language centre and ecotourism venture. It feels, in his words, "like a fairy tale come true." It is a fairy tale founded, however, on the history that is acknowledged in the Foreword to this book. It is essential that readers understand and acknowledge that important history and context because all of the Musgamakw Dzawada̲'enux̲w Nations continue to suffer its impacts.

Much of their homelands, which do not enjoy the level of environmental protection that the north and central coast region has received in the twenty-first century, continue to be logged and desecrated in various other ways. K̲wik̲wa̲sut̓inux̲w hereditary Chief Ol Siwid (Mike Willie) emphasizes this in blunt terms: "Because we were not part of the LRMP process, our territory ended up effectively as an industrial zone." The Nation's access to funding for conservation work and sustainable economic development has been hugely constrained by colonial approaches and unacceptable conditions tied to that funding.

Facing page: Looking down Kingcome Inlet to Wakeman Sound.

The K̲wik̲wa̱sut̓inux̱w Ha̱xwa'mis Nation, in whose homelands Nawalakw is located, gave their permission to include this story in the book on the basis that these facts are emphasized, understood, and acknowledged.[41]

Those facts resonated strongly with many of the foundational funders of Nawalakw, reflects K'odi, and still do. "When they hear this history they really gravitate toward us to support our efforts. They also recognize the importance of funding the vision without placing a colonial framework around it. That has been so valuable and so positive in the outcomes we are seeing already." As both private sector and government funders begin to better understand Indigenous approaches, vision, and leadership, such as that illustrated by the creation of Nawalakw, it is K'odi's hope that they will come forward to support more and more initiatives like Nawalakw in the same way.

The K̲wik̲wa̱sut̓inux̱w Ha̱xwa'mis have shown remarkable resilience and leadership in working toward healing and a better future, one in which experiences such as theirs become a thing of the past. It is that leadership that led to the creation of the Hith'alis Agreement[42] with the government of British Columbia, setting out principles for ecosystem-based management in their territory. The K̲wik̲wa̱sut̓inux̱w Ha̱xwa'mis are also continuing to educate private funders about the need to change colonial approaches to funding and working to reach further agreements with the provincial government on the recognition of their Indigenous Rights and Title, amongst many other initiatives that they are leading. As Chief Councillor Rick Johnson says, "We are on our way. These are exciting times."

This beautiful story is presented in the powerful and loving voices of the people in it, with all of this important context behind it. Gilakas'la.

For the people of the K̲wik̲wa̲sut̓inux̲w Hax̲wa'mis First Nation, a place they call Hada, in Bond Sound, is as old as the beginning of time.

"Hada is where our first ancestor, T'sek̲a̲ma'yi (man born as cedar), was guided by the bumble-bees to Mit'apdzi (Viner Sound)," explains K̲wik̲wa̲sut̓inux̲w Chief Rick Johnson. The K̲wik̲wa̲sut̓inux̲w Hax̲wa'mis are now based at Gwa-yas-dums, on Gilford Island, but for Chief Johnson and his fellow citizens, Hada remains the place to which the descendants of T'sek̲a̲ma'yi are connected like no other in the world: by time, blood, and memory. On that hallowed ground, says Nax'na'gam (Tamara Alfred), in the place where T'sek̲a̲ma'yi gave life to K̲wik̲wa̲sut̓inux̲w people like her, the presence of her ancestors is always tangible. "When I stand on the beach there, I feel the touch of their hands upon me welcoming me home."

Dzawada̲'enux̲w hereditary Chief Maxwiyalidizi (K'odi Nelson) at Hada with K̲wik̲wa̲sut̓inux̲w hereditary Chief Ol Siwid (Mike Willie) to his right.

Located near the mouth of the Hada River, not far from Gwa-yas-dums, Hada lies south of Gwayi (Kingcome Inlet), home of the Dzawada̲'enux̲w Nation, and southeast of Heghums, home to the Gwawa'enuxw Nation. The K̲wik̲wa̲sut̓inux̲w Hax̲wa'mis, the Dzawada̲'enux̲w, and the Gwawa'enuxw are all members of the Musgamakw Dzawada̲'enux̲w Tribal Council, whose territories encompass Gilford Island, Watson Island to the west, and the watersheds of Kingcome Inlet, Wakeman Sound to the north, and Thompson Sound to the south. For the citizens of these Nations, the places within this territory, from which each of their origin stories spring, and the lands and waters on which their history is written, are held deep within their hearts.

When Dzawada̲'enux̲w citizen Hank Nelson was a little boy he lived in Gwa-yas-dums. His family frequently visited a place called Mit'ap in Viner Sound, an hour's boat ride away. Hank is now living in 'Na̲mgis Nation territory, in 'Yalis (Alert Bay), on Cormorant Island, but rarely a day passes when he does not think about Mit'ap and the happiness he experienced there decades previously. "It warms me up to go back to that time. It was before they took me away to residential school. My mother had passed and my aunt G̲ug̲we', who I used to call my mom, started taking care of me. Her English name was Pearl Smith. She and my uncle Sam took me to Mit'ap with them. Those are the

K'odi Nelson's father, G̱usdidzas (Henry Nelson), also known as Hank, has fond memories of spending much of his early childhood in Mit'ap, in Viner Sound, an hour's boat ride away from his home in Gwa-yas-dums.

safest times in my life that I can remember, being in that place. To me it was home."

Life at Mit'ap was spartan, but to the small boy it was also heaven. Hank's aunt and uncle took care of several children, and he had plenty of playmates. Accommodation at Mit'ap, which was only used seasonally, was basic but comfortable. "It was a smokehouse made of long cedar planks," reminisces Hank. "It also had cedar siding, and the joints and knotholes in the walls were lined with cardboard and paper that kept it warm, even in October during the salmon run." The children slept on a cedar bed covered with a thick feather mattress in one corner of the room. "Every night I would go to sleep watching the fire crackling away in the middle of the floor and G̱ugwe', who would be preparing the next day's food. There would be a large pot sitting by the fire with duck soup in it or salmon. Sometimes she would be making bannock in a large black frying pan by the fire. We always had plenty to eat."

His aunt and uncle were responsible for the chum salmon harvest in the creek flowing by the smokehouse. The little boy loved watching them at work. "Each day, after catching the fish, they would cut the heads and tails off. Next they slit the back of the salmon and removed the bones and the guts. The open-faced salmon was laid on its back to have thin fillets cut off each side. The fillets, called K̓awas, and what was left of the salmon, called X̱a̱'mas, were hung in the smokehouse. Once they were smoked and dried, the fish would be bundled and bound together so they could be stacked and transported back to Gwa-yas-dums for us to live on in the winter."

He also recalls playing on the beach and games with the other children and even remembers with fondness an anecdote that G̱ugwe' told him later in life. He was too young to remember the incident himself, but G̱ugwe' was laughing hard as she told him about the time he accidentally hit one of the girls, Da Yi (Mary), in the face when the chewy piece of dried K̓awas he was tugging at with his teeth broke off and his fist flew backwards. "According to G̱ugwe'," says Hank, chuckling, "the fight was on! Mary wound up and punched me right in the face and gave me a good black eye."

K̲wik̲w̲asut̓inux̲w hereditary Chief Ol Siwid (Mike Willie)

Ironically, Hank's family was considered poor back then. "Now, I would be considered rich for being brought up in that time, eating salmon, and ducks, and seals in Mit'ap. Historically as many as 100,000 chum salmon would come to spawn annually there. These days fewer than one thousand fish come back every year. We were also cared for and healthy and well-fed. We were rich with culture, our Kwak̓wala language, and in our knowledge about our territory. The ultimate dream for me," he says, "is that all of us can be out on our lands and waters again like that, enjoying that richness and culture and doing what we used to do."

Hank's son K'odi was born in 1973. Like his father, K'odi grew up immersed in his Dzawada̲'enux̲w culture and loving every aspect of it: the language, the songs, and the stories. Kingcome Inlet, where he was often taken as a child, always felt like a place where his spirit was in tune; a place with ancient and palpable energy that vibrated through the old village sites, the sheltered coves, and in the fragrant cottonwood forests.

Like many of his peers, as he grew older K'odi battled the demons of colonization. Although he did not have to go to residential school, the damage the schools had done to his Elders and community reverberated throughout his childhood. He enjoyed a short and successful career as a professional soccer player in his youth but succumbed for a time to alcohol, becoming lost in a cycle of abuse and denial. In his darkest moments he endured the deaths of a close friend and of a much-loved cousin, both within a short space of time. Inevitably, K'odi hit a wall. He realized that he could no longer run from his problems and made the deliberate decision to put those days behind him.

As an adult, K'odi, a Dzawada̲'enux̲w hereditary Chief, worked as a K'wakw̲ak̲a̲'wakw language and culture teacher at the Gwa'sala-'Nakwaxda'xw school at Tsulquate, near Port Hardy, with K̲wik̲w̲asut̓inux̲w Chief Ol Siwid (Mike Willie), and as a professional guide with Mike's tourism business, Sea Wolf Adventures. By 2021 K'odi was also doing his best to make his father Hank's dream of reconnecting Musgamakw

Mike Willie guiding one of his Sea Wolf Adventures Indigenous tours in 2017.

Dzawada̲'enux̱w people with their homelands come true at last.

That year, ground was broken at Hada to begin building the Nawalakw Lodge and Healing Village. When complete, Nawalakw (which means "supernatural" in the Kwak̓wala language) will comprise a Musgamakw Dzawada̲'enux̱w-owned centre delivering traditional healing programs and a youth camp where children can be reconnected with and taught about their ancestry, culture, language and territory. The centre will also incorporate an ecotourism lodge, welcoming visitors from around the world in the summer to learn about Musgamakw Dzawada̲'enux̱w history, culture, and stewardship of the territory. The profits from the lodge will pay for the cultural and healing programs.

The seeds of the idea were sown several years earlier through K'odi's work with Mike Willie at Sea Wolf Adventures. Mike first set up the company because he had an overwhelming desire to reconnect with Dzawada̲'enux̱w lands and waters, his culture, and his ancestry. "This is where I am from," says Mike. "It is my home, and I was really missing it. I missed connecting with my family, I missed the river, I missed the sound of the birds. That is what Dzawa̲da'enuxw means, 'the sound of the birds.' I missed it all. I really needed to find a way to spend more time here."

Mike spent a few days alone in the forest fasting in accordance with spiritual and traditional protocols and meditating on his future. He emerged with the idea of establishing a water-taxi business in the territory. "That was how Sea Wolf began," he says. He quickly expanded into tourism after realizing that his customers, especially visitors from other parts of the world, greatly enjoyed the stories that he told them about the territory en route to places like the U'mista Cultural Centre at 'Yalis. His next step was to add grizzly bear viewing into the mix, also a hit with his customers. Sea Wolf Adventures eventually became a full-time wildlife and cultural tourism business.

It was a business, however, with a significantly different bottom line from a standard commercial venture. Mike believes strongly in maya'xa̲la, a Kwak̓wala expression meaning "respect." Viewed through a K'wakwa̱ka̱'wakw lens, the tenets of respect contained within the meaning of maya'xa̱la are all-embracing, he emphasizes. "Maya'xa̱la is an action word, not just an action between humans, but an action that takes in everything around us, including the land and the animals and the trees we depend on. One aspect of maya'xa̱la is self-respect—taking care of ourselves spiritually, feeling good about who we are and where we come from. It is also about looking after our territories, making sure that our lands are able to produce and look after us. All of that is maya'xa̱la, the true meaning of taking care of each other and loving one another."

Hada River estuary, an ancient Musgamagw Dzawada̱'enux̱w village site, prior to the Nawalakw Healing Centre being constructed.

Mike also embraces sustainability and philanthropy, both concepts ingrained in his DNA. "Our Chiefs were always philanthropists. Wealth was not measured in terms of what you put in your pocket but what you gave away. You harvested salmon so you could give them away to those who needed food." That philanthropic approach was sustainable because people only took what was necessary and no more. "Indigenous people coined the word 'sustainability,'" emphasizes Mike. "That is part of our whole culture. It goes back to this point: if you take care of the land, the land will take care of you. It is a circle that never stops."

Maya'xa̱la, philanthropy and sustainability are embedded in Mike's approach to Sea Wolf. "The company gave us a vehicle to start training our youth, for example. It started with Kingcome, but we also have people working with us from Fort Rupert, Alert Bay, and New Vancouver," he says, "so it is growing. I really feel proud about that, that we could inspire our young people this way." Company profits are used to generate a fund for language revitalization. "There have been other positive spin-offs. The young guides are typically so shy when they first start work, but when they realize that tourists genuinely want to learn about them and from them, they become so confident and proud. You can see them standing taller as ambassadors for our people. It is nice to witness that." These were aspects of Sea Wolf Adventures that attracted K'odi to working with Mike at Sea Wolf. "I loved his vision and wanted to be part of something positive like that."

These pictographs were designed by Musgamagw Dzawada̱'enux̱w artist Marianne Nicolson and painted by youth and community members. They are located on a cliff in a group of islands referred to as Lixi, but also known as Na'nawalakwe or "Supernatural Ones."

That decision would lead to the next chapter in the Nawalakw story. K'odi and Mike arranged to take the Gwa'sala-'Nakwaxda'xw students they had been teaching out into the territory with Sea Wolf for a few days of hands-on learning about their history and culture. "We brought some Elders with us to share their memories about when they lived out there as kids," recalls K'odi. It was a beautiful trip, enjoyed by Elders and children alike. "It gave the Elders life to tell stories about when they were young, and the kids were very engaged with them." K'odi was also fascinated to observe that the children had learned more language in five days out on the land "than we could teach them in a month in the classroom. There was something about being out in the territory—the kids were in a natural environment and having fun and because they were having fun they retained more information more easily."

That experience started K'odi thinking. Like Mike, he had witnessed how being out on the land was a catalyst for renewed pride and wellbeing in the young trainee guides at Sea Wolf Adventures. "You could see their personal growth from when we hired them in June through to the end of the season in September. It was amazing." One summer, he recounts, an intensely shy twenty-five-year-old Dzawada̱'enux̱w woman named Sherry Moon joined the Sea Wolf team. "At the end of that first season guiding tourists, Sherry was a completely different person," marvels K'odi. "She was walking about six inches taller and was very confident."

Sherry, who had initially taken the job as a temporary break from her studies, decided to stay on with Sea Wolf at the end of the summer. "I felt so good about myself. I was a good guide, I could operate the boat,

Sherry Moon, Dzawada̱'enux̱w citizen and guide for Sea Wolf Adventures

and I felt like a real role model for success for our own people, on our terms, in our world." For K'odi, it was yet more proof that something like Nawalakw was needed to get more people like Sherry back out on the land. "I thought, 'Wow, this is what can happen when you are out in your territory and people genuinely interested in your culture are asking questions about your way of life.' How do we get more of our people out on the land and water to experience that?"

K'odi had a personal interest in the answer to that question. He desperately wanted to create a place out in the territory that his father Hank could visit and reconnect to the happiness and wellbeing he had enjoyed as a child. "When I took those Gwa'sala-'Nakwaxda'xw kids out, I thought about my dad's stories about growing up smoking fish with his aunt. Listening to him made me want to build something like that again for him, in a place like Mit'ap that could give him the same feelings of comfort and safety and connection."

Then, during the summer of 2015 while working for Sea Wolf, K'odi and Sherry dropped into Hada one day. To their horror, they discovered a helicopter logging operation in full swing at the sacred spot. "It hurt our hearts so much to see the destruction," remembers Sherry sadly. "We felt so helpless." Staring at the falling trees, K'odi started talking urgently to Sherry about his dream of reconnecting his father and other Musgamakw Dzawada̱'enux̱w people, especially the children, with places like Hada. "I told him that I shared the vision," says Sherry. "He said to me, 'Then we just have to do it.'"

That day, says K'odi, "was when the wheels really started to turn in my brain. I started thinking about wellness, which I ran away from in my own life for so many years. Having seen what being out on the land and doing the healing work did for me, I wanted to share that with as many people as I possibly could." Through his experience at Sea Wolf, he adds, "I had also seen the benefits of ecotourism and what it was doing for our people employed in the industry. Adding to that my experience with bringing those kids out to Blunden Harbour and how that was doing something so positive for them, I really started to think. If we built a little shack at Hada for the kids to camp out in, what else could we use it for? We could bring adults out there too—adults would benefit just like the kids would. That is when the ideas all really started to flow. That is when it all really started."

K'odi had no money, no backing, and no plan, but he didn't let that stop him. First, however, to do anything at Hada he needed the approval of the K̲wik̲wa̲sut̓inux̲w Haxwa'mis. That permission, says Chief Rick Johnson, was easy to give. "Prior to K'odi coming to the Nation and asking for support for Nawalakw, the Nation already had a similar vision in our community plan. But we hadn't really begun the work required to achieve it. There was so much to be done, sometimes it felt like a house that's been turned upside down: where do you start to put it back up the right way? It felt overwhelming. But if you start at one corner, it feels possible. When K'odi came along with his vision and his energy, he offered us that corner to start on. It leapt us ten years ahead in our plans."

For Chief Johnson, K'odi's vision reflects what is important about K̲wik̲wa̲sut̓inux̲w culture, including maya'x̲a̲la. "The foundation of our culture is love and respect," he says. "I see Nawalakw as building that foundation again to get us back out there in our traditional lands and start the healing. To bring the children back, to revive the language, revive the songs and to instil in our kids where they are from. There is tremendous hope there. I am really excited about it." He also could not think of a better place for that to happen than at Hada, a place of such power and beauty that just being there is healing. "Something unbelievable happens to us when we go there. It is so calming." The people and the place simply belong together. "Our people occupied these territories for thousands of years in direct relationship with these places. The concept of our people coming back to Hada is meant to be."

K̲wik̲wa̲sut̓inux̲w Ha̲xwa'mis Chief Rick Johnson

Turning Nawalakw into reality still seemed a long way off. But despite having only a handful of change in his pocket and a few volunteers behind him, K'odi was undaunted. He talked energetically about the idea to everyone he met wherever he went. "I just kept putting Nawalakw out to the

Tła'yi (black bear) in the Hada River estuary

universe." As he did so, something magical began to happen. First, on the recommendation of someone he bumped into while grocery shopping, K'odi contacted Community Futures British Columbia, an organization funding small start-up businesses, and received enough money to develop a business plan for Nawalakw. He talked to logging companies and started to line up donated timber. Next, the federal government put in enough money to get a feasibility study done. Hamish Rhodes, a friend who happened to be an architect, heard about the feasibility study and offered to draw some designs. "All of a sudden," says K'odi, "the vision went from a shack on the beach for the kids to dreaming big about a wellness and cultural centre and a real lodge."

A feasibility study was one thing; the money to actually build Nawalakw another. But magic was still in play. One particularly fine day, K'odi took a group of K̲wik̲w̲asut̓inux̲w children on a day trip around the territory with an organization called Sea to Cedar, a network of community leaders, local business owners, and conservation scientists working together to support youth and community initiatives on the coast. Program director Scott Rogers was captivated by what K'odi was telling the children about their history and by his father Hank's stories from Mit'ap. She was also intrigued by the vision of building a cultural centre at Hada. "I remember I asked the kids if they would like to come out to a place like that, and they all said yes.

Paddle camp participants at Hada, 2021

They were so excited about the idea," says K'odi. "What I didn't realize was that Scott was listening to me the whole time."

That encounter led to the final piece falling into place. "About six months later, Scott called me and convinced me to come to a retreat at Nimmo Bay Resort, where she said there may be people interested in helping with Nawalakw. That," says K'odi, still shaking his head in awe more than three years later, "is when all of this turned into a fairy tale come true."

One of the people at Nimmo Bay was Tim Cormode, the chief executive officer and founder of the non-profit foundation Power to Give. Tim had met K'odi several years previously in a chance encounter at an old village site where K'odi was teaching a group of students. Tim, who was also the CEO of Power to Be, a foundation helping people overcome barriers to connecting with nature, had been struck by K'odi's efforts to give the children a hands-on experience in their homelands. He subsequently arranged for donations of camping clothes and equipment for the children and stayed in touch with K'odi from time to time to see how he was getting on.

Dzawada̱'enux̱w Chief Willie Moon

Tim was listening carefully as K'odi made his pitch about Nawalakw to a crowded room. "Everyone else left when I was done," remembers K'odi, "except for Tim. He looked at me and said, 'We should talk some more.' He said he managed a family foundation and the wellness aspect of Nawalakw fit right within their mandate." One thing led to another; before he knew it, K'odi was holding a cheque that would cover the cost of the start-up phase for Nawalakw. His dream had suddenly, wondrously, gone from plans on a paper to something very real; a fairy tale, indeed, and one that everyone could believe would finally have a happy ending.

Musgamakw leaders like Sherry Moon's father, Dzawada̱'enux̱w Chief Willie Moon, were ecstatic. "When K'odi first talked about his vision, I was very excited about it," recalls Chief Moon. "When we heard about the funding, I almost couldn't believe it was true." Chief Moon was only nine years old when he, too, was taken away from his home to residential school. When he became a father, he was determined his children would never experience that kind of disconnection from their territory. "When they were young, I took them wherever I went, fishing or deer hunting or clam digging, whatever I was doing. When I look at them now, I see what I did back then is paying off. My children are going through our territory and looking after it for us." Nawalakw, he says happily, will make that possible for other Musgamakw Dzawada̱'enux̱w children who have not been so fortunate.

His daughter Sherry appreciated her father's gift of connection to the land beyond measure. "I was very lucky to grow up in Kingcome Inlet, in one of the last remaining villages that is still inhabited by the original people. I had a good childhood there. I played outside and in the bush. I explored the territory around the village. My dad took us to see old village sites. I was so blessed to have that."

As an adult, having a job that takes her to places like Hada is immensely fulfilling. When she first went to these areas, recalls Sherry, it had been like a welcoming home. "I felt completely at peace with where I was, knowing that this is part of who I am and where I come from, who we are as Musgamakw Dzawada̱'enux̱w people." Being out in her territory has allowed her to become more fully who she is as a human being. "It's like the

Nax'na'gam (Tamara Alfred)

land and water there gives me breath. That's why we must all reconnect with the land. If we don't," she says quietly, "it's as if we cease to exist."

One of Sherry's contemporaries, Nax'na'gam (Tamara Alfred), was sitting on K̲wik̲wa̱sut̓inux̱w Council in 2015 when K'odi came to Gwa-yas-dums to make his case for creating Nawalakw at Hada. As a child, says Tamara, her community's leaders had encouraged the youth to learn and practise their cultural traditions, something she remains immensely grateful for as an adult. "We did cultural camps, we performed for our Elders in our gukwdzi (Big House). We went to Kingcome for gatherings. We went to Knight Inlet to learn how to make grease. We went to Gilford to try and help our people. That is what I want for our youth now," she continues. "Nawalakw is going to make that dream come true."

Tamara and other leaders in the K̲wik̲wa̱sut̓inux̱w community had begun inviting their children to annual events they called Yayuma (youth play potlatches), bringing them home from as far away as Vancouver to learn about where their ancestors came from. "It's all about making that connection, making it real for them to touch and see their homelands. It's pride. It's an emotional connection. It's medicine, knowing your history, your traditions, your legends," says Tamara. It is also an experience in human connection. Throughout the play Potlatches on Gilford Island, she says, "every door is open, because you're walking into your home, where everybody's accepted, everybody's cared for, everybody's loved. There's no judgement, there's not anything but happiness, the sense of belonging, the sense of being Musgamakw, of being one with a place."

On the last day of the Potlatch, the children are invited to showcase everything they had been taught. "The adults step back and the kids take the floor. They let their hearts shine, they let their spirits soar. It is the most beautiful thing I've ever witnessed. Nawalakw is going to do that for all of our children," says Tamara, who in 2021 became Nawalakw's training and employment program manager. "At Hada, they, too, will feel the touch of their ancestors welcoming them home as they arrive on the beach. They will take a deep breath and open their eyes and know they are meant to be there, where 'Tsekama'yi started life for all of us. They will know they are home."

K'odi's uncle Alex was also sent to residential school as a young boy. Alex was delighted when his nephew showed him the plans for Nawalakw and he realized what that meant for the next generation. "The sole purpose in life is for our children. My older brother, Chief Frank Nelson, would have said, 'And also for the children yet unborn.' I see Nawalakw and this wonderful story about who we are, this healing of the scars left by the residential schools and what they did to us, the empowerment and self-value from showing the world who we are and telling our stories, just growing and expanding, including more and more children, more and more families and communities as time goes on."

Gwawaenuk hereditary Chief Kwankwanxwalege Wakas (Robert Joseph) speaking in the Big House at Gwa-yas-dums, Gilford Island, at the inaugural convening of the Nawalakw Healing Society.

For Alex, there is nothing compared to the experience of being in the places his ancestors came from. He remembers vividly the first time he visited Wakeman Sound, west of Gwayi, as an adult. Although he had fished in the area as a child with his father, he had never previously set foot on the landscape. "When I stepped on the ground something happened I couldn't explain. It was like I was left breathless just for that moment. Then I realized this is me, this is our land, where I'm standing—that's what is happening." Later, eager to re-experience that feeling, he returned with K'odi. "We went partially up the river in Wakeman Sound that time. The beauty of it—it had this great spirit about it. It was indescribable. I had such a sense of belonging."

Revered Gwawaenuk hereditary Chief Kwankwanxwalege Wakas (Robert Joseph) was born in 1939 and grew up in Kingcome Inlet and on Gilford Island with his paternal grandmother. By 2021 Chief Joseph had become a cultural ambassador for Reconciliation Canada, a non-profit organization he cofounded to promote awareness and understanding of the need for reconciliation in Canada. He, too, had suffered the abuses of residential school and the impacts later in life of that abuse and is widely recognized for his grace and courage.

Chief Joseph remains immensely grateful for his early upbringing by his grandmother and remembers Kingcome Inlet with great fondness. "Our little settlement was cradled by the forest behind it and the ocean in front.

You could go down to the beach and watch whales and otters or go to the forest and watch deer and other animals. It was a special place for little boys to grow up." The children were kept safe with cautionary tales that discouraged them from venturing too far. "If we were going to play in the back woods the parents would say, 'Watch out for Dzunuk̓wa, the wild lady of the woods. She eats little children if they don't behave.' If we wandered too far or if we went to the beach, they would say, 'Be careful of Bak'was. He is the wild man of the woods, but he hangs around the beaches, too.'"

He recalls, "One time my grandmother and I were drifting down the river in a canoe. There was a cluster of salmonberry bushes hanging over the river's edge. She edged the canoe in and wedged it against the bank so that she could pick the berries. As she was doing that she thanked the Creator for the salmonberries, which she called our dłidła̱dłola or 'na̱mwiyut, our relatives. That was the first sense I had that we are connected."

In his culture, says Chief Joseph, people grew up with a consciousness of oneness, the wholeness of all of creation and humanity, one with each other. "As human beings, we're part of the absolute wonder of creation, as far and deep and as wide and powerful and as beautiful as it can be." He is happy about Nawalakw, not only for the hope it represents for the children but for these places that not only belonged to them but to which they in turn belonged. The rivers in Musgamakw Dzawada̱'enux̱w territory, he says, were never meant to be alone. Reconnecting the children to them through Nawalakw will be healing for both people and place.

Despite the challenges the worldwide pandemic has thrown at them, K'odi and his team are still fully focussed on the endgame for Nawalakw. "This whole concept is about getting our people back on our land, creating much needed employment and a place where healing can happen, where we are present on the territory, where conservation and stewardship programs can be implemented, and where we are teaching our kids about traditional food harvesting and sovereignty," says K'odi. "Nawalakw is going to be our university, building strong-minded and strong-spirited young people. That has been my thinking the whole way along, to provide a place where we could do all these wonderful things."

K'odi's imagination is also brimming with ideas to combine the reconnection of his people to the landscape with the ecotourism side of Nawalakw. "There is a genuine interest in tourism now that steps outside the traditional sense of tourism. People want to learn something when they

are on vacation or they want to have hands-on experiences with people who know the land better than anybody else, who know the stories and can be totally authentic."

Osprey in action above Hada

For example, says K'odi, his people traditionally "planked" cedar trees, carefully removing a few slabs of wood rather than falling the whole tree. "There is a great example of one of those trees here in Alert Bay. It looks like at least six planks were taken out of this cedar tree and that tree is still alive. At Nawalakw, in the architecture of our lodge, could we plank some cedar trees with our kids, in the traditional way? Maybe we could build a sauna using planks from trees around the lodge and build trails for guests to walk by the trees and educate them about how we always harvested cedar that way. We could show them the sauna and the trees where we got the wood, and tell them about maya'xa̱la, how we asked permission from the trees before we planked them, just as our ancestors would have done."

At Hada, visitors will also see spectacular scenery, grizzly bears walking along the shore, seals, sealions, eagles, ducks of all sorts, hummingbirds, and ravens, says K'odi. "There are endless trail opportunities and sightseeing points. On the river they are going to be able to see and understand how our people were fortunate to live in this part of the world where traditional roots grow abundantly and clams and cockles are plentiful. Once

Dzawada̱'enuxw hereditary Chief Maxwiyalidizi (K'odi Nelson) with his father G̱usdidzas (Henry Nelson) and sons K̲angwidayu (Dallas), centre, and Wa̱dzidaga̱m (Zayden), at front, on June 8, 2020, at the blessing of the Hada site.

the tide is out they will understand that the supermarket is open, whether that is for crabs, clams, cockles or mussels. We could do food foraging with the guests and our chef could use those ingredients in meals so they can partake in the bounty they gathered."

In the fall of 2020, machinery was moved onsite at Hada to begin breaking ground for the cultural camp. Before that happened the site was formally blessed in the traditional way, although not by those who would traditionally have done it. "All along we have been telling the world that Nawalakw is for our children and our children yet unborn," explains K'odi. "So when it came time to plan for the blessing, I asked the Chiefs and Elders if we could get the kids to do it and we would just support them. So the children did the blessing. In my lifetime I have never ever seen that before."

K'odi has also never before seen boatloads of his people landing on the shore at Hada, the children running onto the beach, laughing, full of energy and joy. His heart was full. "I thought that from this day forward, Hada is going to be alive again. It seemed so fitting that our children would do the blessing, so they could start to take ownership of Nawalakw and to let them know that this is theirs and they were a part of it from the beginning."

There are many beautiful words in his language, says K'odi, but some of the most powerful that come to his mind are k̲'wa̱la'yu (my reason for living) and hasda̱x̱a̱la'yu (my reason for breathing), words often used in reference to children. "What would we be without our children? What would our purpose be? We are constantly thinking of our grandchildren's grandchildren, the children that are yet unborn. I think that is a really beautiful thing." When the children doing the blessing become Elders, he muses, "they will tell their grandchildren, 'I was one of those kids that helped bless the grounds for this place.' They are the ones who will carry on this vision, long after we are all gone."

Nella Nelson and 'Ok'wilagame' (Alex Nelson) co-hosting a 2019 University of Victoria Faculty of Education recognition event for outstanding members of the education community. Both Alex and Nella are also University of Victoria Distinguished Alumni Award recipients.

For K'odi's uncle Alex, the blessing ceremony was, in a way, also a family reunion. He spoke to those present about the wonder of family relationships and about Xa'nayus, who was also known as "Art Bond Sound," a K̲wik̲wa̲sut̓inux̱w trapper who was the last known previous occupant of Hada, along with his wife Tłapa. The couple had two daughters, Ruth and Kathleen, and a son, Art, Junior. "Ruth told us that her father, who was known as 'Bon,' was very careful never to over-trap any species. He was very environmentally conscious." Kathleen married Alex's uncle, Peter Coon. "And Ruth's daughter Nella married me," smiles Alex. "So it was beautiful to be there, bringing our family together that way." It was a beautiful day altogether, he recalls, and highly emotional. "While we were in the forest, I started looking around and saw these tall trees that grow straight up and I thought my ancestors are all around us, cloaking us with their love and their care. The wonderment that came with that was indescribable."

The dream had finally become real, the fairy tale fact rather than fiction. As he watched the children singing, one thought kept running through K'odi's mind. "I was thinking," he recalls with quiet satisfaction, "that our ancestors must be very happy today."

Gugwilx'ya'ansk— We Are Living It

CHAPTER TEN

The Ts'msyen expression "gugwilx'ya'ansk" is both simple and extraordinary in the depth of its meaning. In one sense, gugwilx'ya'ansk is both the cradle of a vast catalogue of collective Ts'msyen knowledge, accumulated over the millennia since Ts'msyen people first walked the earth, and the vehicle by which it is transmitted. But in its truest sense, gugwilx'ya'ansk cannot be easily explained in the culturally impoverished lexicon of English.

Broken down literally, says Gitga'at scholar Spencer Greening, gugwilx'ya'ansk roughly translates to "for all time walking" or "continuously distributing gifts." In this sense, says Spencer, "it is a verb, a philosophy and law that is action-based, ensuring that stewardship responsibilities, Indigenous Title, and traditional ecological knowledge are groomed and taught to all generations in the community, with the faith that younger generations will continue this action."

One practical way to think about it, he suggests, is as a methodology for how the Gitga'at structure their approach to pedagogy or education. As an expression, "for all time walking" metaphorically represents how the Gitga'at combine experiential place-based learning with Gitga'at Title and stewardship laws. These are laws, says Spencer, that have embraced the idea that continuous circulation and sharing of communal knowledge within and throughout the community are necessary. "All of this weaves together Ts'msyen people and the places to which they belong, take care of, and have been inseparable since time immemorial."

"Indigenous people have experienced massive environmental change, floods, wildfires, and all kinds of other natural crises over ten thousand years of stewardship of our territories and learned how to deal with them. Through that deep, deep history of learning, the values, spiritual teachings, rituals and laws we developed have helped us not only survive, but thrive."

—La'goot (Spencer Greening), Ganhada pdeex, Gitga'at First Nation, April 20, 2020

Facing page: Mountainscape in Gitga'at territory, near the village of Txałgiu (Hartley Bay).

La'goot (Spencer Greening)

Gugwilx'ya'ansk is a term imbued with pragmatism, culture, spirituality, and history. Multidimensional in its definition and its application, gugwilx'ya'ansk is both process, says Spencer, and a fundamental way of being. "Gugwilx'ya'ansk speaks to what resilience means. It is about knowledge that has not only helped us survive but thrive over millennia. As a process, gugwilx'ya'ansk also recognizes that as Ts'msyen individuals we have a role to play in continuing to accumulate that collective knowledge, learn from it, adapt as needed, and pass that gift of knowledge and learning down to all future generations."

Based on their accumulated wisdom, Ts'msyen people have formed age-old societal relationships with each other, with their territories, and with all the species within those territories that they depend upon for sustenance. Those relationships have in turn laid the foundation for structures and systems of stewardship responsibility and decision-making that then formed the basis for laws, governance and management practices founded on sharing, respect, long-term sustainability, and the wellbeing of both land and people.

"Gugwilx'ya'ansk is just this beautiful term that encompasses all of that and which speaks to an alternative way of understanding the universe, the world, and our time here." Spencer reflects that "everyone is talking now about climate change. People are worried about what their grandchildren are going to do as their environment and their ecosystems are changing, but that is something that Indigenous people have always considered. How do we walk on the earth in a way that ensures that in a thousand years from now, in ten thousand years, our people will still be here, still strong, and

still thriving? As Indigenous people we will do it as we have always done. That," he says, "is gugwilx'ya'ansk."

Spencer hiking in the mountains in Gitga'at territory.

Spencer was born in 1989 in the town of Burns Lake, a small municipality in north-central BC. Burns Lake is nearly 250 kilometres in a straight line from the Gitga'at village of Txałgiu (Hartley Bay), his Ts'msyen mother's community. His father, of German settler heritage, worked in town, while his mother had a job in nearby Lake Babine Nation, where Spencer attended school. As a young child, it was a confusing time. "I had a very hazy understanding of who I was. I had an Indian status card. I knew that I was Indigenous. I understood that I was part of some sort of collective, but I also knew that I did not belong in Lake Babine Nation, which is not a Ts'msyen Nation."

As he entered his teens, Spencer's love of music would be the catalyst that connected him with his culture for the first time in a meaningful way. "I formed a band with a cousin from Txałgiu who was also living in Burns Lake. We were both typical angst-ridden teenagers," recalls Spencer. "We got into extreme death metal, the angriest music there is." But Spencer also characterizes his time in the band as opening the door to exploring who he really is. "We started to write our own music and realized we wanted to write about who we are, about being Ts'msyen, being Gitg'a'at men, and we wanted to do that in our own language. That really was the start of my journey into identity."

The two youngsters called their band "Gyibaaw," which means "Wolf" in Sm'algya̲x, their Ts'msyen language. They also set about learning how to write songs that would speak to their culture and history. The experience was powerful and transformative. "It is an intense process for the Ts'msyen to make songs. Some songs are very sacred, some take years to write and only certain people can sing them. Some of them only come through ritual and ceremony and dreaming and fasting and vision. We worked with our Elders on how to incorporate all of that into our music," recalls Spencer, "and took a deep dive into our culture and spirituality."

Gyibaaw met with extraordinary success. The teenagers were touring before they had even left high school, heading across the country and to South America to play gigs, and opening for some of Canada's biggest names in metal. Despite that, Spencer and his cousin decided to call it quits. Both of the young musicians had enrolled in university and touring was getting too much to handle. The white supremacist underbelly of the genre was also increasingly hard to stomach. In any event, says Spencer, "the music had given us what we needed by then."

He had learned to express his culture through his songs in a way that was healing and inspiring. One of the deepest aspects of growth through his music, says Spencer, was exploring his connection to the spiritual world. "We were so hungry for that!" Not least of all, in the harsh arena of the heavy metal world, he had learned to hold his own with confidence, confronting sometimes violent situations. It was a valuable attribute in the world he was entering as an adult, one in which he quickly learned that Indigenous people had to fight hard and constantly to uphold their rights.

Spencer had elected to study Indigenous history at the University of Northern British Columbia (UNBC), in Prince George. As he completed his undergraduate degree, he was thinking a great deal about being a Ts'msyen man and what that meant to him. Eventually, encouraged by a circle of close Indigenous friends and mentors, he decided to go to Txałgiu and try to find out. There he was welcomed by a community eager to help him learn.

Village of Txałgiu (Hartley Bay)

Spencer returned to Txałgiu as often as he could over the next few years, absorbing as much information as possible on every visit.

During the course of one of his visits, a luulgit (Potlatch) was held, at which Spencer was given his Ganhada pdeex (Clan) name, La'goot. The name carried great significance, says Spencer. "A Clan name comes with responsibilities that everyone who has ever held that name over the thousands of years that it has been passed down has carried out. You become a steward of the territory that the Clan is related to. You join the traditional political system. You attend meetings, you help disperse wealth to the Clan, all of these things.

"The Elders made it clear to me that I was entering a 'give and take relationship,'" continues Spencer, "in that the community was saying, 'We will take care of you for the rest of your life, but you must do the same for us.' It hit me that this was something like a marriage in that sense, to my community and to my Clan and my lineage that my name comes from. My actions going forward would be based on the standpoint of the collective rather than individual preference. Behind that concept is this deep, ancient understanding that if we base our actions on collective wellbeing, for the most part we will be more resilient and will be a healthier, thriving human society."

He felt a strong and immediate responsibility and a huge desire to live up to his name. "My community had committed itself to me, and I wanted to honour that. I wanted to understand what I had become reconnected to and to be taught about governance, traditional structures, about our laws and our oral history. I wanted to understand what it all means." He turned to the Elders. They told him that the only way to truly learn and understand was to start practising the teachings.

"Instead of just telling me what it was all about, they made me do everything myself. They took me to hereditary political meetings and expected me to contribute. They made me act as master of ceremonies at luulgit and at memorials. That was their way of showing me what gugwilx'ya'ansk is, by showing me that I am part of a cycle that keeps going and going, and I had to actively participate in it. That's when I really understood for the first time that the only way to truly honour gugwilx'ya'ansk," says Spencer, "is by living it."

As Spencer continued his education with his Elders, he also began work on a master's thesis at UNBC in which he would endeavour to untangle for himself the essence of Ts'msyen identity and values. As he worked to increase his understanding of gugwilx'ya'ansk, his appreciation grew for the Gitga'at people's place-based system of oral histories, laws, and relationships, in all its elegance, sophistication, and sustainability, both remarkable in its design and incomparably beautiful in its approach.

Ts'msyen governance and territorial stewardship responsibilities, he writes in his completed thesis,[43] are not about artificial lines on a map but part of an age-old system that incorporates wil'naat'ał, bloodlines that connect all fourteen of the Ts'msyen tribes both physically and politically. It is a system of relationships between the families and the pdeex, Clans that form those tribes, and the hereditary names, like La'goot, that families hold and pass down to the next in line.

Under Ts'myen law, no one may kill a seal lying on an exposed rock.

The responsibilities that belong to those relationships and names, also inherited, are manifested and implemented through adaawx (oral history passed down from generation to generation) and ayaawx (laws that have evolved from the stories). The responsibility of humans is to implement the ayaawx within these structures, devised to ensure sustainability, collective wellbeing, and—to the extent that any human beings are capable of it—peace among their respective Nations. "Our ayaawx," wrote Spencer, "are derived out of our relationship with the land and tell a narrative of our relationship with all things living on it...to follow our ayaawx is to follow a way of life that keeps order."

As he went deeper into his understanding of the ayaawx that truth became increasingly clear to him: that in his history, and that of many, if not all, Indigenous Peoples, it is the natural world that defines these laws. In giving expression to the laws, humans merely act upon what the lands, waters, and animals effectively tell them is necessary for their sustainability and wellbeing, and therefore for the wellbeing of the humans who rely upon them. It is a perspective that requires a mind open to the concept that trees, creatures, and even the elements have sentience and agency in their own right to demonstrate what works and what doesn't; and that working with that concept, rather than trying to control it or fight it, results in far more effective and sustainable outcomes for all concerned.

"I'll give you an example," says Spencer. "There is a Ts'myen law that prohibits killing a seal lying on an exposed rock. There is a reason for that law, and the natural world provides it. If you kill a seal on a rock, it taints their sleeping area with blood. The southeast wind has to come and pound that rock with rain to wash it so they have a place to live and sleep again. Until it does, the seals will avoid that place. In that sense, it is both the seals and the wind telling us how to live, giving us this law." Break the law, and there will be no more seals to eat until after the next storm. Conversely, respect the law, and everything remains in balance: the place, the seals, the weather, and the people.

It is an approach that Spencer embraces completely. "The more I engage with our oral history and our teachings, it becomes a lot clearer that the ecosystems we live in control us, not the other way around. It is the natural world that dictates how we should live on the land and therefore our stewardship and resource management laws and practices. That is very powerful." It is also much more sustainable than trying to manage ecosystems to suit what human beings think they need or want, which is the prevailing approach in non-Indigenous resource management systems. Dramatically declining biodiversity and ecological crises occurring worldwide indicate that these approaches have failed to serve humanity or our planet well.

"At the foundation of this and of all of our laws that tell us how to behave in the world," adds Spencer, "is the fact that our ancestors were open to understanding how the natural world works and delivers us the rules that we abide by. We have always known we cannot control nature, that it tells us what to do. As a result, over the last ten millennia so much knowledge has come from the non-human world and been incorporated into our institutions as Ts'msyen people. In such a time of ecological chaos, this is something I believe all of humanity should understand and be thinking about embracing."

In 2015, Spencer was elected to the Gitga'at First Nation Council. One of the youngest citizens of Gitga'at ever to be elected to that office, he hoped to contribute positively to his community in the role. But he also struggled to reconcile being an elected Councillor under the *Indian Act*—an artificial

Spencer near Laxgalts'ap (Old Town)

and highly constrained political governance system barely 150 years old, largely confined to the Gitga'at reserve at Txałgiu—with the natural authenticity of the Ts'msyen people's ancient and sovereign system of territory-wide relationships between human beings and ecosystems, and laws and governance practices in which people, animals, trees, and the lands and waters they depend upon within those ecosystems, all thrive.

By then Spencer had started work on his doctorate and was researching a place called Laxgalts'ap (Old Town), located not far from Txałgiu. "This is an important cultural place, a sacred and spiritual seasonal village of the Gitga'at people," says Spencer. "It is the longest consistently occupied place that we know about in our territory, for at least ten thousand years, almost certainly more than that." Laxgalts'ap is a place that he feels in his blood and in his bones. It is somewhere that his grandfather once accompanied his parents and grandparents to live in the summertime, and where their forebears always spent their summers in a continuous line stretching back into history so old that it is almost inconceivable. Gitga'at people, says Spencer, "have never stopped living and breathing our ways of being here."

Spencer chose Laxgalts'ap as the subject of his doctoral research because of what this special place and its history can offer not only Gitga'at

Following spread:
The rare white or spirit bear is sometimes seen in Gitga'at homelands.

people, but everyone, in very practical terms of understanding our relationship with the earth. "If you want to understand how humans should deal with climate change and potential environmental disasters or even pandemics, you should look to places like Laxgalts'ap, where people have consistently lived and experienced those kinds of events for millennia and still come out thriving. We have had such a long practice of learning to live as human beings in this place. These are lessons that resonate with human society in a time of deep vulnerability with the environment. We need to look to these places for those lessons."

Like the concept of nature setting down our laws, it is a way of thinking about our relationship with the natural world that is not typical in non-Indigenous systems. In those systems, "resource management" is usually equated with over-exploitation of increasingly scarce natural resources and increasing use of fossil fuels, despite the evidence of their negative impacts on the planet, and long-term sustainability is rarely given anything more than lip service. This reality and the importance of the research that Spencer had been undertaking came into stark focus for the Gitga'at in 2014.

That year, the federal government approved the Northern Gateway project, a proposed twin pipeline from Alberta to Kitimat, at the head of the Douglas Channel. Enbridge Inc., the Canadian company behind the proposal, estimated that when completed, the 1,170-kilometre dual pipeline would carry 525,000 barrels a day of diluted bitumen to Kitimat for export to Asia and 193,000 barrels a day of hydrocarbon condensate (a natural gas by-product used to mine bitumen) back to the tar sands. The tankers would have to traverse not only the island-strewn Douglas Channel but the stormy waters of Hecate Strait, one of the most dangerous bodies of water in the world.

For First Nation communities who have depended on the seafood harvested from those waters for sustenance for millennia, the very real prospect of an oil or chemical spill in their back yard was horrifying to contemplate. The Nation had already experienced one disastrous ship sinking when the provincial ferry MV *Queen of the North* ran aground on rocks not far from Txałgiu on the night of March 22, 2006. The Gitga'at community were able to save all but two of the passengers, but nothing could save the local waters from the impact of oil leaking from the vessel's damaged fuel tanks.

In 2012, prior to the approval of the Northern Gateway project, a federal review panel tasked with hearing submissions from interested parties about the proposal visited Txałgiu. Among the people who spoke to the panel were head Ganhada and Gitga'at Chief Wii Hai Waas (Arnold Clifton) and Man Gis Haytk (Marven Robinson), also on Council and at that time head of the Nation's environmental stewardship program. Cameron Hill (who holds two names—Ha'gwil laxha and Ka'gwaays), principal of the Txałgiu school, also made an oral presentation. These were all individuals with whom Spencer has experienced gugwilx'ya'ansk in action, all mentors from the generation before him whose knowledge and experience he has benefitted from, respected highly, and is endeavouring to live up to in accordance with his hereditary responsibilities.

Gitga'at Chief Councillor Wii Hai Waas (Arnold Clifton)

Chief Arnold Clifton was born in Txałgiu and raised by his grandparents to take on his inherited name and role as a Chief in due course. "My grandfather Lewis was a hereditary Chief," says Arnold. "He was also raised by his grandparents. They taught him all our ayaawx and our adaawx, and in turn, as I would eventually become a hereditary Chief, he taught me." An experienced commercial fisherman, Lewis frequently took his small grandson with him on his boat to teach him his history and to show him important places in Gitga'at territory that had sustained his people for thousands of years, and which still did. He was taught the importance of ritual and to be thankful for the resources available to him in the territory. He learned that it was his responsibility to share those resources with those in need in the community, putting their needs above his own.

As a fisherman, says Arnold, as well as a harvester for his community, no one understood wild salmon better than Lewis Clifton. Apart from anything else, he was famous for his accuracy in predicting the wild salmon runs each year, using his people's ancient practice of observing the movement of the sun and the moon to forecast not only when the fish would arrive in Gitga'at territorial waters but how many. In doing so, he repeatedly proved wrong the forecasts of non-Indigenous government officials in the Department of Fisheries and Oceans (DFO), whose disastrous management of BC's wild fisheries had resulted in their dramatic decline over the decades DFO had been in charge. "His famous saying," recalls Arnold with a chuckle, "was 'White men are crazy. They think they can rule nature and that's one thing they will never do.'"

Man Gis Haytk
(Marven Robinson)

Arnold's grandfather indelibly impressed upon the younger man the importance of taking his marching orders from the lands, waters and creatures in Gitga'at territory in the same way his ancestors had done. "Everything he told me in that regard is still relevant in how I approach my responsibilities and my work every day," says Arnold, who followed in his grandfather's footsteps to become a commercial fisherman as well, running his own seine boat for more than fifty years. Arnold had his grandfather's saying at the front of his mind when he decided that Enbridge could not be allowed to develop the Northern Gateway pipeline, the most unnatural endeavour he could imagine. "When we were asked if there were any Nations willing to take on Enbridge," recalls Arnold, "right away I said, 'We'll fight it.'"

At the time, Arnold had been at a meeting of the Coastal First Nations in Vancouver, where lawyer Joseph Arvay spoke to the group to ask if they would consider joining a court case that was under way. The legal action was challenging agreements between the governments of Canada and BC that had eased the way for regulatory approval of the pipeline. If successful, the case would be helpful as one of the steps to stop the pipeline from proceeding altogether. "As I sat there," recalls Arnold, "all I could think about was my ninety-three-year-old aunt who was dying from cancer, who despite being so ill had come to speak to the review panel and tell them they could not let this happen in our territory. So many of us spoke that day. They did not listen to a single one of us or pay any attention to our concerns. That's why I decided to fight. I told the lawyer, 'Yes, we'll do this.'"

The next day Arnold met with Joe Arvay and spent nearly five hours telling him about what he had learned from his grandfather Lewis. "At the end, he said to me, 'You know, I didn't have much hope that we could win this case. Now I think we have a chance.' I went back the next day for another three hours and told him even more. At the end of that session, Joe said, 'Yesterday, I thought we had a chance. Today, I think we will win.'" The case, taken in the name of the Coastal First Nations and the Gitga'at, ultimately went to the Supreme Court of British Columbia.[44] To Arnold's immense relief, Joe Arvay's prediction proved correct: "We ended up winning." In 2016 it was Arnold's turn to accurately predict another win, this time a new case in the federal Court of Appeal[45] in which the Gitga'at participated along with a number of other Nations. The court overturned the pipeline's approval once and for all. "I am very proud," reflects Arnold, "that this little Nation was part of making that happen."

Ha'gwil laxha / Ka'gwaays (Cameron Hill)

Many Gitga'at people had stood shoulder to shoulder with Arnold in opposing the proposed pipeline, including Marven Robinson and his then fourteen-year-old daughter, who both told the review panel in 2012 how fundamentally wrong it would be to allow the pipeline to be built through their territory. What they and their fellow citizens said gave vivid meaning and significance to the concepts that Spencer described in his research work.

Marven told the panel that when he was young he never had to worry about the environment or whether he would still be able to go fishing when he was an old man. It was a dreadful thing for him to watch his daughter crying in front of the panel, panic-stricken at the irreparable harm the proposed pipeline would do to her heritage and to her future. "To see her so afraid was very difficult," he recalls, the emotion thick in his voice. When it was his turn to speak after listening to his daughter, Marven was unequivocal. "I will fight to protect our future generations, culture and way of life," he said adamantly. "I will not sit here and let someone else impose a different future on Gitga'at."

Cameron Hill, who most people simply call Cam, had lived his whole life in Txałgiu. Like Marvin, Cam also had a young daughter who had previously presented to the panel. It was an equally wrenching experience to hear her speak. He told the panel, "You will never know the hurt and the anger and the sadness I felt as my daughter stood before you having to basically defend who she is." Cam also told them, "I am a Gitga'at harvester. I have been harvesting traditionally since I was eight years old, when my father first took me out on a boat to teach me. I use what the land and the sea provide to me...If there were to be a spill, my way of life would be lost.

Following spread: La'goot (Spencer Greening) believes that the ancient adaawx and ayaawx, and the Indigenous relationship with ecosystems manifest in those stories and laws, can be the answer to long-term sustainability of the coast's wild salmon fisheries.

The food that I share will be lost. We should not have to live with that cloud hanging over us. My generation is on the verge of switching from learner to teacher. We cannot jeopardize our lands and seas. If we do, we will have nothing to hand down but memories. I am not going to let that happen."

Cam describes his personal story as a Gitga'at man as one of "being born and raised in the community I love." He recalls his grandmother's words as clearly as when he first heard them as a child. "She would tell me, 'Cam, we know who we are.' I always remember that. All of her knowledge gave me such a sense of security as to who I was. One of my most intimate teachings from her was simple: 'Take what you need and use what you take. Don't waste anything.' That meant if you look after your surroundings, this place will always be there for you. It makes me feel good to be able to practise what I have been taught," he continues. "I truly believe that if the rest of the world thought and behaved like this we would be in a far better place than we are right now."

In his own way Cam is a living embodiment of gugwilx'ya'ansk. "When I am out in Gitga'at territory, I can feel my ancestors, knowing that they were out there doing the same things in the same places. I can imagine my aunts and uncles and grandparents walking those same beaches and doing the same things. I feel an overwhelming sense of security when I'm out there, that I'm being watched over. My ancestors are looking after me and they're guiding me, they're showing me the proper ways to do things. Now it's my turn to keep that tradition going and to teach other people about what it means to be Gitga'at and look after our territory and harvest from it."

When he became principal of the Txałgiu school, Cam was following in his father Ernie's footsteps. After completing high school, says Cam, "my dad was passionate about becoming a teacher. He graduated from Simon Fraser University and immediately came back to teach in his own community so that he could try and further the education of his own people. Then I took over. First, I was just teaching because he was still the principal, but when he retired I went back to university, got my master's degree in education, and came back so that I could be principal here in my own home."

Cam decided to combine the traditional teachings he had learned from Ernie and his grandmother with the contemporary curriculum in a way that would set up Gitga'at children for the best chance of success in their lives. He wants them to achieve whatever they want and believes strongly that the kind of place-based learning that Spencer is pursuing

in his gugwilx'ya'ansk journey is as important in his twenty-first-century classroom as all the other mainstream subjects. "I teach all the academic subjects to my students—maths, science, English, and the arts—but while these are all important to further anyone's educational endeavours, I think they need more than that. They need place-based learning in which they can really identify with the territory they are in and be respectful and honour it in every way, shape, and form that they can. That's what I try and get across to my students and support them in being able to learn."

Orca in Gitga'at waters

Sometimes, for example, students show up for class late the day after a harvesting trip with their families. Cam never penalizes those children. "That is real learning. That's my people pushing forward and realizing their histories, their norms, their beliefs, their values, and that's so important. To me, that walks hand-in-hand with the traditional academics of learning." Cam also brings traditional teaching and Gitga'at history into his classroom. "Whether it's weaving, art, cooking traditional foods, gathering medicinal plants, I want that always going on in my school to show the kids how important their history is. I want them to experience how important it is to learn about their culture and the land they come from."

Gitga'at laws require the careful and sustainable stewardship of their homelands.

The Gitga'at have, of course, incorporated their traditional knowledge into everything they have done for thousands of years. They are also building on that knowledge through a range of diverse contemporary initiatives, everything from traditional Sm'algyax lessons on computer tablets, connected through high-speed internet, to high-tech research on the impacts of marine noise on whale populations in their waters, based around Gitga'at knowledge of seasonal whale activity and migration through their territory.

Marven Robinson brings a similar approach to the diverse roles he has undertaken for the Nation over time, including being a director of Gitga'at's economic development arm. "The thought process as a First Nation regarding economic development is very different," explains Marven. "We always think about the environment first. That's just automatic. We didn't ever know the word 'conservation.' We were just doing it. It's like Spencer says, we were just living it every day in everything we did. We still do."

Spencer is still hard at work at Laxgalts'ap, continuing his research. He is also applying what he has already learned in practical terms, having co-authored an article[46] on salmon sustainability that describes how the ancient adaawx and ayaawx, and the Indigenous relationship with ecosystems manifest in those stories and laws, can be the answer to long-term sustainability of the coast's wild salmon fisheries. The work is a neat example of gugwilx'ya'ansk in practice. "We are in a unique position whereby striving to live as we always have in the past, we can forge a structure and a direction in how we engage with the future," says Spencer. "How do we deal with securing at-risk salmon populations, for example? What we can do is look at how we did it for the past several thousand years. How did we engage with salmon to last that long? When your culture's way of being inherently leads to good management and ecological sustenance, it offers a great opportunity for where we should go in the future."

In the conclusion to his master's thesis, Spencer reflects, "As I write this final chapter, I am in my home village of Txałgiu, working on the order of events of an upcoming luulgit. As we plan the Ganhada business that is about to take place, the house is also ensuring I understand my role as the speaker/master of ceremonies for this event. I would like to contrast this to where I was when I first began this thesis. At that time, I had just received a name, had little experience carrying out a feast, or being a speaker for that matter. I carried little understanding of adaawx, ayaawx, gugwilx'ya'ansk, and how to express those ways of living in Sm'algyax...In my eyes, [what] I have experienced is the essence of gugwilx'ya'ansk, the essence of cultural continuity and the passing down of knowledge...Receiving the teachings of how to live within my community, outside of my academic life, is when my true education began."

Spencer is hopeful that these ancient laws and ways of being might one day be embraced not only by Ts'msyen people but more broadly in the world. "When your lineage, your language, your spirituality, and the laws and institutions of your society all derive from the landscape that you continue to live on," he observes, "and when a society has a way of being through thousands upon thousands of years, human ingenuity and brilliance just pour out of that, out of these Indigenous ways of being. That is gugwilx'ya'ansk. That is how we could and should imagine our future."

For the Generations Yet Unborn

CONCLUSION

When I started work on this book I asked a remarkable group of Indigenous individuals to speak about how people, place and wellbeing are linked, and the ways in which their own connections to the places they are from are reflected in the different paths in life that they are following and the work they are doing to take care of those places, each other, and their communities.

I expected a wide-ranging conversation. After all, the group included scientists, tourism operators, businesspeople, politicians, hereditary Chiefs, executives and administrators, environmental stewards and monitors, fisheries workers, cultural and language workers, students, academics and teachers, artists and photographers, journalists and writers, youth and youth workers, Elders, engineers and handymen, housing managers, and more (many of them wear several different hats, working long hours in a number of roles in their communities).

Indeed, all of them reflected on the theme of connection in different ways. They have all taken different approaches to improving the wellbeing of their homelands and their communities, depending on their location, circumstances, challenges and opportunities. But they also, without exception, talked about the many things that they have in common, threads that ended up weaving themselves through the fabric of every story in the book.

Of course, everyone spoke about the impacts of colonization. They said that without understanding the history and the severity of those impacts, it is impossible to

"Everything we do today is for the generations not yet born and to uplift and empower our children and our youth: through connecting them with the land and their culture and through learning our languages and the old values we were taught as children by our Elders."

— Ts'xwiixw (Megan Moody), (Nuxalk) 2022

Facing page: The connection of Indigenous Peoples to their homelands is ancient and unbroken. This beach is located near Laxgalts'ap, in Gitga'at territory.

Taking care of the land, water, and wildlife in the homelands is not only a profound responsibility but a way of life and being.

appreciate the extent of what they have to do to heal themselves and their families and communities and just how hard it is—and how important—to work toward reconnection with their lands and each other. Most are still on that healing journey. But they also made it clear that they are not defined by colonization and its legacy. Instead, they are defining themselves on their own terms. In whatever role they happen to be, they are reviving the values, laws, and the old ways of being of their ancestors in these places and applying them, to the best of their ability, in a twenty-first-century context.

It is a journey as much about reclaiming cultural autonomy as it is about exercising age-old governance responsibilities and rights that were never forgotten or willingly relinquished. As these stories demonstrate, although every community and Nation has different approaches to restoring and improving the wellbeing of their places and their people, the same fundamental principles underly all of those approaches: the inseparability of people and the landscapes in which they live; holding onto values that have been passed down the generations, such as respect for all things, including all living creatures; and ensuring the sustainable use of natural resources while protecting the territory.

These are ways of living and being that we can all learn a great deal from. In "Gugwilx'ya'ansk—We Are Living It," La'goot (Spencer Greening) points out, "Indigenous people have experienced massive environmental change, floods, wildfires, and all kinds of other natural crises over ten thousand years of stewardship of our territories and learned how to deal with them. Through that deep, deep history of learning, the values, spiritual teachings, rituals and laws we developed have helped us not only survive but thrive...when a society has a way of being through thousands upon thousands of years, human ingenuity and brilliance just pour out of that, out of these Indigenous ways of being. That is how we could and should imagine our future."

Snxakila (Clyde Tallio) agrees that we can all learn from each other. "In the next chapter of the human story we are entering an era of globalization of Indigenous wisdom. This is a pivotal time in history," Snxakila believes. "We are learning about how generations of being in these different places around the world have formed all these different languages and cultures and Nations, and how amazing that human experience is, all these ways of being and doing things. I think our role as Indigenous people is to bring that to light and to bring these ways of thinking forward to the human species to share and learn from."

People also spoke about mother tongue fluency as a cornerstone of cultural strength. The Indigenous languages of the people in this book include Nuxalkmc, the Ts'msyen language of Sm'algya̱x, Nisg̱a'a, Haíłzaqvḷa, X̱aad kil and X̱aayda kil, Sgüüx̱s and Xai'xais, Kwak̓wala, the Bak̓wa̱mk̓ala dialect of the Gwa'cala language, Nak'wala, Haisla (a Wakashan language) and Liq̓ʷala. It is a roll call of dialects and language groups that not only personify identity, but with infinite grace and beauty form a structure for every aspect of daily life in all its permutations: whether it be family relationships, community work, education, governance, protocols, or ceremony.

The words in these languages cannot be translated into English or French equivalents. They have values inherently embedded within them that govern how people should behave. For example, the words and phrases used to convey the instructions to collect medicinal or food plants include a litany of principles and practices to follow while doing so, incorporating ecological, spiritual, and cultural values. These are not separate concepts but embedded in the words themselves, in much the same way the languages are embedded within the identities of the people who speak them. Being fluent in the language, in other words, carries much greater significance than simply knowing the words. Indigenous language fluency is a way of being and behaving, imbued with confidence in identity and awareness of ancestral laws and values.

It is unsurprising then that everyone spoke about their overwhelming desire for their children and grandchildren to grow up learning their mother tongues from infancy, including Haíłzaqv mother Jess H̓áusṫI (Housty) in "Haíłzaqv Unfettered." As I wrote in that chapter, "In early 2021 Jess wrote on Twitter: 'My five-year-old just crawled into my arms and said: H̓íkúx̌vs ẇiúł, mommy. I think my heart just exploded.' The significance of that simple but fundamental exchange in Haíłzaqvḷa between mother and son could not be overstated. 'Noen and Magnus,' says Jess, 'are part of a generation that will truly be, for the first time, Haíłzaqv unfettered in every sense of the word.'"

The desire that their children reconnect to their languages this way is reinforced by the fact that so many people did not have that opportunity when they were young. The importance of uplifting and empowering their young people, including exposing them to their languages, resonates in every story. They are the ones, after all, who will inherit the legacy of all of the hard work and unflagging commitment of their Elders—including the people in this book, and so many others—to reclaim and protect their homelands and ensure a sustainable future for them. They are the ones who will, in turn, carry on that legacy.

The children are "hasda̱xwa̱la'yu," or "my reason for breathing," says Dzawada̱'enux̱w hereditary Chief Maxwiyalidizi K'odi Nelson. "What would our purpose be," he asks simply, "without our children?"

—Katherine Palmer Gordon, 2022

Timeline

The following points in both ancient and contemporary history came up in many of the conversations I had with the people in this book. These are not comprehensive, of course. To learn more about the history and the contemporary unfolding of the stories, see "To Learn More: Resources" on page 227.

PRE-SETTLER CONTACT: Evidence is beyond dispute of occupation and implementation of political, economic, resource management and cultural frameworks by Indigenous Peoples, for millennia, of the territory known in the twenty-first century as British Columbia. The Haíłzaqv, for example, hold both original and contemporary archaeological knowledge establishing ancestral presence in their territory at least fourteen thousand years ago.

SEVENTEENTH CENTURY: The "Doctrine of Discovery"—a Catholic Church principle developed in the fifteenth century that became enshrined in international law (which is still the case)—denied the prior occupation by Indigenous Peoples of their lands and waters in North America (and later in other countries, like New Zealand). Invading European nations deemed lands that had no European inhabitants to be vacant. Based on this, they claimed they had "discovered" such lands and had sovereignty over them.

EIGHTEENTH CENTURY: The 1763 Royal Proclamation issued by King George III claimed British territory in North America. It stated that all land would be considered First Nations land until "ceded" by treaty and that only the Crown could sell such land. The Proclamation slowed down the pace of settlement but only temporarily. Even in unceded territory—most of modern BC, for example—the Royal Proclamation appears to have done little to reduce the impact of settlement on Indigenous Peoples.

NINETEENTH CENTURY: Indigenous Peoples continued to exercise ancestral responsibilities for stewardship of their lands, but this became increasingly difficult as colonial governments asserted increasing power and settlers pre-empted land for homesteading:

- Between 1850 and 1854, and in 1899, a handful of treaties were made in BC, but they provided little immediate benefit to the First Nations involved. Indeed, the Crown was slow to implement and quick to retract many of its commitments under those treaties—even more land was removed, for example, and government-to-government relationships and agreements are still being negotiated.

- In 1862, the colonial government of the future province of BC made it illegal for "status Indians" to pre-empt land, a system which allowed settlers to occupy a block of unsurveyed Crown land and, after developing it for agricultural use, receive ownership of the land at no charge. The prohibition was lifted in 1948.
- In 1876, the first iteration of the *Indian Act* defined "Indians" and "Indian Bands," and established Indian reserves. The legislation also introduced a raft of discriminatory provisions preventing "status Indians" from engaging in their cultural practices as well as a wide range of commercial, legal, and other activities.
- In the late 1800s, residential schools were established. Tens of thousands of Indigenous children were taken from their families and sent to the schools, where many suffered horrific abuse. Thousands did not survive. Under the guidance of Indigenous communities who knew that their children had died and been buried in unmarked graves at the former schools, those grave sites began to be uncovered in 2021 through the use of ground-penetrating radar and other techniques. The publicity associated with the uncovering of the graves sparked an unprecedented level of awareness by non-Indigenous Canadians (and internationally) of the actions of colonizing governments and churches and the impacts of those actions.
- In 1884, the Potlatch was banned by statute, with a penalty of imprisonment. Many First Nations people kept potlatching in secret despite the risk.

TWENTIETH CENTURY:

- Thousands of Indigenous men and women volunteered in both the first and second world wars (and other wars) but did not receive any benefits as returning veterans unless they renounced their Indian status.
- In 1945, Indigenous people were permitted to vote in provincial elections in BC.
- After the end of World War II industrial development and resource extraction activity increased massively. Indigenous people, however, were largely excluded from economic investment opportunities associated with major resource industries.
- In 1951, the Potlatch ban was lifted after nearly seventy years. Indigenous people were permitted to hire lawyers, enabling them at last to defend their human and land rights in court.
- In 1960, Indigenous people were permitted to vote in federal elections.
- During the "Sixties Scoop," which occurred while the residential school system was still ongoing, thousands of children were forcibly removed from their families, this time by social services, and given away for adoption to

non-Indigenous families, many of them outside Canada.

- In 1969, the Government of Canada introduced the *White Paper on Indian Policy*. The paper denied the existence of Indigenous Title and dismissed treaties as irrelevant in the context of modern Canada.
- In 1973, the Supreme Court of Canada in *Calder v British Columbia* acknowledged for the first time in Canadian law that Aboriginal Title existed prior to the colonization of the continent.
- Just over a decade later, in 1982, the new *Constitution Act* recognized the existing Rights and Title of the Indigenous Peoples of Canada, and Supreme Court of Canada (SCC) case law began to increasingly endorse Indigenous Rights.
- In 1984, Tla-o-qui-aht and Ahousaht First Nations on the west coast of Vancouver Island established Wah'nah'juss Hilth'hoo'iss (Meares Island) Tribal Park, a form of what had, by 2022, become commonly referred to as an Indigenous protected and conserved area (IPCA). Tla-o-qui-aht subsequently established three additional tribal parks, Ha'uukmin, Tranquil, and Esowista, collectively known as the Tla-o-qui-aht Tribal Parks.
- In 1991, a contemporary treaty negotiation process began with the creation of the British Columbia Treaty Commission. Some First Nations embraced the new process; others did not.
- In 1996, the Royal Commission on Aboriginal Peoples issued a damning report on abuse by the Government of Canada of Indigenous Peoples and its genocidal behaviour toward them.
- Finally, in 1997, the SCC observed in the *Delgamuukw v British Columbia* case that Aboriginal Title constitutes an ancestral right protected by section 35(1) of the *Constitution Act*, 1982.

TWENTY-FIRST CENTURY:

- In 2000, the Nisg̱a'a Treaty came into effect.
- In 2006, the BC government offered to protect up to eighty-five per cent of the central and north coast of the province and seventy per cent of old growth in the area over time and enable ecosystem-based management of the region. The commitment was contained in what have become known as "the Great Bear Rainforest Agreements," which were implemented in the *Great Bear Rainforest Land Use Order* and *Great Bear Rainforest (Forest Management) Act*. Legislation to give effect to that agreement would come into effect in 2017.
- In 2007, the United Nations adopted the *Declaration on the Rights of Indigenous Peoples*, a "universal framework of minimum standards for the survival, dignity and wellbeing of the Indigenous peoples of the world and existing human rights standards and fundamental freedoms as they apply to the specific situation of Indigenous peoples."
- The same year, Coast Funds was established in the names of the 'Na̱mgis

Nation, Coastal First Nations, Da'naxda'xw Awaetlala First Nation, Dzawada̱'enu̱xw Nation, Gitanyow Nation, Gitga'at Nation, Gitxaala Nation, Gwa'sala-'Nakwaxda'xw Nations, Gwawa'enuxw, X̱aayda/Haida Nation, Haíłzaqv (Heiltsuk) Nation, Haisla Nation, K'ómoks Nation, Kitasoo/Xai'xais Nation, Kitselas Nation (or Gitselasu), Kwiakah First Nation, Kwik̓wa̱sut̓inu̱xw Ha̱xwa'mis Nation, the Allied Tribes of Lax Kw'alaams, Mamalilikulla First Nation, Metlakatla Nation, Na̱nwak̲olas Council, Nisga̱'a Nation, North Coast Skeena First Nations Stewardship Society, Nuxalk Nation, Tlowitsis First Nation, Ulkatcho Nation, We Wai Kai Nation, Wei Wai Kum Nation, Wuikinuxv Nation, and Xwémalhkwu (Homalco) Nation.

- Contributions to Coast Funds of $30 million each by the governments of Canada and BC toward a sustainable economic development fund (the Coast Economic Development Society) were negotiated and matched by $60 million for a conservation fund (the Coast Conservation Endowment Fund Foundation) from the Nature Conservancy, the William and Flora Hewlett Foundation, the Gordon and Betty Moore Foundation, the David and Lucile Packard Foundation, the Rockefeller Brothers Fund, and Tides Canada Foundation (now operating as Make Way).
- In 2010, X̱aayda Gwaay's original name was restored by legislation (as Haida Gwaii).
- In 2011, K'ih tsaa?dze Tribal Park was declared by Doig River First Nations.
- In 2012, the Idle No More movement, an Indigenous-led social movement, was founded among Treaty People in Manitoba, Saskatchewan, and Alberta, protesting the Canadian government's dismantling of environmental protection laws that endangered First Nations who live on the land.[47] Many First Nations people in BC, particularly Indigenous youth, embraced the movement.
- In 2014, the SCC confirmed that the Tŝilhqot'in Nation held unextinguished Aboriginal Title to lands in their territory in BC. Nexwagweẑʔan-Dasiqox Tribal Park was established by Yunesit'in and Xeni Gwet'in, Tsilhqot'in communities, the same year.
- In 2015, the Truth and Reconciliation Commission of Canada (TRC) on the legacy of residential schools issued ninety-four Calls to Action to governments and other institutions in Canada for action to support reconciliation efforts.
- In 2018, under pressure from many Indigenous Nations and environmental groups, the provincial government ended the grizzly bear trophy hunt in BC.
- In 2019, the government of British Columbia became the first province to pass the *Declaration on the Rights of Indigenous Peoples Act* (*Declaration Act*)[48] into law. The Act established the United Nations' Declaration as the province's

framework for reconciliation as directed by the TRC's Calls to Action.

- On June 20, 2021, the government of Canada passed the *United Nations Declaration on the Rights of Indigenous Peoples Act*[49] into law.
- In August, Gitanyow hereditary Chiefs unilaterally declared 54,000 hectares of their territory to be an IPCA.
- On September 30, Canada observed the first National Day for Truth and Reconciliation. However, BC did not observe the day as a statutory holiday.
- On November 29, Mamalilikulla First Nation declared more than 10,000 hectares of their territory in Knight Inlet to be an IPCA, affirming the Nation's Title and Rights and its inherent responsibilities for the land, sea and natural resources in the area.

Endnotes

1 The full title of the essay is "From Conflict to Collaboration: The Story of the Great Bear Rainforest." https://coastfunds.ca/resources/conflict-to-collaboration/. Arthur William Sterritt is a northwest coast artist and co-founder of Coastal First Nations-Great Bear Initiative. Merran Smith is the executive director of Clean Energy Canada.

2 www.coastalfirstnations.ca.

3 https://nanwakolas.com/ha-ma-yas-stewardship-network/.

4 Readers can learn more at The National Centre for Truth and Reconciliation: nctr.ca; ReconciliationCanada.ca; and Indigenousfoundations.arts.ubc.ca/the_residential_school_system. Also see "To Learn More: Resources," page 227.

5 The environmental movement would later coin the term "the Great Bear Rainforest" for this region.

6 In *Delgamuukw v British Columbia*, [1997] 3 SCR 1010, the Supreme Court of Canada confirmed the existence of Aboriginal Rights and Title in British Columbia, providing a more even playing field for First Nations at tables such as the LRMP consultations.

7 Richard Schuster, et al., "Vertebrate biodiversity on indigenous-managed lands in Australia, Brazil, and Canada equals that in protected areas," *Environmental Science & Policy*, vol. 101 (November 2019).

8 Spencer Greening, et al., "Indigenous Systems of Management for Culturally and Ecologically Resilient Pacific Salmon," *BioScience* XX (2020):1-19.

9 Nancy J. Turner, et al., "From Invisibility to Transparency: Identifying the Implications," *Ecology & Society*, 13(2) (2008): 7.

10 Others include Kw'alhna (Kwatna), Ista-Sutslhmc Suts'lahm (Kimsquit), Ista (King Island), and Nusxiq' (Green Bay). The People of the four Territories of Nuxalk Nation are the Nuxalkmc (Bella Coola), Talyuumc (South Bentick), Kw'alhnamc (Kwatna inlet), and Ista-Sutslhmc (Dean Inlet, Kimsquit).

11 "ẃahlin" is used in referring to a Nisga'a who has passed who bore a Nisga'a name, i.e. the "late" Dr. Gosnell. Dr. Gosnell was also a Sim'oogit, a Chief.

12 Speech delivered to the Vancouver School of Theology at the University of British Columbia, 2011.

13 Pronounced something like "Hrrem-sim," with the "Hrr" coming from the back of the throat.

14 Generally, "hee" and "dee" are understood to be masculine expressions, i.e., expressions used only by males to each other. "Hee-eey" could also be referred to as a cheer.

15 Literally: aim (one's gaze) at the sun/moon: i.e., a Nisga'a astronomer.

16 Hadiks means to swim, an affectionate term for salmon because they are skilled swimmers. Hee indicates that a male is speaking to the salmon.

17 The test fishery that year estimated a return of 269,000 sockeye. The actual return was 635,000. Bocking, 1993: A comparison of two gillnet test fisheries operated on the Nass River in 1992. Prepared by LGL Limited, Sidney, BC, for Nisg̲a'a Lisims Government, New Aiyansh, BC.

18 A similar discrepancy occurred in 1993.

19 Joint management is shared with the provincial government for provincial fish species such as steelhead and trout and for managing freshwater habitat.

20 In *Calder v British Columbia*, the Supreme Court of Canada acknowledged for the first time in Canadian law that Aboriginal Title existed prior to the colonization of the continent.

21 Noen's name is a contraction of "No Enbridge," the campaign slogan; he was born at the height of the protests.

22 Also spelled Kvai, and pronounced something like "Kway" or, according to some Elders, more correctly "Kwee-ay," Koeye translates as "bird sitting on the water."

23 To say "to speak Haíłzaqvḷa" is redundant as that is what Haíłzaqvḷa means.

24 Noen said: "Good morning, mommy."

25 The name Haida Gwaii is an Anglicized version of the archipelago's name in both X̱aad kíl (the northern X̱aayda dialect) and X̱aayda kil (the southern dialect). Both names are used throughout the chapter to recognize both dialects.

26 To say "X̱aayda people" or a "X̱aayda person," says K̲ii'iljuus (Barbara Wilson), is redundant: the word "person" or "people" is inherent in the word X̱aayda.

27 Thom Henley, *Raven Walks Around the World: Life of a Wandering Activist*" (Madeira Park, BC: Harbour Publishing, 2017).

28 During the infamous Sixties Scoop (1961 to the 1980s) thousands of Indigenous children were removed from their families in Canada without consent and adopted out to non-Indigenous families, many of them outside Canada. Learn more at https://indigenousfoundations.arts.ubc.ca/sixties_scoop/.

29 Scott Steedman, et al., ed., *That Which Makes Us Haida* (Haida Gwaii, BC: Haida Gwaii Museum Press, 2011).

30 The story of Lyell Island and the refusal of the X̱aayda to accept continued logging in Gwaii Haanas is told in Athlii Gwaii: Upholding Haida Law on Lyell Island, ed. ng, Nika Collison Jisgang (Locarno Press 2018).

31 Although it is a Ts'msyen word, "Kitamaat" is the name in common usage for the village.

32 Ecotrust Canada is a non-governmental organization "working with rural, remote and Indigenous communities to build sustainable and resilient local economies in a healthy natural environment" (www.ecotrust.ca).

33 The full Kitlope Declaration was published in the Western Canada Wilderness Committee's Educational Report, Vol. 10, No.5, spring 1991 (Vancouver), https://www.wildernesscommittee.org/publications/save-kitlope.

34 John Charles Pritchard, *Economic Development and the Disintegration of Traditional Culture Among the Haisla*. Doctoral thesis (University of British Columbia, 1977).

35 Ellis won a seat in the provincial legislative assembly for the District of Skeena in 2017, becoming Minister of Natural Gas Development

and Minister Responsible for Housing while in government. He was re-elected in the 2020 election.

36 The proposed pipeline did not receive regulatory approval, much to the relief of the Kitasoo/Xai'xais and many other coastal communities in the region.

37 SEAS is a program supported by Nature United, Tides Canada, the Moore Foundation and Coast Funds across several coastal First Nation communities.

38 The film *Great Bear Rainforest* was screened in Canada and internationally in 2019.

39 Profile in "Stories from the Coast," September 2020, newsletter of Coastal First Nations/Great Bear Initiative.

40 https://www.natureunited.ca/what-we-do/our-priorities/investing-in-people/mercedes-robinson-neasloss-interview/.

41 Readers wishing to understand more about this story may contact the K̲wik̲w̲asut̓inux̱w Hax̱wa'mis Nation via their website, https://khfn.ca/.

42 https://coastfunds.ca/news/province-of-b-c-partners-with-kwikwasutinuxw-haxwamis-first-nation/.

43 Spencer Greening, *Raven Bloodlines, Tsimshian Identity: An Autoethnographic Account of Tsimshian Wil'naat'ał, Politics, Pedagogy and Law* (Prince George: UNBC, 2017).

44 *Coastal First Nations- Great Bear Initiative Society and Gitga'at First Nation v. British Columbia (Environment)*, 2016 BCSC 34.

45 *Gitxaala Nation vs. Canada*, 23 June 2016, 2016 FCA 187.

46 Spencer Greening, et al., "Indigenous Systems of Management for Culturally and Ecologically Resilient Pacific Salmon," *BioScience* XX (2020): 1-19.

47 idlenomore.ca/about-the-movement/.

48 https://www.leg.bc.ca/parliamentary-business/legislation-debates-proceedings/41st-parliament/4th-session/bills/third-reading/gov41-3.

49 https://laws-lois.justice.gc.ca/eng/acts/U-2.2/.

To Learn More: Resources

The stories in this book touch on history, law, ecology, culture, spirituality, economics, and so much more. For those wishing to delve into more detail on any of this subject matter, the following set of resources, though only a tiny fraction of those available, may be helpful.

General Resources

Coast Funds. "Coast Opportunity Funds." www.coastfunds.ca.

Coastal First Nations-Great Bear Initiative. "Our Stories." www.coastalfirstnations.ca.

First Peoples Cultural Council. "First Voices: Explore Languages." www.firstvoices.com.

Joseph, Bob. *21 Things You May Know about the Indian Act: Helping Canadians Make Reconciliation with Indigenous Peoples a Reality*. Vancouver: Page Two Books Inc., 2018.

Library and Archives Canada. *Royal Commission on Aboriginal Peoples, Final Report*. October 1996. https://www.bac-lac.gc.ca/eng/discover/aboriginal-heritage/royal-commission-aboriginal-peoples/Pages/final-report.aspx#shr-pg-pnlShareMain.

Mathews, Darcy L., and Nancy J. Turner. "Ocean Cultures: Northwest Coast Ecosystems and Indigenous Management Systems." In *Conservation for the Anthropocene Ocean*. Elsevier, 2017.

Moss, Wendy, and Elaine Gardner-O'Toole. *Aboriginal People: History of Discriminatory Laws*. Law and Government Division, Government of Canada. November 1987.

National Centre for Truth and Reconciliation. "Reports and Calls for Action of the Truth and Reconciliation Commission of Canada, 2015." https://nctr.ca/records/reports/.

Nature United. "Indigenous Guardians Toolkit." https://www.indigenousguardianstoolkit.ca/.

Turner, Nancy J., and Fikret Berkes. "Coming to Understanding: Developing Conservation through Incremental Learning in the Pacific Northwest." *Human Ecology*. New York: Springer Science+Business Media, Inc., July 2006.

Turner, Nancy J., R. Gregory, C. Brooks, L. Failing, and T. Satterfield. "From Invisibility to Transparency: Identifying the Implications." *Ecology and Society*, 13(2), 2008.

Vowel, Chelsea. *Indigenous Writes: A Guide to First Nations, Métis & Inuit Issues in Canada*. Winnipeg: Highwater Press, 2016.

Gitga'at

Canadian Legal Information Institute. *Coastal First Nations v British Columbia (Environment)* 2016 BCSC 34 (CanLII). https://www.canlii.org/en/bc/bcsc/doc/2016bcsc34/2016bcsc34.html.

Greening, Spencer. *Raven Bloodlines, Tsimshian Identity: An Autoethnographic Account of Tsimshian Wil'naat'ał, Politics, Pedagogy, and Law*. University of Northern British Columbia, 2017.

Marsden, Susan. *The Gitk'a'ata, Their History, and Their Territories: Report Submitted to The Gitk'a'ata*. January 2012.

McDonald, James A. "Tsimshian Wil'naat'ał and Society: Historicising Tsimshian Social Organization. In *Of One Heart: Gitxaala and Our Neighbours*, vol. 8, no. 1. University of Northern British Columbia, 2016.

Thompson, Kim-Ly, and Natalie C. Ban. "Turning to the territory: A Gitga'at Nation case study of Indigenous climate imaginaries and actions." *Geoforum*. November 2021. https://www.sciencedirect.com/science/article/abs/pii/S001671852100292X.

Website of the Gitga'at First Nation. "About us..." www.gitgaatnation.ca.

Gwa'sala-'Nakwaxda'xw

Culhane, Dane. "Tsulquate: The Demographic Story." Unpublished manuscript, 1984. Tsulquate Band Council, Port Hardy, BC.

Emery, Cliff, and Douglas Grainger. "You Moved Us Here—A Narrative Account of the Amalgamation and Relocation of the Gwa'Sala and 'Nakwaxda'xw Peoples." In *Royal Commission on Aboriginal Peoples Final Report Vol. 5*, 1996.

Gwa'sala-'Nakwaxda'xw Nations. https://www.gwanaknations.ca/.

Jackson, Lisa, director. *How a People Live*. Bliss Pictures Inc., 2016.

Jamaine Campbell Videography. "My Work: Gwa'sala-'Nakwaxda'xw." Elder interviews and KEDC profiles. https://jamainecampbell.com/gwasala-nakwaxdaxw-work.

k'awat'si Economic Development Corporation. "Realizing revenue, prosperity, skills and development for the community." www.kedc.ca.

Library and Archives Canada. *Royal Commission on Aboriginal Peoples*. 424-500. October 1996. https://www.bac-lac.gc.ca/eng/discover/aboriginal-heritage/royal-commission-aboriginal-peoples/Pages/final-report.aspx#shr-pg-pnlShareMain.

Haíłzaqv

Artelle, K.A., J. Stephenson, C. Bragg, J.A. Housty, W.G. Housty, M. Kawharu, and N.J. Turner. "Values-led Management: the guidance of place-based values in environmental relationships of the past, present, and future." *Ecology and Society* 23(3): 35, 2018.

Brown, Frank, and Y. Kathy Brown. *Staying the Course, Staying Alive–Coastal First Nations Fundamental Truths: Biodiversity, Stewardship and Sustainability*. Bioversitybc.org, 2009.

Haíłzaqv Tribal Council. "Bella Bella, BC—Home of the Haíłzaqv." www.heiltsuknation.ca.

Waterfall, Hílistis Pauline. "For First Nations, These are Precedented Times." *The Tyee*, May 22, 2020. https://thetyee.ca/Opinion/2020/05/22/First-Nations-Precendented-Times/. First published April 24, 2020.

Waterfall, Hílistis Pauline. "Healing Through Culture." In *Memory*, edited by Philippe Tortell, Mark

Turin, and Margot Young. Peter Wall Institute for Advanced Studies, 2018.

Waterfall, Hílístis Pauline, Lisa Glithero, Mary Simon and Wendy Watson-Wright. "The Heart of the Biosphere: Exploring Our Civic Relationship with the Ocean in Canada." Ottawa, Ontario: Canadian Commission for UNESCO's IdeaLab, 2020.

Haisla

Haisla Nation. "Welcome to Haisla Nation." www.haisla.ca.

Paul, Cecil, with Briony Penn. *Stories from the Magic Canoe of Wa'xaid*. Victoria, BC: Rocky Mountain Books, 2019.

Pritchard, John Charles. *Economic Development and the Disintegration of Traditional Culture Among the Haisla*. Doctoral thesis. University of British Columbia, 1977.

Wolfhard, Eric. *Historical and Documentary Corroboration Regarding the Haisla Nation's Occupation of its Traditional Territory*. Haisla Nation Council, December 19, 2011.

Kitasoo/Xai'xais

British Columbia, Indian Advisory Committee Project. *Klemtu Stories: Told by the People of Klemtu*. Recorded by Susanne Storie. Edited by Susanne Storie and Jennifer Gould. Victoria, BC: Indian Advisory Committee Project, 1968–1969.

CCIRA. *Kitasoo/Xai'xais Heritage Database: Bringing wisdom and stories home*. Central Coast Indigenous Resource Alliance, 2017. https://www.ccira.ca/2017/03/kitasooxaixais-heritage-database-bringing-wisdom-stories-home/.

Halpin, Marjorie M., and Margaret Seguin. "Tsimshian Peoples: Southern Tsimshian, Coast Tsimshian, Nishga, and Gitksan." In *Handbook of North American Indians: Northwest Coast*, vol. 7., edited by William C. Sturtevant. Washington: Smithsonian Institute, 1990.

Kitasoo/Xai'xais Nation. "The Kitasoo Xai'xais village of Klemtu in the heart of the Great Bear Rainforest." www.klemtu.com.

Spirit Bear Lodge. "Spirit Bear Lodge—The Heart of the Great Bear Rainforest." www.spiritbear.com.

Musgamakw Dzawada̱'enu̱xw

Dzawada̱'enu̱xw First Nation. www.kingcome.ca.

Kwik̓wa̱sut̓inux̱w Ha̱xwa'mis First Nation. https://khfn.ca.

Musgamagw Dzawada̱'enu̱xw Tribal Council. www.mtdc.ca.

Nawalakw. "A wellspring of inclusive healing, learning and renewal." https://nawalakw.com/

Wildman, Bobbie (Musgamakw Dzawada̱'enu̱xw), S. Williams. C. John, B. Helin, L.M. Dorion, M. Corneau, C. Aleck. *Strong Stories: Kwakwa̱ka̱'wakw*. Nanaimo, BC: Strong Nations Publishing Inc., 2018.

Nisga̱'a

Editorial committee of Nelson Leeson, Chief Alvin McKay, John A. MacKenzie, Rod Robinson, Alex Rose, Edmond Wright. *Nisga̱'a: People of the Mighty River*. Nisga̱'a Tribal Council, 1992.

Harper, Joan. *He Moved a Mountain: The Life of Frank Calder and the Nisga̱'a Land Claims Accord*. Vancouver, BC: Ronsdale Press, 2013.

Nisga'a Nation. "Nisga'a Lisims Government." Nisga'a Nation. www.nisgaanation.ca.

Rose, Alex (editor). *Nisga'a: People of the Nass River*. Direction from Nisga'a Tribal Council. Co-published Madeira Park, BC: Douglas & McIntyre Ltd., 1993.

Turner, Nancy J., F. Berkes, J. Stephenson, and J. Dick. "Blundering Intruders: Extraneous Impacts on Two Indigenous Food Systems." *Human Ecology*. New York: Springer Science+Business Media, Inc., June 9, 2013.

Nuxalk

Bella Coola. "Nuxalk Heritage." https://bellacoola.ca/portfolio/first-nations/.

Beveridge, Rachelle. *Standing up for sputc: The Nuxalk Sputc Project, eulachon management and well-being*. Victoria, BC: University of Victoria, 2019.

Hanuse, Banchi, director. *Cry Rock*. Smayaykila Films, 2010. https://smayaykila.com/films/cry-rock.

Hilland, Andrea. *Extinguishment by Extirpation: the Nuxalk Eulachon Crisis*. Vancouver: University of British Columbia, 2013.

Moody, Megan Felicity. *Eulachon Past and Present*. Vancouver: University of British Columbia, 2008.

Wei Wai Kum

Boas, Franz. *Kwakiutl Ethnography*. Chicago: University of Chicago Press, 1966.

Curtis, Edward. *The North American Indian: Volume 10*. Michigan: North American Book Distributors, LLC, 2015. First published 1970 by Plimpton Press.

"Laich-Kwil-Tach Nation Our Lands and Stories." Laich-Kwil-Tach Treaty Society, 2015. YouTube video, 23:41. https://www.youtube.com/watch?v=_Odyng8DmjU.

Wei Wai Kum First Nation. www.weiwaikum.ca.

Wilson Duff: Lekwiltok in the Wilson Duff Collection at the Royal BC Museum Library, File 91 (undated).

X̱aayda

Davidson, Robert, and Sara Florence Davidson. *Potlatch as Pedagogy: Learning Through Ceremony*. Winnipeg: Portage & Main Press, 2018.

Haida Nation. "Council of the Haida Nation." www.haidanation.ca.

Hart, 7idansuu James. Conversation at the Audain Gallery, Whistler, BC. January 6, 2021. https://www.youtube.com/watch?v=MijlDudCntk

Jisgang, Nika Collison, editor. *Athlii Gwaii: Upholding Haida Law on Lyell Island*. Locarno Press, 2018.

Jisgang, Nika Collison, and Scott Steedman, editors. *That Which Makes Us Haida*. Haida Gwaii, BC: Haida Gwaii Museum Press, 2011.

Turner, Nancy J. *Plants of Haida Gwaii: Third Edition*. Madeira Park, BC: Harbour Publishing, 2021.

Yahgujaanas, Erika. *My First Solo [at T'alaan Stl'ang Rediscovery Program camp]*. South Carolina: CreateSpace Independent Publishing Platform, 2018.

Acknowledgements

I thank each and every one of the people in this book who so generously shared your stories, unflinchingly, kindly, and passionately; first for your time in speaking with me, then for reading the transcripts of your interviews, followed by the summaries of the stories, and the drafts of the chapters (sometimes more than once).

Writing a book like this is a labour of love, trust and good relations. It takes longer than it might otherwise because of the fundamental importance of every person in the book being comfortable with the way their voice and story have been portrayed. Seeking that comfort was time very well spent and priceless in terms of the generosity of spirit of everyone I have come to know in the process and the warmth of your responses. I will always treasure these three years of learning from all of you. Your care and thoughtfulness in every aspect of the work was so gratefully received. Haw'aa/hawaa, g̱ilakas'la, ğiáxsix̆a, t'ooyak̲siy̓ ṅiin, ap luk'wil t'oya̲xsut 'nüün!

Many other people supported the creation of the book, starting with former Coast Funds chair Merv Child back in 2015. Gilakas'la, Merv, for enthusiastically supporting the idea of the book right from the start. The staff team at Coast Funds, including former executive director Brodie Guy, Eddy Adra, Raine Playfair, Stephanie Butler and former communications manager Laura Hope, lent me their organizational support, wise advice, and introductions to some of the people in this book, for which I am immensely grateful. I am also very thankful for the anonymous third-party sponsor which Coast Funds arranged, helping make an impossible dream reality by covering a portion of the cost of publishing the book. In appreciation of that support and the support of all those who have participated in the book, all royalties will be donated to the Coast Conservation Environmental Endowment Fund for use by the First Nations with whom Coast Funds works.

Many other people supported the completion of this book. They include a number of interviewees who do not necessarily get a mention in the actual text but who provided valuable background, insights, and history: Richard Alexander R.P.Bio., Conrad Browne, Elodie Button, Tim Cormode, Cliff Emery, Mike Jacobs, UBC associate professor Jennifer Kramer, Lucy Neville, Danny Robertson, and Michael Ross. Renowned ethnobotanist and

University of Victoria emeritus professor Nancy J. Turner, who has worked with many of the people in this book, offered wise advice, compelling commentary, and many useful resource suggestions. The Haisla Nation’s Gail Amos helped me to connect with her husband Gerald and reviewed the draft chapter with him. Brenda Bouzane ensured that I was able to speak with Mike Jacobs. Art Sterritt and Merran Smith kindly agreed to the use of abridged excerpts from their essay, “From Conflict to Collaboration.”

A number of photographers graciously offered to donate their work. They include Philip Charles, Jerry Daoust, Chris Darimont, Barb Dinning, Alisson Gamero, Alex Harris, Rachel Hill, Kimi Hisinaga, Paul Joseph, Loni Leblanc, Courtney Louie, Jack Plant, Angela Sterritt, the Swan Bay Rediscovery Camp (Rachel Singleton-Poster) and the University of Victoria’s Faculty of Education. Raine Playfair at Coast Funds snapped a beautiful portrait of Ḵii’iljuus Barbara Wilson. Erica Roberts photographed Edith Wilcox. Na̱nwaḵolas Council and Nawalakw provided images for use. Not least of all, former Coast Funds executive director Brodie Guy also happens to be a wonderful photographer and generously provided many images.

Kim Winslow, a Canadian expatriate transcriber living in New Zealand, went above and beyond in her professional, careful, and respectful transcription of nearly one hundred interviews for me. Kim wrote to me at one point to say that she had learned a great deal from the work, to express her dismay at how little she had previously understood about her country’s shameful history regarding Indigenous Peoples, and to commit to educating her family and her friends about that history. Thank you, Kim, for your good heart and great work. Way With Words Ltd., who transcribed the balance of the interviews, also ensured the highest standard of professional care and diligence in taking care of the often-sensitive material they were entrusted with.

My gratitude goes also to the two editors of this book, Alicia Hibbert and Shari Narine, for the same reason. Their professionalism, skills, sensitivity and understanding were greatly appreciated.

Not least of all, my usual round of deep thanks to my family: Marc, Juliette, Michael, Caroline, and Hugo, my greatest fans and unflagging cheerleaders. Aroha ana ahau ki a koutou katoa.

Photography Credits

Tamara Alfred, p. 186

Mike Ambach/From The Treehouse Photography, p. 205

Taylor Burk Photography, pp. 177, 181

Jamaine Campbell, pp. 46, 48, 53, 62

Tavish Campbell, pp. 15, 78, 89, 208 – 209, 226

Jerry Daoust, p. 67

Coast Funds/Raine Playfair, pp. 122

Chocolate Dog Photography, p. 242

Barb Dinning, pp. 18, 131, 132, 134

Alisson Gamero, p. 151

Walter George, pp. 60–61

Jeffrey Gibbs, p. 106

Ǧvu̓í (Rory H̓áusṫI)/Robin Humchitt, p. 96

Brodie Guy, pp. vi, viii–ix, 26, 37, 38, 44, 54, 57, 58, 64, 66, 69, 73, 76, 98 – 99, 102, 105, 107, 111, 116, 126, 136, 138, 150, 157, 163, 164, 167, 169, 172, 175, 179, 180, 183, 187, 199, 201, 211, 212, 214, 216

Alex Harris/Raincoast Conservation Foundation, pp. 82, 88, 95

‘Cúagilákv (Jess H̓áusṫI), pp. 94

Haíłzaqv Tribal Council/Tavish Campbell, pp. 85, 87, 90

Rachel Hill, p. 207

Kimi Hisanaga, pp. 70, 79

Tim Irvin, pp. 202–203, 206, 223

Paul Joseph, p. 140

Loni Leblanc, p. 118

John Lehmann/The Globe and Mail, p. 80

Deirdre Leowinata, pp. 93, 156

Courtenay Louie, p. 101

Laurie MacBride, pp. ii–iii, 2, 63, 124

Na̱nwaḵolas Council, p. 8

Nawalakw, pp. 184, 189, 190

Nicole Morven, pp. 77

Nisg̱a’a Lisims Government, pp. 71

Douglas Neasloss, pp. 154, 158, 159, 161, 162, 165, 166, 170

Justin Neasloss, p. 168

Katherine Palmer Gordon, pp. 74, 129, 143, 146, 148, 152, 197

Qqs Society, p. 100

Christopher Roberts, p. 135

Erica Roberts, p. 133

Robin Rowland, pp. 144, 149, 153

Marilyn Slett, p. 91

Jennifer Nelson Smith, p. 178

Angela Sterritt, p. 92

SuavAir Aerial Imaging Ltd., p. 128

Swan Bay Rediscovery Camp (Rachel Singleton-Poster), pp. 108–109, 119, 123

Snxakila (Clyde Tallio), p. 33

University of Victoria, Faculty of Education, p. 191

Michael Wigle, pp. 24, 27, 29, 31, 32, 35, 41

Ol Siwid (Mike Willie), pp. 176, 182, 185

K̲ii’iljuus Barbara Wilson, pp. 104, 112, 113, 114, 115, 117, 120, 121

Mark Wunsch, Greencoast Media pp. 192, 194, 195

Index

Note: Page numbers in **bold** indicate photographs or information in captions.

About the Author

The author of eight non-fiction books, Katherine Palmer Gordon has been writing for publications in both Canada and New Zealand since 1995. She was in England in 1963, and her much-travelled French/Scottish family eventually settled in New Zealand when she was eleven. She has spent most of her adult life in Canada, living in the city of Toronto for several years before relocating to the city of Victoria, in the unceded territory of the Lək̓ʷəŋən (Lekwungen) people, known as the Esquimalt and Songhees Nations, in late 1999. In 2004 she moved to Gabriola Island, in the unceded territory of Snuneymuxw First Nation in British Columbia, working both as a writer and in Indigenous-governmental relations. Along the way she acquired the love of her life, Marc, and a labradoodle named Hugo, who comes a very close second.

Her first five books were published under the name Katherine Gordon. With the publication of her sixth book, *We Are Born With the Songs Inside Us* (Harbour, 2013), Katherine re-introduced her original name, Palmer, to her readers. Including a Foreword by Shawn A-in-Chut Atleo, *Songs* profiles a number of young Indigenous men and women talking about their lives in twenty-first-century British Columbia and the importance of cultural connection to the diverse paths they are following.

You can read more about Katherine at https://abcbookworld.com/ and https://www.writersunion.ca/member/katherine-gordon.